Shattered Nation

Shattered Nation

*Inequality and the Geography
of a Failing State*

Danny Dorling

VERSO
London • New York

This edition first published by Verso 2024
First published by Verso 2023
© Danny Dorling 2023

1 3 5 7 9 10 8 6 4 2

Verso
UK: 6 Meard Street, London W1F 0EG
US: 388 Atlantic Avenue, Brooklyn, NY 11217
versobooks.com

Verso is the imprint of New Left Books

ISBN-13: 978-1-80429-584-7
ISBN-13: 978-1-80429-328-7 (UK EBK)
ISBN-13: 978-1-80429-329-4 (US EBK)

British Library Cataloguing in Publication Data
A catalogue record for this book is available from the British Library

The Library of Congress Has Cataloged the Earlier Edition as Follows:

Names: Dorling, Daniel, author.
Title: Shattered nation : inequality and the geography of a failing state /
  Danny Dorling.
Description: Brooklyn, NY : Verso Books, 2023. | Includes bibliographical
  references and index.
Identifiers: LCCN 2023006249 (print) | LCCN 2023006250 (ebook) | ISBN
  9781804293270 (paperback) | ISBN 9781804293294 (ebk)
Subjects: LCSH: Equality – Europe. | Poverty – Europe.
Classification: LCC HM821 .D675 2023 (print) | LCC HM821 (ebook) | DDC
  305.094 – dc23/eng/20230414
LC record available at https://lccn.loc.gov/2023006249
LC ebook record available at https://lccn.loc.gov/2023006250

Typeset in Fournier by MJ & N Gavan, Truro, Cornwall
Printed and bound by CPI (UK) Ltd, Croydon CR0 4YY

Contents

Part I. Borders

1. The Roundabout   3
2. Growing Divides   22

Part II. Giants

3. Hunger   51
4. Precarity   80
5. Waste   110
6. Exploitation   136
7. Fear   163

Part III. Mountains

8. A Failing State   193
9. Conclusion   221

Acknowledgements   244
Notes   246
Index   275

To Karen Shook – and the fight
against the shattering

Part I.
Borders

1.
The Roundabout

Where did you grow up? For the first few years of my life, I lived in a house on a road between a cemetery and a shopping centre. I don't remember much of those years, and I suspect that I was too young to really know where I was living within the city. I now know that there was near full employment around me, and that my rose-tinted recollections of smiling faces fitted the mood of the times. People had never had it so good. Britain had never been so equal. Life chances had never been as fair as they were then, and they were better for more people than they had ever been before, even for those who fared worst.

When I was aged six, in 1974, my family moved to a house close to a major roundabout on the east of the city. In the 1970s, which neighbourhood a child lived in mattered far less for their life chances, and which local school you went to was less important than it is today. House prices varied far less between areas, and children who grew up in private housing and council housing more often played together, largely unaware of whose parents paid rent or had a mortgage.

There were two general elections in 1974. These were becoming turbulent times, but the turbulence had not yet affected my neighbourhood. I later learnt that in the shipyards of Belfast, on the Clyde and on the Tyne, people were losing their jobs.[1] But the car factories in the city of Oxford were still employing thousands. I had no way of knowing that the children in my school year would be the final cohort taken on in such large numbers to work in those factories. The wave of manufacturing unemployment that swept down from the North did not reach Oxford until my later teenage years.

The ravages of the 1980s swept away most well-paying jobs in the city's car factories. Deindustrialisation was masked by gentrification as the two local universities expanded. The cheaper neighbourhood on one side of our roundabout had begun to be gentrified. The more affluent neighbourhood on another side had become unaffordable for most people who worked locally. When the manual work began to dry up, the first to lose their jobs were the parents living on the council estate beside a third segment of the roundabout. Many school-leavers could not find work. The reputation of the council estate began to fall, while estate agents talked in ever more glowing terms about the wonderful houses in the more affluent neighbourhood.

The lives of the teenagers I went to school with became increasingly determined by what side of that roundabout they had grown up on. Place mattered much more in the 1980s than it had done in either the 1960s or 1970s.[2] The borders of the local primary school catchment areas became more rigidly defined and apparently important. Children played a little less freely across those borders. A tiny few of us went away to university. Almost without exception, those who did so lived in the 'better' segments. I was one of those few.

I came back in my forties to live again in the same city. Recently a local councillor told me that there were over 200 places available on Airbnb in the council estate next to the roundabout. I checked on the website, and at first it appeared he had exaggerated. However, whenever I zoomed in to any part of the estate, a few more Airbnb offers would appear; and not just in the estate, but all around the roundabout.[3] It can be a shock to see that so many of the homes your friends grew up in have been sold on, and bought not by a family to live in, but just to be rented out to tourists.

The Oxford neighbourhood that once had the cheapest private housing – where the majority of homes were originally owned by car-factory workers – is now too expensive for most university academics to afford. Today, it's increasingly inhabited by London commuters, including political reporters and business folk, many benefiting from being able to work from home while in theory working in London. The most expensive enclave in the neighbourhood has become an investment opportunity for overseas buyers and more up-market buy-to-let landlords. What was once the local pub is today a drive-through McDonald's. Fields that I played in as a child are now fenced off. There are also fewer children playing outside; and fewer children overall. Today, children mix far less with other children.

If you grew up in Britain, think of what has now become of your home neighbourhood. Very few areas of the country have become less divided over time. Those that have tend to be places that have been abandoned by money and are becoming more similar because poverty is rising more uniformly. They are now areas of increasingly widespread and severe deprivation. Conversely, many cities now thought of as affluent have some of the greatest local social inequalities within their boundaries.[4]

I left Oxford at the age of eighteen, and lived for ten years each in Newcastle and Sheffield. The place I grew up in is hardly recognisable to me now. Most buildings are the same, but the city has become a completely different social world. A similar story can be told of almost anywhere in Britain, but the story of what has happened to Oxford illustrates how nowhere has escaped the crisis of a shattered nation. The city of Oxford is a far more unaffordable, tense, anxious and restless place than it was in my childhood. There are far more students now, many of them coming from overseas and featuring as part of the 'export earnings' of the nation.[5] Those who are not from the United States are normally shocked to see how many homeless people sleep on Oxford's streets. People hardly ever had to sleep on the streets of the city during my childhood.

Of course, the University of Oxford students of my childhood could be annoying, but there were fewer of them, and they were greatly outnumbered by local teenagers and young adults. Thirty years later there are far fewer local children than there were then, and even fewer young adults who are not students. The students still occasionally wear their silly gowns in public, but do so with what appears to be less embarrassment and a little more smugness than they did in the 1980s. When I was a teenager, I assumed that Oxford students' public displays of arrogance were soon going to end – surely they would be too embarrassed in future, I thought. How wrong I was.

In 2019 Oxford made national news when it was revealed that the city had one of the UK's highest rates of homelessness as well as of deaths among homeless people. What most shocked local officials was just how many of those who had died had grown up in the city, had gone away, and then come back. What most shocked me was that many were around my age, and I even recognised some of the names of those who had died. In one case, I was able to provide a name when shown a photo of a deceased person the authorities were trying to identify. He had attended my school.[6]

If you live in the UK, it is easy to believe that everything must be getting worse everywhere. But in most of the world, most things to do with human lives and livelihoods are getting better. People are living longer. Life expectancy is rising steadily almost everywhere, except in the UK (and the US). Almost everywhere, infant mortality is falling faster than in the UK. Almost (but not quite) everywhere, people are better off than their parents were. Economic inequality is falling in the majority of countries, and population growth is slowing even in the poorest nations. The social statistics suggest that elsewhere in Europe people have never had it so good, although in the most equitable and advanced European countries folk tend to be sceptical about social progress and are far more vigilant in tracking signs of a lack of progress than we are in the UK. Other parts of the continent have experienced the socio-economic decline of which the UK is an extreme example, but they are the parts that have more often followed the UK policy mantras of privatisation and individualisation. These mantras are now being questioned more intensely than before.

We now expect the global human population to peak in number within the current century. Educational opportunities are widening, and that is linked to the global population slowdown, as well as rising rates of equality in so many countries. There is terrible poverty in much of the world, but it is now more often falling than rising. Other economic inequalities are also falling worldwide, although falls in income inequality, and states becoming more stable and safer, never seem to make the news headlines. I can show students hundreds of statistics from all over the world that suggest we are not travelling towards hell in a handcart. But I can find hardly any social statistics about the UK that are particularly positive, and I spend much more time looking for them than most people do.

Climate change, our great global concern, is now being taken far more seriously than it was a decade or two ago. Carbon emissions per person are lower in more equitable countries as compared to the more profligate unequal ones, and especially the most unequal richest countries. We can see what we have to do to reduce pollution. Much may have been left too late to avoid serious harm, but some good things will be achieved. Even the numbers of people directly involved in wars have been falling for decades, although we are rightly shocked by each new war. The threat of nuclear war, something we once thought would be almost impossible to avoid, has fallen over recent decades, although it rose again as a concern after the Russian invasion of Ukraine in 2022.

I am not pessimistic when it comes to global trends. It is just that closer to home the statistics are all a great deal less rosy. As a nation, we have travelled down a road that people in other nations have almost always been far more successful in avoiding. That has brought us to a particular point and resulted in a particular human landscape in the UK, one that is hard to summarise but perhaps can be best described as *shattered*: people feeling shattered. Hopes shattered. Much of the fabric of society shattered. The ability of our schools to educate our children well, of our social housing system to cope with need, of the National Health Service to care for us, and so much else – all shattered. Many of those previously just coping can no longer cope. Food banks are proliferating. Levels of debt have increased for millions of people, while a very few of the extremely wealthy have seen their riches soar. So many people are feeling shattered by all of this.

Capitalisms Plural

> People talk about capitalism as if it were just one thing, but the truth
> is that we live in a global system of capitalisms plural, with a chunk of
> ideology in common but considerable differences in local emphasis.[7]

In the UK capitalism has taken on a particularly cynical form. This
has allowed inequality to grow to levels higher than can be found
almost anywhere else in Europe. In fact, it is possible that, in 2022,
the UK became the most unequal country in Europe in terms of
income inequality. Elsewhere on the continent development in
the opposite direction can be seen, and in between there are now
huge variations.

With the words quoted above, the British journalist and novel-
ist John Lanchester opened his investigation into how fraud has
become such a significant problem in a number of countries in
Europe. He began with the £15 billion-plus lost due to fraud and
error during the UK government's Covid response, a loss he
described as simply 'off the scale'. Writing during the first 2022
Conservative Party leadership contest, Lanchester commented
on how remarkable it was that one of the two candidates, Rishi
Sunak, had been head of the Treasury – the government department that both supervised and failed to control these huge levels
of fraud and error – and that this was not being held against him.
Was it just seen by the public as a lamentable part of what it means
to be in power?

Lanchester argued that, even among the rich nations, the UK is
unusually cynical. Its bankers do not worry too much about where
the money they launder comes from. He could have added that UK
universities appear to have little concern over whom they accept

donations from. According to Lanchester, while financiers in other countries suffer from complacency, in the UK that complacency was replaced some time ago by outright cynicism. And, yet, this is indulged. One of the first acts of the brief Truss government was to allow bankers to be paid unlimited bonuses, which only encourages them to gamble more.[8]

Perhaps British bankers cannot now afford to be anything other than cynical; perhaps they have to be in order to survive, given the environment they work in. People with dirty money come to them because they know they are cynical. People with somewhat 'cleaner' money are less and less keen to be associated with London or Britain. Cynicism may be the key asset that brings money into the UK today.

Lanchester is far from alone in making this assessment. Dozens of books have been published in the past few years about the current state of London's financial services. Oliver Bullough's *Butler to the World: How Britain Became the Servant of Tycoons, Tax Dodgers, Kleptocrats and Criminals* became a bestseller in 2022. There is money to be made out of describing the rise of dodgy money. Sam Bright's *Fortress London: Why We Need to Save the Country from the Capital* was published in the same year, as was Caroline Knowles's *Serious Money: Walking Plutocratic London*.

While these books now come thick and fast, London has been identified as a centre of financial corruption for years. In 2017, Anna Minton's *Big Capital: Who Is London For?* made the case that the London housing market is out of control because of who invests there. A year later Nicholas Shaxson's *The Finance Curse: How Global Finance Is Making Us All Poorer* was published. Rowland Atkinson's *Alpha City: How London Was Captured by the Super-Rich* appeared in 2020. So why, even as the criticism mounted, did such behaviour become even more brazen? One answer is that the cynicism was still rising, among both the financiers and some of the politicians of their favourite political party.

Lanchester put it very neatly: we now live in a world of capitalisms plural. Most versions of capitalism are far less socially damaging than that found in the UK. At the other extreme to the UK is Finland. That most benign version of capitalism has resulted in the lowest level of infant mortality ever recorded, almost zero homelessness, the lowest recorded income inequality anywhere in the world, the highest rates of educational achievement and the best work–life balance (choosing what hours you work) for all social groups ever measured.[9]

This is a book about the UK at a potential turning point: about the realisation that we are shattered, and how that realisation might well be essential to understanding how to move forward. What could be done is suggested at many points. What has already been tried and failed is described, and what is constantly suggested but not possible is also touched upon, but only where it is most relevant, rather than at the very end of the book. To make the necessary turn, we first have to realise that we must change direction, because doing the same thing over and over again and expecting different results is – as Albert Einstein was once thought to have observed – madness.

The argument I try to sustain in the pages that follow is that the UK has been heading in the wrong direction for a long time. We cannot continually privatise and individualise as much as possible and still expect some positive aggregate outcome. Eventually the truth has to dawn. Geographical comparisons are very helpful here: by comparing the UK to the countries it is nearest and most similar to, we can see that our experiment has failed. No single event resulted in the shattering. Many events have been blamed, and many of those are as much symptoms as causes.[10]

As a nation shatters there is a tendency to see each new crack as being the most important issue of the day. Often the retaliatory response is to say that each such event is just part of a global process that happens to be a little worse for the UK than elsewhere. But there comes a time when bad luck strikes too often, in the same place and repeatedly, for all of it simply to be blamed on bad luck. Geographical comparisons show that most places have not been as badly affected by so-called global processes as Britain has. In fact, many of those slow-running processes have had benign or even beneficial effects elsewhere.[11]

Britain reached its current peak of overall income inequality a very long time ago, in the mid-1990s, and has remained extremely unequal every year afterwards. Ever since then changes have taken place that were not seen elsewhere in Europe. By the time the Labour Party led by Tony Blair came to power in 1997, no other European social-democratic party had placed itself and its policies so far to the right. People joked that Blair was doing things that the right-wing Conservative prime minister Margaret Thatcher would never have dared to attempt.

At a private dinner in Hampshire in 2002, Thatcher was asked what her greatest achievement had been. She replied: 'Tony Blair and New Labour. We forced our opponents to change their minds.'[12] This may be a little unfair on Blair, and is certainly unfair to many of the MPs in his governments. But, partly in order to outmanoeuvre New Labour, the Conservative Party was subsequently pushed even further to the right. Indeed, in the European Parliament in 2014, British Conservative Party MEPs left the large centre-right European People's Party group to instead ally themselves with a small far-right group that included the German political party Alternative für Deutschland.[13]

What had pushed the Conservatives so far to the right? It

was the rightwards shift in Labour during the thirteen years the Conservatives were out of office. New Labour introduced university tuition fees of £1,000 a year in 1998, raised them to £3,000 a year in 2004, and then set the stage for them to be increased again to the highest levels seen worldwide by 2012 (the average US state university fees are second highest). Most importantly, the Labour governments of 1997–2010 did not bring inequality levels down.[14] Britain went on to suffer more severely from the global economic crash of 2008 than almost any other nation. This was because the Blair government, seeing financial services as paramount and seeking to avoid upfront payments by government, had made financial sleight of hand central to its plans, such as by massively extending what was then called the Private Finance Initiative. New Labour had become reliant on the continued growth of the City of London.

Austerity, imposed from 2010 by the Conservative–Liberal Democrat coalition government, was deeper and longer in Britain than anywhere else in Europe.[15] This was partly the result of decisions made by Labour between 1997 and 2010, and not simply because the coalition government, and the Conservative government that succeeded it in 2015, was so callous, although that callousness significantly exacerbated the suffering. Britain was shattered as a result of the actions of all three main political parties. And while the leaders of all three opposed Brexit in 2016, it still happened, eventually, in January 2020.

The key ramifications of the shattering of the UK are threefold. First, we are growing spatially and socially further apart from each other. Second, the five giants of poverty first identified in the 1940s – want, squalor, idleness, ignorance and disease – are returning in new forms. Third, we have growing internal political divisions. These spreading cracks in the social structure are all classic signs of a failing state.

Cracks

When a state begins to fail, attempts are made to suggest that claims of its shattering are exaggerations. Typically, a list of apparent problems faced by other countries will be produced whenever their people are said to be doing better than the British: 'What about suicide rates in Finland?', 'What about Germany's reliance on Russian gas?', 'What about the rise in "populism" in the US, Brazil, Hungary, Turkey and Russia?' This response is so common that it now has its own label: 'whataboutery', which itself dates back to responses to the Troubles in the shattered province of Northern Ireland in the 1970s.[16]

One of the functions of whataboutery is to paper over the cracks by diversion and subterfuge. It draws people's attention away from what they should be looking at by attempting to make false comparisons or confusing the terms of reference. In June 2021 it was revealed that 'British diplomats [are] being told to change the way they speak about the UK, referring to it as "one country rather than the four nations of the UK"'.[17]

In fact, hardly anyone tries to present the UK as a single nation, but the decision by the government to refer to it as such is another illustration of an attempt to paper over the expanding cracks. The United Kingdom is nothing of the sort. It is actually becoming increasingly disunited.

When London-based Conservatives mention 'this nation', for them there is only one. At the very least, it encompasses all of Great Britain and Northern Ireland as a sacred indivisible whole. For some of them, Gibraltar (whose residents were allowed to vote in the Brexit referendum), the Falklands and a myriad of other rocks and islands dotted around the world are also part of their imagined British nation. One idea of a nation is of a place or a people worth fighting for. The few shattered remains of a once vast empire are clutched close to the hearts of a particular group of people who would happily send others to fight to defend every remaining offshore holding.

Moderate Conservatives are more accommodating. The BBC still talks of the UK's nations and regions, but it also now obeys the government mandate to categorise the UK as a single country. The BBC's motto, 'Nation shall speak peace unto Nation', was dreamt up in 1927, in the aftermath of the war that was supposed to end all wars. The BBC still retains the distinctions between the nations, but all are prefixed by one acronym to rule over them: BBC English Regions, BBC Cymru Wales, BBC Northern Ireland and BBC Scotland. In BBC vernacular, the UK is a single country comprising these four nations. The ten English regions are then further subdivided into forty-two areas.[18]

Those at the top of the BBC think their role is to hold the pieces together and celebrate the imagined unity. As they recently stated at the unveiling of their latest five-year plan: 'We celebrate the UK's creative strength, telling stories from every part of the country. We have a responsibility to nurture the UK's democracy, and we seek to do so with trusted, accurate and impartial programming.'[19] The BBC is key to papering over the cracks. Its problem is that the cracks are getting wider, while at the same time its budget to produce such content is repeatedly being cut. In September 2022 it resorted to showing hour upon hour of people filing past the Queen's coffin.

The BBC's role in nurturing the UK's version of democracy involves presenting it as if it were normal, even though it includes the monarchy, the unelected House of Lords, the first-past-the-post voting system, and Scotland and Wales being described as nations (rather than countries). Despite all this, the BBC repeats the mantra that it is being accurate, impartial and trustworthy. However, the director general responsible for the latest five-year plan,[20] Tim Davie, was the deputy chairman of the Conservative Party in the London borough of Hammersmith and Fulham in the 1990s. It was his job to put a brave face on things and, as he puts it, 'celebrate the UK's creative strength'.

The more shattered the fictional nation, the more papering over the cracks will be required. More new myths will be created, and more talking up of our creativity.[21] The young, however, increasingly tend not to watch the BBC, getting their information and news from elsewhere. Most BBC fodder, as a result, is being prepared for the old.

In a shattered state the invisible walls separating areas grow ever higher. But those walls remain mostly invisible because we are repeatedly told that they don't really exist, and that there is opportunity for everyone out there. Lip service is paid to levelling up, even as most people are being beaten down. A peculiar map emerges as a result, a geography of places with decaying fortunes encroaching on the enclaves of success.

Those enclaves are found in the more affluent streets of London, but also in the country retreats concentrated mostly within rural parts of Oxfordshire and Gloucestershire, and in pockets close to the roundabout I grew up beside. The few people who have done well for themselves increasingly occupy the enclaves. In my childhood the better-off were more evenly spread out geographically. However, no enclave of affluence is now very far from other places that are going bankrupt.

Nostalgia

In May 2022, a stone's throw from Eton College, the borough of Slough was ordered to sell off all its assets in the wake of being forced to declare bankruptcy over outstanding debts of £760 million. These assets included the town's public libraries, all of its children's centres, its community hubs and what remained of its council housing stock.[22] The story received very little media coverage. This had already happened in so many other places. It was also becoming clear that the same fate was about to befall more and more local authorities facing escalating fuel bills and eviscerated by decades of central-government policy designed to privatise public goods and services. Most secondary schools had been transferred out of local authority ownership long ago, and most primaries more recently. At least they could not be sold off, but they would now have to face the coming storm on their own.

The pillaging of the state has seen the numbers of UK public sector workers – in other words, people working for the public good – plummet from 23 per cent of all those in work in 1992 to just 17 per cent of the much larger total national workforce today. The proportion is redefined over time by the Office for National Statistics (ONS) to allow for changes in definitions of who is a public servant. The most recent large fall in the share of public sector employment began under the New Labour government in 2005 and has continued ever since, despite a temporary halt when the Covid-19 pandemic arrived in 2020.[23] Overall, UK public spending as a proportion of GDP fell below that of Spain in the 1980s, and below that of Greece in the 1990s. It was already lower than almost every other Western European nation following the cuts that began in the late 1970s.

It is worth reflecting on the fact that it was only the least democratic of Western European nations that spent less on public goods after 1980: Spain was still recovering from the dictatorship of Franco, and Greece from the junta of the generals.[24] While the UK continues to be an outlier in the paucity of its spending on public goods, both Spain and Greece are now much more democratic and more like the rest of the European mainland in having larger public sectors than the UK.[25]

A country's spending statistics are presented by the International Monetary Fund (IMF) as a proportion of GDP. The IMF also reports on what countries plan to spend in the future. The current UK government has said it intends to spend less than almost everywhere else in Europe,[26] even though it will allocate a higher share of its public monies to its military than any other Western European country, and a huge amount to its debt repayments. Here are the percentages for 2023: France and Belgium will spend 55 per cent of their GDP on public services, followed in descending order by Finland, Greece, Austria, Denmark, Norway, Sweden, Germany and Spain, and finally both Portugal and the Netherlands at 45 per cent, with the UK way below at only 41 per cent. While the IMF's projection for the UK for 2023 is two percentage points higher than the 39 per cent spent in 2019, that is a reflection of the rising costs of debt repayment and the projected further increase in military spending, rather than representing any rise in spending on public well-being.

The position of the UK is even worse than the numbers above suggest because in recent years its GDP has not risen as much as that of other European countries. Meanwhile the pound has fallen in value. By the first quarter of 2022 the Institute for Fiscal Studies (IFS) was reporting that average real earnings per person in the UK were a massive £11,000 lower than they would have been had the slow upward trend seen through 1990–2008 continued.

Perhaps we do not see this change for what it is because we are deluded about our past. There is a type of nostalgia that labels certain historical periods as good and others as bad, but this almost never stands up to scrutiny. We often forget when things were actually getting better for most people.

Looking back at the past through a particular lens focused on particular places is a very British trait. There are, for example, far more news reports about Hong Kong produced in Britain than almost anywhere else in the world. The BBC appears determined to perpetuate some kind of collective memory with its frequent reporting on events in former colonies that long ago gained their independence, as if those places were still partly British. Reports from India, Zimbabwe, South Africa and even the United States are often tinged with a little wistfulness that all these were once 'ours'. There was less enthusiasm, though, for providing much coverage of Barbados electing its first president, Sandra Mason, in 2021, to replace the Queen as head of state.

In the UK, nostalgia can act as a sedative. Politicians feed on this, but it is less effective on the young. In May 2022 a large poll of the general public was taken about their views on the monarchy.[27] Opinions varied not by social class but by age. The proportions who said that the monarchy was good for Britain were: aged 18–24, 24 per cent; 25–49, 49 per cent; 50–64, 67 per cent; and 65+, 74 per cent. Of course, as people age their opinions may be changed by the stories they are fed, but it becomes harder to do that with age groups that hardly watch mainstream TV channels any more. Between 2019 and 2021 support for retaining the monarchy plummeted among younger adults.[28]

You can still find parts of the UK to visit that have picture-postcard looks and which on the surface appear impervious to change. But even there, when you scratch beneath the surface, all is not well. Behind the Regency facades of Chelsea and inside the barn conversions of the Cotswolds there is growing anxiety. Very affluent people now ask me, much more frequently than they used to, what I think will happen when most people realise what has happened to the UK. I do not have a simple answer for them.

The decay is clearest in the suburbs, where families now increasingly rent a home that a generation ago they would have owned. In Middle England neighbourhoods like the one I grew up in, I get asked to give public talks about how people might cope with the latest cost-of-living crisis. In poorer areas, where things have been so bad for so long, there is less of a sense of crisis and more one of bitter resignation. The crisis of 2022/23, as mortgage rates rose, was very much a middle-class affair, affecting almost everyone who had got on the housing ladder in the current century. It was no longer among the poorest where the pain was most concentrated.

The children of the winners from Thatcher's Britain are now losing out. They face unprecedented spikes in their energy bills, pay rises below inflation and, if lucky enough to have them at all, the prospect of their private pensions becoming increasingly insecure. That was partly why Liz Truss tried to offer them Thatcher Mark II, and why Rishi Sunak presents a re-spinning of Tony Blair–like enthusiasm. But the deeper the malaise becomes, the more any solutions will need to go in the opposite direction to Thatcherism, and the more the question arises: when will so few benefit from the system, a system that already fails so many, that it ceases to be tolerated?

The multiple crises that afflict Britain are worse and have deeper roots than those affecting other European states. The UK is now very likely to be the most economically unequal country in Europe (although until early 2022 it was ranked just slightly more equal than Bulgaria). The repercussions are widespread. It really matters that Britain has the most divisive education system in Europe, tainting our institutions and affecting individuals for life. It matters greatly that the UK has the most expensive and poorest-quality housing, the most precarious and often lowest-paying work for so many people, the lowest state pension and the stingiest welfare benefits. Recently Britain has also experienced the sharpest declines in health in all of Europe, especially in the health of its children. A whole state is being plunged ever deeper into poverty. This is failure. It is not surprising that even the rich are now worried.

As the crisis deepens, geographical inequalities grow and, cruelly, these disparities help to sustain the crisis because they serve to hide the exploitation it involves. The very rich increasingly live apart from the rest of us, leading parallel lives. But so too do the fairly rich, who control most of what is left of the opposition (both within Parliament and the mainstream media), and who tell us that the only rational alternative to our shattered present is a watered-down version of more of the same.

This book is not utopian. Its core argument is that sooner or later Britain's divisions will have to be addressed because they are now so great that they are becoming unsustainable: too few people now benefit. However, addressing these divisions will not result in a sudden arrival at the sunlit uplands.

Nonetheless, we have been this shattered before, and other states have been too. In every case it took decades to put the pieces back together again. We can choose now either to cultivate hope, so that we have the energy to persevere, or to burn out in exhaustion at the collective trauma that the shattering induces, and allow those who have divided us to continue to do so. This is the choice we face.

2.

Growing Divides

Last stop on round would be Old Ma Bigoty's place; 'twas like taking bread to the top of the world; 'twas a grand ride back though. I knew baker would have kettle on and doorsteps of that Hovis ready. 'There's wheatgerm in that loaf', he'd say. 'Get it inside you boy, and you'll be going up that hill as fast as you come down.'

Can you recall the Hovis boy on a bike – often called Britain's favourite advert? The quote above was most of its short script. It was filmed in 1973 and recounts the story of a young boy struggling to push his bike up a steep street to deliver bread to the last of the baker's early morning customers in a small town. The advert was a little deceptive. It was not shot in a northern mill town, but on Gold Hill in Shaftesbury, Dorset, a small market town in the south-west of England. Those watching it usually presumed the town was in the North, not just because of the steep hills, cobbled streets and flat caps, but because the voiceover was delivered in a strong regional accent.

Perhaps the man who directed the advert thought that a regional English accent in the 1970s implied trustworthiness, wholesomeness and tradition. The director had grown up in the North.

However, just before the end of this forty-five-second-long masterpiece of advertising, the actor doing the voiceover switches to someone very different, someone with a southern-English received pronunciation voice.

Having established trustworthiness using the voice of a regional working-class man, the southern upper-middle-class professional then delivers the supposedly final authoritative advice: 'Hovis still has many times more wheatgerm than ordinary bread. It's as good for you today as it's always been.'[1] What ordinary bread might have been, or what wheatgerm is, or does, could not be explained in those forty-five seconds. Especially not if there were to be dramatic pauses in the narrative for the volume on Dvořák's *New World Symphony* to rise and stir the emotions.

The advert clearly worked. It was played on TV for many years and, when polled forty-six years later, people voted it their 'most heart-warming and memorable advert'. But what were the public doing voting so positively for a vignette about child labour? One thing many of them were probably doing was remembering their own childhoods. We tend to think of the past as having been a better place, a place in which community existed and life moved more slowly and safely. Although not everyone had that experience, in many ways it was true.

I do wonder whether the director of the advert decided to call the woman whose house the boy was riding up the hill to 'Old Ma Bigoty' as a signal that all was not well in this fictional northern town. But I suspect he was not as insightful as that, and when you replay the ad today, it is hard to make out the name clearly. The director was a thirty-five-year-old unknown, born in South Shields and educated in Stockton-on-Tees and Hartlepool.[2] In 1979, six years after shooting the Hovis advert on Gold Hill, his first successful feature film, *Alien*, was released, quickly followed by *Blade*

Runner in 1982 and then a stream of other famous movies and groundbreaking adverts, including one for the Apple Macintosh personal computer. His name was Ridley Scott.

Scott had an eye for creating dystopian futures which, when we look back now, were as much a reflection of the troubles of their era as portents of what was yet to come. His dark films warned of the threat of corporations and the rich becoming too powerful. In the UK, 1979 and 1982 were desperate years marked by growing corporate power, mass unemployment, rising social division, and economic impoverishment for millions.

In contrast to what came later, 1973 – when the Hovis advert was shot – was a time of low corporate power. Although there was a great deal of bigotry, much was improving. The school leaving age had been raised to sixteen the year before. Two years earlier, in 1970, the Equal Pay Act, for men and women in the same or equivalent jobs, had been passed. Between those two progressive moves, however, a step backwards had been taken. The 1971 Immigration Act had made it harder for mainly black and brown Commonwealth citizens, mostly former British subjects who had enjoyed automatic right of entry, to move to Britain.

When we look back, we see there never was a golden age of unrelenting progress. Even in the best years, clear bigotry could be found spliced between progressive incidents and actions. However, 1973 did mark the beginning of the end of an era in which there had been the most remarkable social progress in Britain. Today, it is often painted as a time of strife, but the many strikes and protests of the time were attempts to preserve what had been won, and to maintain progress. Those attempts failed, and more spectacularly in the UK than anywhere else in Europe.

Statistical analysis confirms that 1973 was the high-water mark. The New Economics Foundation (NEF) is a transparently funded British think-tank, founded in 1986, that promotes 'social, economic and environmental justice'. According to the NEF, measures of domestic social progress peaked shortly after 1973 and fell relentlessly from 1977 onwards.[3] In the early 1970s, people were well paid and there was near full employment. This meant that they could tell their bosses to shove it if they did not like how they were being treated. There were always jobs to be had, especially for able-bodied white men, but greater equality was being won by other groups too.

In 1973 UK income inequality was at an all-time minimum – almost the lowest that had ever been measured anywhere worldwide. British wealth inequality had been shrinking for decades, education was being extended and access widened, poverty was being reduced more and more every year, and health improvements were rapid.[4] And then, in the summer of 1973, Britain joined the European Community, the preparation for which was partly responsible for that racist Immigration Act (fortress Europe). Nevertheless, on balance it was a good time, a time of Britain becoming less arrogant and more inclusive, a time for joining in rather than trying to be special and superior to everyone else.

So what happened?

Crisis after crisis hit the UK, and with each new setback divisions grew. Some of these crises were global, others home-grown. Inflation, unemployment, poverty, inequality, homelessness and much more worsened. Even when the crises were global, often the effects were worse in the UK than elsewhere because few serious attempts were made to heal the growing divides. One exception to the progress of the early 1970s was in Northern Ireland, where the Troubles became much worse after Bloody Sunday (1972), and it was only much later that the divisions there were reduced.

However, the Good Friday Agreement of 1998 was seriously undermined two decades later by Brexit.

The greatest crisis came with the banking crash in 2008, after which the UK experienced its worst pay squeeze since the Napoleonic era, when it had taken some twenty-four years, until 1822, for average pay to return to the level it had reached in 1798. The Trades Union Congress (TUC) compared the real-pay crisis post-2008 with all the others that had occurred in the past 200 years and showed that it was worse than any of these. In spring 2022 the TUC used forecasts from the Office for Budget Responsibility (OBR) to suggest that the effect of the 2008 crisis could be expected to last seventeen years, until 2025.[5] This, however, was before it became clear just how high inflation could rise. The possibility of the current crisis outrunning that of 1798–1822 is now a very real one.

Crises come and crises go, but if a substantial proportion of your life is spent living through them, they start to become part of what defines that life. Gold Hill in Shaftesbury, the setting for the 1973 Hovis advert, has seen all the wage crises ever measured come and go. Its cobbled streets and cottages pre-date the building of Eton College.[6] Deprivation maps show in which areas most people are poor and where there are fewest poor people. Today, if you zoom in to the town of Shaftesbury on the deprivation map of the UK, you'll see that the town is now socially divided.[7] You'll also find Shaftesbury today sitting amid a more recently socially fractured patchwork of Middle England villages lying between Salisbury and Yeovil, places where the cost of petrol and the energy needed to heat homes have become key issues for most people, but not all, living in these enclaves. The deprivation map also shows that the poorest people in Middle England live in neighbourhoods that are usually not too distant from the best-off areas. Some people living there may still have pitchforks, but rebellion in the twenty-first century will not involve storming the castle gates. It will most likely come when rural England votes differently, no longer doffing its cap so dutifully in the Tory shires.

In 2007, just before the financial crisis, I took part in a project to map changes in poverty and wealth in the UK since 1968.[8] My colleagues and I found that geographical inequalities were lowest between 1968 and the early 1970s. Britain really was a more equal place then – that is not some rose-tinted fiction. When we looked at trends in mental health and the use of antidepressants, we saw that the past was also a happier place. We charted how the divides between areas increased in every decade after 1971. The period since 2007, on which this book mostly focuses, has only seen those divides widen further towards the shattering point.

The Hovis Gold Hill advert that launched Ridley Scott's career was remastered for a relaunch in 2019. The company that released it gave the following reasons for the relaunch: 'Hovis said it hopes to introduce the advert to a new generation who still appreciate its "core message of hard work, family and the strength of community".' The marketing director at Hovis went on to say: 'We are seeing a mass movement across the country celebrating craftsmanship, traditional products and UK produce, and this advert is one of the most iconic examples of a brand celebrating the ties that bind us as communities and as a country, drawing on tradition but informing our future.'[9]

The reimagined advert renamed Old Ma Bigoty as Old Ma Peggoty. It made no mention of wheatgerm or the apparent deficiencies of other breads. Presumably Advertising Standards Authority rules have changed. But few people viewing the advert today would recognise it as the UK they live in now, or the idea that hard work pays off, or that communities are strong, or that craftsmanship is high, or that the traditional products and produce of Britain are selling well on world markets. They might, however, recognise a brand trying to sell its bread to a population increasingly having to choose between cheap bread or no bread, energy for heating or petrol for the car, or the rent for a place to call home.

Decline

Sadly, the good times did not last. Analysis has shown that 1974 was the peak year for UK living standards overall, especially when taking into account factors such as pollution and the depletion of natural capital.[10] For many ethnic-minority groups, and for women, this will not likely have been the best year, but in general, for children, families and the population as a whole, it was.

Why did the measures of social progress peak in 1974 and begin to fall after 1976? If you look at the combination of measures the NEF assembled in its analysis, the factors said to have caused living standards to drop were rising levels of crime, rising family separation, and the harms associated with each. However, crime had been rising since the late 1950s, and family breakdown since the 1960s, so the turnaround after 1974 had causes other than those factors. The index the NEF constructed included many components. Those that brought the index down included the net international position of the UK economically; the effects of rising inequality including a small rise in spending on private health and private education; the growing costs of commuting; the number of car accidents and the social costs of pollution (including rising noise pollution); the loss of natural habitats; and the depletion of other resources.

In the UK it is very common to say that everything went wrong in the 1970s, but actually more was going right than wrong. People too young to remember the 1970s have to rely on the accounts of others. Liz Truss was derided for so many things during her Conservative Party leadership campaign and brief premiership that each of her many failings began to blur into one. But at one point she was mocked for her account of the 1970s in the book *Britannia Unchained* that she co-wrote in 2012 with four other relatively young Conservative MPs, including Kwasi Kwarteng, the (very temporary) chancellor of the Exchequer in Truss's administration. In short, they accused the average British worker of being lazy. Their evidence was mostly sourced from a single 1979 article in the *Economist* and five pages of a book by Dominic Sandbrook.[11] A third source was two pages from a book by Matt Ridley, a journalist and former chairman of Northern Rock.[12] These Conservatives tended to have a very narrowly informed view of the past, based on a limited archive of sources.[13]

The *Economist* article that Liz Truss repeatedly referred to is worth looking at in more detail. It was published on 2 June 1979 under the title 'Britain's decline: its causes and consequences'.[14] It was in fact a highly confidential memorandum from the man who was then Her Majesty's ambassador to France, written for the secretary of state for foreign and Commonwealth affairs. Only partially published at the time, the memorandum was eventually fully declassified in 2006, twenty-seven years later. It begins by explaining the long-term trend with these words: 'we have been in relative economic decline since the middle of the 19th century (when we were still producing two-thirds of the world's energy, and half its iron and cotton cloth and when per capita income in the UK was over twice that in Germany and one-third greater than in France)'.

Nicholas Henderson, the author of the memorandum, lamented how those whom he saw as 'the best people' in the UK sought work in finance in the City of London or as top civil servants (presumably like himself) rather than in industry.[15] What he found particularly hard to bear were the attempts by the French press in the late 1970s to find something good to say about Britain, repeatedly falling back on praising British humour for lack of any other laudable qualities.[16] Towards the end of his memorandum he wrote: 'The British people do not give the impression that they are fully aware of how far Britain's economy has fallen behind that of our European neighbours or of the consequences of this upon living standards.'

Could it be that, more than four decades later, and following a continuation of many of the trends Henderson outlined, the British people are today finally becoming a little more aware? If they are, it is no thanks to the many governments in power between 1979 and 2023, all of which continued the long tradition of talking Britain up and ignoring the long decline.

This fall in the economic position of the UK had two key drivers. One was the loss of captive imperial markets as the empire shrank. The other, which came later, was the growth in income inequality in the UK, which meant that poorer people had less money to spend in ways that would have supported many local businesses. Instead, each year in the quarter century after 1973, the better-off saw their incomes grow by more than the average. A disproportionate share of that money stoked up housing booms, was invested in private pensions and other savings, or was spent on private healthcare or schooling. It was also spent on frequent holidays abroad and consumer goods made abroad. After income inequality peaked in the late 1990s it never significantly fell again in a single year, and so the inefficiency of so much selfish consumption by the better-off continued at what was by then a very high annual rate.

Henderson was right to say that the nation's descent from the very top ranks had been going on since the middle of the nineteenth century, when its rise due to amassing a huge empire peaked. Even so, for most people in Britain, living conditions in the middle of that century were dire, and often much worse than for many people elsewhere in the world, even in some of the countries we colonised. This, despite Britain then being the richest country on the planet.

In the middle of the nineteenth century infant mortality in Britain was so very high, and adult health so bad, that the average age of death for people born into the labouring classes was fifteen in Liverpool, seventeen in Manchester and nineteen in Bolton and Leeds. In rural Rutland it was thirty-eight.[17] The ravages of infectious diseases in the newly industrialised cities were terrible, and the importance of providing clean water was very poorly understood. While most people were born into the labouring classes, in Liverpool and Bolton even members of the highest professional classes had life expectancies below that of agricultural labourers in Rutland!

You might have thought such shocking statistics would have disappeared over the nearly 200 years that followed, but while infant mortality did plummet, some of the other inequalities of the nineteenth century actually widened. People do live longer now, but not more equitably. By the start of the twenty-first century, Rutland, which in the nineteenth century had been in good health because it was a remote rural area, had become a safe, affluent enclave for the better-off. By 2011, of every 2,174 women aged sixteen to seventy-four in the highest social class in Rutland, one died each year on average.[18] In contrast, in Manchester, men in the same age band but from the lowest social class were twenty-two times more likely to die, and those in Leeds and Liverpool fourteen

times more likely. When you look at adult mortality, the risk of
death in England was more unequal (albeit much lower) in the
twenty-first century than it had been in the nineteenth, whether
we consider it by class, gender or geography. The borders between
areas and groups matter far more now than they used to.

It is not hard to find statistics that reveal how terrible the state
of things now is. Nor is it hard to produce graphs similar to those
at the end of Nicholas Henderson's 1979 memo showing the UK
falling down the international ranks. What is harder to explain is
why it has taken people in Britain so very long to accept that there
has been such a great deterioration in their circumstances relative
to people living in other quite similar countries, and why they are
so easily taken in by promises from most of their politicians that
all this can be quickly and easily remedied just by voting for them.
Many voters are of course more cynical than that, and in most
constituencies their vote makes very little difference anyway, but
there is still something unusual about the constant message given
to the British that better times lie just ahead.

By 2015 the UK had become unique among the affluent countries of the world. Like most countries its GDP had grown a little
since 2007, after falling due to the financial crash of 2008. However,
unlike any other country in which GDP had grown, the wages of
people across the UK were 1 per cent lower in 2015 than they had
been in 2007! This put the UK in the company of Italy, Portugal
and Greece, which had also seen wages fall in real terms. But the
UK was not really in the same league as those countries, because
they had had no choice given that their GDP had fallen. In Britain,
what recovery there was in terms of GDP had all been taken
advantage of by those who owned companies and shares, with the
bosses and the wealthy taking a little more on top of that for good
measure.[19]

Break-Up

More than any other state in Western Europe, the UK is currently on course to disintegrate politically. The UK was never a happy union of four countries. The union arose through conquest, with England seen as the aggressor controlling its smaller siblings with antipathy and sometimes open contempt. Wales was the first to be conquered in battle, and Ireland was the first colony in what became the British Empire. Scotland joined the union at the beginning of the eighteenth century in a marriage of convenience that is no longer so convenient. The peripheral regions of England declined when the triangular trade – textiles and other manufactured goods to Africa, whence slaves to the New World, and cotton back to England – declined, and again much later with deindustrialisation and centralisation. Since then, London has ruled, and more often in its own interests, with the peripheries increasingly living off the scraps.

Devolution for Scotland, Wales and Northern Ireland was introduced in an attempt to move to a more federal structure similar to that of Germany. But the UK can never reproduce that model while England remains so dominant and no English regions are devolved administrations. Today, the Scottish National Party (SNP) is the third-largest party in Westminster. The last time anything similar happened was in 1918, when the third-largest party was Sinn Féin, just before most of Ireland broke away. The SNP proposes independence for Scotland as supposedly the fastest way to secure policies to end the shattering of society there. Northern Ireland is now one of the poorest parts of Europe, and relies for much of its infrastructure, such as electricity and water supply, on cross-border cooperation. Wales has had relatively little to show for having returned a majority of Labour

MPs at every election for over 100 years. Devolution has not been enough.

One very crude way of measuring the growing clamour for break-up is the rate of change in the number of nationalist MPs elected. The first nationalist MP elected in Scotland was Robert McIntyre, in a by-election held in Motherwell in 1945, although he lost the seat at the subsequent general election a few months later. The next Scottish-nationalist MP, elected in 1967, also won a by-election; one more was elected in 1970, the fourth in 1973 and then a further eleven in 1974. There was then a hiatus until three more victories were recorded in 1987, followed by a steady trickle of further victories until the SNP landslide of 2015, and the general election of 2019 when the party won forty-eight of Scotland's fifty-nine Westminster seats.[20] Over the decades there has been a rise in economic, political and cultural arguments for Scottish independence, but it will be through parliaments and the courts that the decision is eventually made.

In 2014 the first Scottish independence referendum returned a 55–45 'No' vote. However, the much narrower Brexit referendum two years later took Scotland out of the EU against the wishes of a large majority of the people living there. This was one of the reasons a second Scottish independence referendum was proposed for October 2023. The Supreme Court of the UK began debating in October 2022 whether that might be allowed and decided in November that it would not be. Support for the SNP in opinion polls in Scotland rose to a new high following that decision. Earlier that year, while on the hustings, hoping to become Conservative leader and hence prime minister, Liz Truss proclaimed Scotland's then first minister Nicola Sturgeon an 'attention seeker' with an arrogance that might well have helped Scotland further along its road to freedom.[21]

Cultural, economic and political issues also underlie the rising calls for independence in Wales, not least concern about the Welsh language. Again the rate of dissent is most easily measured through the ballot box. The Welsh nationalist party Plaid Cymru won its first seat in the House of Commons at the 1966 general election, its second and third in the February election of 1974, and its fourth in the October election of that year. But its fortunes have risen little since then. In the 2022 Parliament the party held only five seats at Westminster.[22] However, without the rise of Plaid Cymru, it is unlikely that Wales would now have devolved government.

Wales has far more powers of self-determination than any region of England, including powers to halt or even reverse privatisation of the NHS in Wales, to prevent any grammar schools being opened, and to triple the council tax on some holiday lets and second homes after April 2023.[23] One reason why the Welsh nationalists have not done as well in elections as their Scottish counterparts is that the Labour Party in Wales has broken away from the strictures of the Labour Party in England and now offers a far more radical option.

The most contested region of the union is Northern Ireland, which has the longest history of struggle for political separation from the mainland. This has been the hope of many since the partition of Ireland in 1921 and before, and the fear of many others. By the 1970s the mainstream British parties no longer put up candidates for Northern Ireland's Westminster constituencies. MPs for Sinn Féin, the Irish nationalist and republican party, have not taken up their seats in Parliament, as they do not recognise its legitimacy. In the 2022 Northern Ireland Assembly elections, Sinn Féin became its largest party for the first time in the history of Northern Ireland. The Northern Ireland Protocol, introduced in the aftermath of Brexit, means that economically Northern

Ireland is now more closely aligned with the rest of Ireland as there are no economic borders within the island. Instead there is now a new border in the Irish Sea. The British government's attempts to weaken the protocol and establish new borders within Ireland have so far failed.[24]

Britain has been splintering into fragments ever since its empire began to dissolve in the 1940s. It is surrounded by islands with weird constitutional arrangements that are not part of its official political body. In almost every case this is primarily for tax avoidance purposes. The Isle of Man, Jersey, Guernsey and some of the smaller surrounding islands are 'crown dependencies'. There are more such islands in the middle of the Atlantic, in both the north and south Atlantic, in the Caribbean, in the Indian Ocean and in the Pacific. There is Gibraltar at the entrance to the Mediterranean and a part of Cyprus that is still British. Even a segment of Antarctica is claimed by Britain as its territory, although this is disputed by both Argentina and Chile. Eventually the islands slip away, but the British try to hold on to them in their hearts and minds.

Within England itself, the regions are pulling further apart from each other.[25] The south-east has been becoming more and more unlike the north-east for decades, and all the regions in between are increasingly dissimilar.[26] Invisible borders marked by house-price cliffs have proliferated within England, between regions and towns as well as within cities. Within each region, even within London, more areas have been losers, increasingly separated from other neighbourhoods. Such divisions are established by the incomes people earn, where they can afford to live and their overall life chances.[27]

The government's 2022 white paper *Levelling Up the United Kingdom* implied that any part of England that so wished could have a devolution deal 'with powers at or approaching the highest level of devolution with a simplified, long-term funding settlement'.[28] However, the same commentator who explained this also suggested that 'as has been the case in Scotland, the result will probably be a "voice" rather than anything resembling sovereignty'.

The union is slowly splintering, like the empire before it. At the end of September 2019, the polling organisation Ipsos MORI revealed that eight in every ten people polled in the UK were dissatisfied with how Boris Johnson's government was running the country. Only two other UK administrations had ever had such bad opinion poll results – the government led by Theresa May just before she was ousted from office earlier in 2019, and the government led by John Major just before he lost power to Labour in 1997.[29] Such comparisons have been made every year since 1977, and only Conservative governments have ever managed to be this unpopular, and then only for a brief period. Liz Truss managed to break all previous records for unpopularity in 2022.

When the 2019 polling information was revealed, I wrote: 'The current Conservative government has the opportunity to take pole position and become the most unpopular government in at least four decades, possibly ever, if it plays its cards right.'[30] Less than three months later, at the 2019 general election, the Conservatives secured one of the largest majorities ever achieved, and then very quickly went on to become the most unpopular government ever – which was quite an achievement. Underlying it all was the shattering of the nation. Desperate for some stability, a majority voted to get Brexit done. They were then rewarded with more instability; and later, by the autumn of 2022, with the most unpopular government ever.

The shattering does now at least get mentioned more often. In the run-up to the December 2019 election, all the England-based political parties included references to the UK's high inequality in their manifestos. The Green Party talked of inequality as being corrosive, but made proposals that even they admitted would take a long time to have any effect. The Liberal Democrats, in their manifesto, mentioned the issue a little more often than the Greens, but mostly in the context of their conviction that staying in the EU would allow them to somehow better (but ever so vaguely) 'tackle inequality'. The Labour Party mentioned it the most, over thirty times, and pledged to raise public spending each year so that, by the end of the fifth year of a Labour government, the UK would be taxing and spending at just under the levels that Germany then taxed and spent – all with a view to making the UK more equitable, fair and just. Unfortunately, Labour did not explain it well enough, or point out that their tax and spending plans were so prudent as to be lower than Germany's.

Of all the 2019 manifestos, it was the Conservative Party's that mentioned inequality the least. The word appeared only twice, so these two references can be quoted in full as they are so brief:

> We are committed to reducing health inequality. We will continue to repair the damage done by Labour's disastrous PFI deals.
>
> The UK Shared Prosperity Fund will be used to bind together the whole of the United Kingdom, tackling inequality and deprivation in each of our four nations. It will replace the overly bureaucratic EU Structural Funds – and not only be better targeted at the UK's specific needs, but at a minimum match the size of those funds in each nation.

The first mention is a criticism of an initiative launched originally in 1992 by the Conservative prime minister John Major, and later expanded by the 1997 Labour government. It had been disastrous, but the Private Finance Initiative had first been introduced as a Conservative idea. Labour's mistake was to continue to use it and accelerate its use greatly to fund investment, rather than using redistribution to make that much-needed investment possible. The ideology behind the PFI was embraced by both New Labour and the Tories. The second mention of inequality in the Tory manifesto was not only a sop to the union, but also disingenuous camouflage for a policy of moving public monies away from poorer areas under the guise of 'better targeting'. This was actually aimed at Tory marginal seats, although it did not help them in the long run, as so many Tory seats had become marginal again by late 2022.

Deception

In August 2022, almost three years after the 2019 election, the Department for Levelling Up produced a prospectus explaining that the policy of a UK shared prosperity fund was, 'fundamentally, about levelling up people's pride in the places they love'.[31] People needed to be more proud of where they lived, so that they would be less disenchanted by the shattering of the nation and not see it for what it was. The prospectus suggested that perhaps a little more money could achieve this, but what it mainly offered was good vibes. The minister who was almost certainly responsible for drafting these words was Michael Gove; however, he had been sacked (reportedly for being a 'snake') a few weeks earlier.

Four days after the August prospectus was released, the former chancellor Rishi Sunak was caught on camera explaining in detail at a hustings that what the Conservatives were actually doing was diverting money away from poorer areas and towards some of the wealthiest parts of England, in order to benefit people like the Tory supporters in Tunbridge Wells that he was speaking to. One of his former ministerial colleagues, Zac Goldsmith, responded: 'This is one of the weirdest – and dumbest – things I've ever heard from a politician.'[32] Goldsmith did not necessarily mean it was dumb to do what Sunak said they were doing. He appeared to mean it was dumb to *admit* to doing it.

A year before the December 2019 general election, when all the monthly opinion polls were averaged, it could be seen that Labour and the Conservatives were neck and neck. But by May 2019 Labour had moved almost 10 percentage points ahead.[33] It was then that any residual loyalty to Labour in the parts of the national media that traditionally supported it fell away – at the very point at which it looked as if it might deny the Conservatives a working majority a second time, or perhaps even win enough seats to form a coalition government if it won those extra votes in the right places.

The prospect of that was too frightening, and so in the spring of 2019, long before Boris Johnson was elected Tory leader that July, what remained of the left-leaning mainstream British press withdrew its already grudging support for Labour.[34] The right-wing press had already poisoned the waters by demonising 'prominent left-wingers as enemies of Western civilisation'.[35] In combination, almost all the newspapers, and the broadcasters they influenced, encouraged many traditional Labour voters to disengage. It was that voter disengagement – Labour supporters choosing not to vote, rather than changing their allegiance – that gave the Conservatives their huge majority in December 2019.

Overall election results are a very poor indication of what is happening within a country. Instead we have to look at factors other than votes. One of the greatest electoral myths of all was that of a 'Red Wall' running across the North of England, an unbroken line of Labour-supporting areas. Local-election results indicated otherwise; in between the Labour cities of the North there were always Liberal and Conservative buffers. Wealthy non-Labour northern enclaves were also found within the cities, such as Nick Clegg's Liberal seat in Sheffield Hallam, George Osborne's seat of Tatton in Manchester and the seat of Leeds North East, which the Conservative Keith Joseph held for thirty-one years from 1956 to 1987.[36] Other than Liverpool, all large northern cities have a longstanding Tory enclave, and much of rural northern England has traditionally been Conservative – typified by Rishi Sunak's seat in North Yorkshire.

The social and economic splintering of the UK has also had an effect on the geography of its politics. Between the late 1970s and early 2010s, young people in Britain were increasingly likely to move south if they could. The population in many parts of the North became older, and usually these areas also became more conservatively inclined. Often retirees from the South of England moved north for cheaper detached houses and bungalows and a quieter life, spending the private pensions they had earned in London or its surrounds. The majority of the North of England did become more solidly Labour over the course of recent decades, but some parts did not, and there never was a Red Wall. Party loyalty, which had once seemed set in stone, was being undermined by demographic changes and migration, including of those who moved in to retire and those who moved away, in most cases initially to attend university.

The geography of where people live by age matters more today because political and social views have become more polarised across age groups. After economic inequalities rose in the 1980s, the Conservatives began to target older voters even more, because they could not rely on the shrinking proportion of the population who were doing well economically. They promised to protect pensions, hold up the house prices of the homes now owned outright by so many who were old, and respect nostalgia. Younger voters

BORDERS

were a demographically shrinking group, and traditionally less likely to vote. But if they could be encouraged to behave more individualistically, those who did vote would be more likely to vote Conservative. This demographic shift in political affiliations had geographical consequences that are still very poorly understood.

People in the South of England are more likely to live longer. Because of this, and because older people were more likely to vote for Brexit, a higher proportion of people in the South voted to leave the European Union than in the North, where more people did not vote at all in the 2016 referendum. The story we have been told of northern working-class leave voters being key to the outcome is markedly at odds with the data. Of all those who voted leave, 59 per cent were middle class (A, B or C1), and 41 per cent were working class (C2, D or E).[37]

One of the early supporters of Brexit was Michael Ashcroft, a former treasurer of the Conservative Party and a businessman with strong connections to the tax haven of Belize. Ashcroft said that voting for Brexit was 'a decision for the long-term future of the country',[38] the country he was presumably referring to being the UK. Ashcroft's polling provided the data showing that more than half of the votes to leave the EU were cast by people who lived in the South of England (home to a minority of the electorate). But his polls provide far more insight than that – often as much in the questions chosen to be asked as from the answers themselves.

As the UK shatters, we see the Tory party losing its composure. Three years prior to the crisis of Liz Truss's leadership in 2022, Ashcroft had arranged for a large opinion poll to be taken in the last week of June 2019, when Boris Johnson was competing with Jeremy Hunt for the Conservative leadership. The poll revealed that the word voters most associated with Jeremy Hunt was 'smug', while with Boris Johnson it was 'arrogant' – very closely followed by 'dishonest', 'dangerous' and 'unreliable', in that order.[39]

Labour lost the 2019 election so badly because (net) 1.2 million people who had voted for the party in 2017 chose not to vote in 2019. It was as simple as that. They mostly chose not to vote in the places that really mattered (that is, marginal seats), which made the outcome more devastating. And, lest we forget, a few weeks after he became Conservative leader, Johnson purged twenty-one moderate MPs from his party.[40] Only four of those twenty-one were allowed, or chose, to stand in the election three months later. It was a changed Tory party that came to power.

How did it happen? I can offer an anecdote that I think is illustrative. A man not much older than myself, who had always lived in the poorer parts of Oxford, told me shortly before the 2019 election that although he had voted Labour all his life, he could not bring himself to do so again. I asked him why not, and he told me he could never vote Labour while Jeremy Corbyn was leader. I asked him how he had voted in 2017 and he told me he had voted Labour then. Jeremy Corbyn became Labour leader in 2015. I didn't want to embarrass him, so I didn't ask him if he knew that. I suspect that in his mind it was a different Jeremy Corbyn, or that he had not really known who the leader of Labour was in 2017. The key question then becomes: what had most influenced this change in view?

The same analysis of the vote data that revealed it was Labour voters not voting that mattered also showed that of the roughly 66 million people living in the UK in 2019, by far the largest group was those who did not cast a ballot. Unlike in elections in Wales and Scotland, sixteen- and seventeen-year-olds are not allowed to vote in UK general elections; 20 million potential voters chose not to vote or were not registered, and a further 3 million adults were not allowed to vote, mostly because they were EU but not UK or

Irish citizens. The UK has never fully accepted that Ireland left the UK, and so, tellingly, all Irish people living in the UK can still vote in UK elections.

The number of people who voted for the Conservatives was 14 million, 9 million less than all of those adults who did not vote at all. Viewed in that way, the Conservatives' win was hardly a stunning victory. The 14 million votes they gained was 3 million less than those who voted for all the other main political parties combined – but in the weird British system of democracy, which does not follow the normal European models, a party can win a huge majority of seats with a minority of the votes. Furthermore, less than 10 per cent of people in any age band below forty voted for the Conservatives.

On 14 December 2019 the *Telegraph* reported:

> In a sign of the damage Mr Johnson's Tories have done to Labour, there are 24 constituencies that have voted Tory for the first time in decades. The new Conservative majorities in three of these constituencies is more than 20 percentage points: Dudley North (31.3 per cent), Bassetlaw (27.6 per cent) and Great Grimsby (22.2 per cent). All of these seats saw double-digit swings from Labour to the Tories. The seat with the longest history of backing Labour is Rother Valley, that had elected a Labour MP since Thomas Walter Grundy won the seat with 55 per cent of the vote in 1918.

However, when you look at the social geography of the four seats mentioned by name, each now contains at least three very affluent neighbourhoods – large groups of people in the least-deprived fifth of the population in England as a whole.[41] It is wrong to paint these seats as prosperous. They did not turn in 2019 because 'private housing estates and comfortable homeowners had crept up on the red wall'.[42] Enough of those estates and homeowners had been there in 2010, 2015 and 2017 too. It was because enough poorer people in those areas were persuaded not to vote at all in 2019. Of course, just by visiting them, you could tell that most neighbourhoods in these areas were not that prosperous and that people were not that comfortably off, as long as your eyes were unblinkered. But the statistics help too.

What we tell ourselves about places we have never been to are mostly myths. In the case of journalists working for London-based newspapers or TV channels and reporting on places outside the capital, they typically visit for a day and go on to tell the stories they came intending to tell. Geographical statistics are one antidote to this echo chamber of familiar narratives. No amount of fieldwork can tell you what lies in the minds of tens of millions of voters and potential voters. Instead you have to look at the polls, the social statistics and the changing geography of the outcomes for clues. But even then people do not always tell pollsters or statisticians what they really think. And they also change their minds and alter their memories.

When a state is failing, areas do tend to flip-flop between political parties. It is almost as if entire places are casting around for a solution, any solution, confused in the morass of decline. In 2019 in those so-called Red Wall seats, what mattered most was people not voting who had voted Labour two years earlier. But just a few years later, in local elections in the South of England, parts of the newly christened Blue Wall began to turn red surprisingly often, or yellow, or occasionally even green.

In the local elections of 2021, the traditionally Tory counties of Oxfordshire and Cambridgeshire saw rainbow alliances take power. This was a shock, because for more than forty years before the 2017 general election, Conservative areas had tended

to become more Conservative and Labour ones more Labour at
each election. At first it was at the local level that a change in the
geographical segregation of voting in Britain was seen, a segregation which had reached its postwar peak in 2015. The segregation
that had risen continuously since the 1970s has now begun to fall.
The 2017 election was the first to mark the change in direction
nationally.[43] There is so much more to see in careful analysis of
the data beyond the crude results. The 2017 election was the real
sea-change election – the one in which the direction of travel we
had been on for decades first measurably altered – when a nation
that had become increasingly politically divided by geographical
area first became less divided. That was continued in 2019.

It is true that in 2019 more people voted to 'get Brexit done' in
most places, often out of exasperation. But before that, it is also true
that, for the first time, more people in more parts of the country
had voted differently to how they had voted before or from how
their parents had voted. Many parts of the South of England saw
Labour votes rise in 2017 in ways that had not occurred since the
1960s, and then *rise again in 2019*. Shattered by the financial crisis
of 2008 and the austerity years that followed, encouraged by a new
more hopeful tone from the Labour leader in 2017, and distrustful
of the Liberal Democrats who had kept the Tories in power for
five of those post-financial-crisis years, people's voting patterns
changed: Conservative voting in the South of England fell and
Labour voting rose.

In 2019 the Conservative share of the vote actually shrank in
London and the south-east. These were the two regions, along
with the south-west, where Labour losses were lowest. However,
a rise in popularity for the Liberal Democrats in every region
also helped to split the opposition vote and secure the very large
Conservative majority. The SNP made huge gains in Scotland – an

extra fourteen Westminster seats – and lost only one seat. Nevertheless, and this was a key deciding factor, turnout was lower than it had been in 2017 owing to so many Labour voters deciding not to vote, and lower than in the landslide elections of 1979 and 1997. Beneath the crude headlines, fundamental shifts were occurring, and 2019 was no great mandate for Johnson.[44] The country he won was in many ways bankrupt.

There is a statistical measure that is used to determine when we are becoming more or less divided: the segregation index. The Conservative segregation index measures the proportion of Conservative voters that would need to be allocated to different constituencies to create an even distribution. The last time the country began to become less polarised geographically, in terms of the segregation index of the Conservative vote, was after the 1918 general election. However, the greatest fall in the segregation index occurred with the general election of 1945. Then it was the areas of the country that had least voted Labour that saw the greatest rise in Labour voting as compared to the previous election. A fundamental change had occurred. Just one factor in that change was the publication in November 1942 of the 'Social Insurance and Allied Services' report, more widely known as the Beveridge Report, after its author, William Beveridge. It made many suggestions, most of which were implemented, and the modern welfare state was created. The Beveridge Report was not radical, but growing equality and the clamour for something far better provided the context in which its arguments came to be seen as urgent and necessary. Central to that report was the identification of the five giants of social evil: want, squalor, idleness, ignorance and disease. Those giants have now reappeared as hunger, precarity, waste, exploitation and fear, and so it is to these and their current geographies that we now turn.

Part II.
Giants

3.

Hunger

There was never a golden age, but during the times when inequalities in the UK fell, a virtuous circle could arise, with each improvement leading on to and reinforcing others. The closest the UK came to achieving this was in its post-empire decline of the 1960s and early 1970s, as it emerged from 1950s austerity and reaped the benefits of the 1940s plan to slay the five great evils of want, squalor, idleness, ignorance and disease.

The five evils were named by an unlikely man, William Beveridge, the master of University College Oxford (1937–45). Beveridge was not a predictable scourge of poverty. Educated at Charterhouse boarding school and Balliol College, Oxford, he briefly became a Liberal MP in 1944. He was no socialist. During the Second World War he chaired the government's committee on Social Insurance and Allied Services, which reported in November 1942. The committee's report established both the need for and the promise of the modern welfare state.

Today, Beveridge's five evils have transformed into hunger, precarity, waste, exploitation and fear (the titles of Chapters 3 to 7 of this book). But before describing each new evil, and suggesting how each might be overcome, we need to know both how we got here and just how bad a situation we now are in. How did we end up with food banks – modern-day soup kitchens – opening up across Britain, half a century after the Beveridge Report sought to end the need for such things?

The Trussell Trust was created in 1997. It did not open its first food bank in the UK until the year 2000, near to its original offices in Salisbury, not far from Shaftesbury. The Trust was never intended to become the largest charity supporting food banks in Britain. Before 2000 it had been supporting children sleeping rough in that other most economically unequal state in Europe, Bulgaria.[1] Bulgaria and the UK now jointly top the Organisation for Economic Co-operation and Development's (OECD) league table for income inequality in Europe. The story of how the Trussell Trust began its operations on the very far side of Europe, but before long ended up concentrating on problems at home, is not as surprising as it first appears.

From the late 1970s onwards, the cradle-to-grave UK welfare state has been substantially dismantled, with the country moving towards a minarchy or night-watchman state, with minimal power over the rich and minimal support for the poorer of its citizens. However, the dreams of a few to create an even more libertarian government have turned out to be impossible to enact – as was seen in the fiasco of autumn 2022, when Chancellor Kwasi Kwarteng's mini-budget was rejected by 'the markets'.

Instead, we now have one of the most cumbersome systems of means-tested benefits in Europe, with outrageous sanctions and administrative delays, and hundreds of state regulators for private industries. The better alternative, as enacted elsewhere on the continent, was to transform welfare states into what many Europeans call 'well-being states'. None are without fault, and many have plenty of flaws. In places like Britain and Bulgaria, however, people have had to rely increasingly on charity when the system fails. There are now almost twice as many food banks in the UK as there are McDonald's outlets.[2] The poorest are increasingly likely to go hungry in the most unequal of rich countries.

The human geography of Europe provides us with a patchwork map of what works better and what doesn't. It is not just Bulgaria that does as badly as Britain. In some international comparisons Estonia also now tops the chart alongside the UK because it also has high income inequality. Furthermore, the UK often does the least to mitigate the effects of that inequality, such as the poorest becoming destitute due to the rising cost of fuel. In August 2022 the IMF singled out the UK and Estonia as the two most problematic states in a study of twenty-five European countries. The IMF researchers recommended immediate action:

> In Estonia and the United Kingdom . . . living costs for the poorest 20 percent of households are set to rise by about twice as much as those for the wealthiest. Putting in place relief measures to support low-income households – who have the least means to cope with spiking energy prices – is therefore a priority.[3]

How did the UK come to be more similar in many ways to some Eastern European countries than to Western European ones? Across the east of Europe, satellite states of the imploding USSR moved in different directions after the fall of the Berlin Wall in 1989. None were very economically unequal to begin with. Some went on to join the group of Europe's most unequal states. Others chose a very different course, and are now some of the most equitable in Europe.[4] Today, the most unequal states, like Estonia, are beginning to look more closely at alternatives (such as in nearby Finland, the Czech Republic or Slovakia) for a more hopeful future, especially in areas such as public transport. Few now consider the UK's exit from the EU to have been a sensible way to address inequality, poverty and discontent.

Poverty is worse in those parts of Europe where inequality is highest. There is no longer a simple divide between a well-off west and a poor east. The UK became one of the most unequal states in Europe during the 1980s, after having been one of the most equal in the early 1970s.[5] By the 1990s income inequality in the UK was even higher than in the 1980s, making poverty in the UK an ever more desperate experience. It then never fell by more than a tiny amount in any year, and always increased again the year after any fall.

Income inequality fell slightly in 2003, and by one measure (from the OECD) it fell again very slightly for a few years after the banking crisis of 2008. But overall, income inequality in the UK has remained stuck on a high plateau since the late 1990s. In contrast, income inequality in Estonia has either fallen or failed to rise every year since it was first measured by the OECD in 2013.[6] But while Estonia has started to change tack, and is becoming more equal, the UK has not. By 2017 the declining quality of nutrition among children in poor families was cited as a key reason for the return of diseases such as rickets in the UK.[7]

The UK became the most unequal country in Western Europe in 2007, after ten years of Labour government.[8] After nine years of Conservative government, it then became the second most unequal country in the whole of Europe, overtaking Latvia in 2019. When there are such pressing problems at home, it no longer makes sense for charities based in the UK to travel all the way to Eastern Europe to 'do good'.

Most people in the UK still imagine that people are, on average, worse off in other parts of Europe, or at least believe that they are better off in an unequal country like the UK than they would be elsewhere. There is a tendency to think this must be the case. But did you ever wonder why today there are ever more pawn shops, charity shops and gambling shops opening up on the UK's high streets?

In 2022 the descent into yet more crises in the UK steepened. As the summer began, research results from the Financial Fairness Trust were released showing that one in six (about 4.4 million) UK households was in serious financial difficulty. This was a much higher proportion than had ever been measured before. Over a third of those households had fallen into difficulties in just the previous nine months. Most had reduced the quality of the food they ate. Some pawned their possessions, often to get money for food. More and more used charity shops for clothes and gambling shops for hope. The majority of those households (60 per cent) had avoided turning on their heating for most of the previous winter and spring. Households with children were especially hard hit. A further 20 per cent of all UK households were not in such severe financial difficulties, but were still struggling financially.

Putting both groups together, 36 per cent of UK households were facing significant financial hardship by the summer of 2022. That proportion rose again by the autumn to 38 per cent in the revised Financial Fairness Trust estimates.[9] According to these, by Christmas a majority of people in Britain were saving money by reducing how much they used their oven or cooker. And then the prices of essentials rose further; at that point, chief among the rising costs was food. Even when inflation eventually comes down, the price of food and other essential goods will still be a major problem for over a third of households. The price rises were not simply the inevitable result of the increase in fuel and other underlying costs. Over winter 2022/23 the UK government did cap the retail price of gas per unit used, although it spread confusion when it suggested that the cap was set at £2,500 per household. This was not true; the figure was just the average projected bill. There was also mounting concern that the UK might not be able to secure an adequate energy supply, despite controlling the price per unit to customers. It would have been better if the government had ensured all households could afford a minimum amount of fuel, and then allowed the cost of usage above that to rise sharply. Similarly, when it comes to food, there is no need for crude price controls such as those Richard Nixon introduced in the United States in 1971, when all prices and wages were frozen for ninety days. Instead, much more subtle interventions can be made, and are being made in other parts of the European continent today.

Food crises are dotted throughout British history. The Act of Union of 1800 that brought the current United Kingdom into being was passed following two years of poor harvests. One of the first decisions of the new UK state was to send its navy to the Baltic shores of Russia to secure food supplies and reduce the chance of a revolution in Britain.[10] The revolution that had recently occurred in France had been triggered by poor harvests. The UK was born out of a food crisis, and its legitimacy as a state is now dying in a food crisis. It is uncanny that the two longest periods of falling wages in the UK were from 1798 to 1822, the period in which the UK was formed, and again from 2008 through to an as yet unknown (but hopefully in the 2020s) endpoint.

We are transfixed by the most recent aspects of the current crisis. As we stare into the headlights of the latest news headlines, we see what is immediately before us as all-important and do not easily notice the slow and general direction of travel.

Most British households have been in crisis for a long time. The poorest fifth of them were already spending over 51 per cent of their income (after housing costs) on absolutely essential goods way back in 2006. That rose to nearly 60 per cent by 2019, and will be even higher now. In contrast, the best-off fifth of households saw the proportion of their spending on these non-discretionary essential items increase by only about 1 per cent of their income (after housing costs) in those same thirteen years.[11] The essential items in that comparison were food, fuel, clothing and (non-leisure) transport costs.

To cope with the crunch, many poorer people have been cancelling or reducing routine expenses that are classed as non-essential spending. These include insurance premiums in case of fire, theft or flood, life insurance, and pension contributions. Those who did not have insurance policies or a pension to cut had to find other ways to save, beg or borrow from relatives, or go further into debt.

The 2022 Financial Fairness Trust report on families in serious financial difficulties referred to above showed that the government's attempt to target people in need was failing. When energy bills rose in March 2022, refunding some groups £150 of their council tax payments was not a well-targeted approach. This payment was said to be targeted because it applied only to people living in properties in council tax bands A to D. It ended up helping a slightly lower proportion of people in serious financial difficulties (40 per cent) than those who were in a secure financial position but received the rebate anyway (41 per cent). In fact, a quarter of households with an annual income before tax of over £100,000 qualified for the rebate because of the council tax banding of their home! These were the households most likely to have savings and least likely to have had to make any significant cuts to their spending in 2022. Furthermore, by August that year it became clear that 3 million eligible households had not actually been paid the rebate at all, because they did not pay their council tax by direct debit. These were the people most likely to be in financial difficulty.[12]

The poorly targeted £150 grant ended up as a farce, with the £450 million supposedly allocated to the most needy in England being much delayed or never reaching many of them. In Scotland, by the same point, the number of households that had yet to receive their payments was only 3,000. The state there was more efficient.

British government policies intended to deal with the various crises of the early 2020s have been utter messes. The Covid-19 pandemic was blamed, but other countries did not report nearly as many instances of fraud relating to furlough payments and other schemes, or anything like the same magnitude of equipment sourcing fraud, as in the UK.[13] However, what caused the most shock during the pandemic was not fraud, but rising hunger.

Food

In November 2020, the Premier League footballer Marcus Rashford managed to get the government in England to change its mind about allowing children to go hungry. The governments in Scotland, Wales and Northern Ireland had already decided that children in the poorest households should not starve during school holidays. On 9 November 2020, the UK prime minister phoned Rashford to let him know that £396 million was to be committed so that children in the poorest families in England could also have a bit more to eat over the coming Christmas, and during the Easter and summer holidays of 2021. This news was reported to children through the BBC's *Newsround* programme.[14]

In my 1970s childhood, *Newsround*'s reporting occasionally mentioned issues of food poverty in faraway places, but never within the UK. By the summer of 2022, government support had been cut to as low as £1.66 a day per child during the summer holidays in England, less than half the amount allocated in Wales, and less than the £4 a day allowed in some parts of Scotland. Unfortunately, no new football star emerged to shame the government into action that year.[15]

The last time food was such a topical issue as it is today was in the 'hungry' 1930s. The great shame then was the prevalence of soup kitchens, and the need for them to exist at all in the fourth decade of the twentieth century. That scourge had been identified as avoidable decades earlier. In 1904 the York chocolate-factory owner Joseph Rowntree established a foundation in his name with the explicit purpose of ending the need for soup kitchens. They had been commonplace for at least half a century by 1904, with Joseph's own father having helped to establish one in York in the middle of the nineteenth century.[16] It would be another fifty years before they were all but gone.

The old evil of want has become the new evil of hunger. We can now say things more directly and use clearer language than the Victorians. William Beveridge was very much a product of the Victorian age. He named two of the social evils 'want' and 'ignorance' after two children in *A Christmas Carol* by Charles Dickens. It was Beveridge's generation that helped usher in full employment and the unemployment insurance that ensured soup kitchens became a thing of the past. It was also thanks to the trade unions ensuring decent pay, and a political party coming into power that was prepared to end the scourge. A civilising influence had altered some of the elite, the William Beveridges and Joseph Rowntrees of the time, such that allowing people to go hungry came to be seen as sinful.

Significant hunger did not reappear until Margaret Thatcher became prime minister, introducing policies that caused poverty to rise quickly in the 1980s. In the early 1970s, one of her first acts as Education Secretary had been to remove the provision of free milk for school children, earning her the nickname 'milk snatcher'. The milk had been given to children to improve their nutrition, and especially their intake of calcium for their growing teeth and bones. The mass unemployment of the early 1980s, which Thatcher thought of as necessary, was accompanied by mass destitution. Eventually the mass unemployment abated, but in its place inequality increased, expanding the group at the bottom of society that had less and less money for basic needs – which often meant less food, and certainly less nutritious food for a healthier start in life.

There were other ways the poor were made even poorer under Thatcher than simply through rising unemployment, inequality and poverty. She is often idolised by her supporters as a tax cutter, but she was not. She did cut the size of the state and public spending, but she did not cut taxes overall. Between 1979 and 1990, the basic rate of income tax was reduced from 33 per cent to 25 per cent, and the top rate slashed from 83 per cent to 40 per cent. But at the same time, Thatcher raised both VAT (from 8 per cent to 15 per cent) and National Insurance contributions. The result was that the overall share of GDP taken in tax hardly changed: it was 30 per cent in 1978–79 and still 30 per cent in 1990–91.[17]

What did change was who paid most of that tax. Everyone has to pay VAT, including the very poorest. It is a regressive tax. And everyone in employment has to pay National Insurance, although those in self-employment pay much less. Thatcher's tax rises for the poor helped ensure that they had less money for food. Her fiscal policy made the rich richer and the poor poorer. This led to a growing need for charity and eventually food banks, at first slowly, and then in ever greater numbers, set up by volunteers – most of them wishing that they did not have to.

If we wish to see food banks disappear, there is much that needs to be done. Taxes need to be changed so that the poor are no longer taxed relatively more than the rich as a share of their income. VAT is a very unfair tax, and it should be minimised. Benefits must be raised above the levels needed to barely survive. Low wages need to be increased faster than the increases in the cost of food. How can all this be afforded? By ensuring that wages rise by fixed amounts across the board, not by percentages; by ensuring that high salaries do not rise when inflation does and that progressive taxes are increased to take up the slack of minimising regressive ones; and ultimately by ensuring that food is not wasted.

You do that by having a more equal society in which the well-off cannot be so profligate. You level, not up, not down, but across. In answer to how we can afford to end hunger: there is no need to import more food into the UK, or grow more, for there to be enough food for no one to go hungry. We waste so much already and would waste much less if its relative cost to the better-off were higher. The inefficiency involved in people with a little more money buying extra cans of soup at the supermarket to put in the trolley for the local food bank is stunningly high, and it does not get the right nutrients to the people who most need them. A more equal society is both a less hungry society and a much better-fed society.

Supermarkets can be taxed depending on how high they price certain goods. They can be incentivised to ensure that basic fruits and vegetables are available and affordable. To do this they would have to pay their shareholders a lower dividend, or increase the prices of other less essential goods. With their monopoly hold over consumers, they now provide a part-public service, so they have to be considered as part of the quasi-public sector, providing an essential service.

In the immediate future, school lunches should be made universally available across the UK all year round, and funded at £4 a meal to ensure they are high quality, because the food that children eat affects their long-term health much more than for adults. The prices of essential foods can be capped and supermarkets taxed or fined if they do not adhere to the cap. What is seen as an essential food differs between countries and is not merely about nutrition. In states more compassionate and equitable than the UK, the need for there to be affordable basic food and drink when you are out and about and mixing with other people is also seen as essential.

In 2014, a cap was successfully introduced on the beaches of Greece to stop greedy proprietors trying to charge more than €1.15 for a cheese toastie.[18] By 2022 simple price controls on basic foodstuffs had been extended to the food and drinks sold in airports, cinemas, theatres, bus stations, hospitals, clinics, archaeological sites and museums, passenger ships, trains, sports grounds, courts, nursing homes, universities and schools.[19] The items affected included bottled water of any kind, which was capped at half a euro for half a litre. A single Greek coffee was capped at €1.20, French filter coffee at €1.30, an espresso coffee at €1.45, a frappé at €1.30 and English tea at €1.30. Passengers travelling in first class could be charged more.

The point of these price regulations was to stop exploitation. By 2022 the price of a toastie in Greece had risen by 10 cents to €1.25, or €1.45 if it also contained ham. These were among the limited set of items that Greeks could always assume would be available at affordable prices when they travelled, and there were other controls for essentials they could buy to eat at home. The price caps kept down inflation, or in the case of the toastie at least slowed its price rise considerably. It is entirely possible to implement such measures – but it is hard to even imagine this happening in Britain.

If the price of cheese toasties on Greek beaches can be capped, a UK government could, if it wanted to, ensure that essential food items are affordable everywhere in Britain. Whenever a British politician says something is not possible, it is always worth checking to see if it is indeed being done elsewhere in Europe. They used to regularly claim that 'EU rules prevented it', but that was rarely true. Basic foodstuffs need not be unaffordable for anyone. We should not have to rely on one of the UK's largest supermarket chains making basic children's meals available for £1 in its cafés out of the kindness of the bosses' hearts (and to attract shoppers). In July 2022 the chain announced that: 'Baby food is also available as part of the initiative, with little ones able to enjoy a free pouch of Ella's Kitchen baby food.'[20] That offer ended on 4 September 2022.

At the very least, a government that wants to ensure we do not live in a country where people go hungry could pass legislation so that basic foodstuffs are not sold at prohibitive prices. If supermarkets and other large shops need to sell more fancy goods at higher prices to cross-subsidise, then so be it. If a government does almost nothing of any consequence to relieve hunger, then you have to assume that it wants a large group of people to be sufficiently hungry to cause them to desperately try to find even more underpaid work in order to quell their own hunger and that of their children.

Benefits

Welfare benefits in the UK used to be far more generous. In the past, those relying on them were fewer in number and much more evenly spread out geographically. But in comparison to average wages, unemployment benefit has halved in value over recent decades. By 2009, after twelve years of New Labour government, the UK had the lowest unemployment benefit for single people in Europe in comparison to average wages; the next most miserly country was Poland.[21] Benefits have continued to fall relative to average wages. This even happened during the fourteen years since 2008 when wages fell in real terms. Despite being a little better protected from rising inflation thanks to the 'triple lock', the British state pension also remains among the lowest in Western Europe.

At least we do now have minimums. There are now minimum hourly wage rates, in contrast to the situation before 1998 when you could pay someone as little as you liked to work for you. But these minimums are lower if you are under twenty-three, and in some areas the minimum wage – which was only £9.50 an hour, including in London, in summer 2022 – has become the most common income.

In many rural areas of Britain, as well as in Teesside, north Manchester, the Black Country, several parts of Kent, Essex and Devon, and in many other local authority areas (other than those to the immediate west of London), more than 10 per cent (and even up to 18 per cent) of the workforce is paid only the minimum wage. Across Northern Ireland it is 9 per cent, across Wales 7 per cent, but across Scotland only 5 per cent.[22] This compares with only 4 per cent in London and the south-east. Since 1998 the proportion of workers on the minimum wage has been rising, and it has become the most common wage for many types of jobs. Worse still, new zero-hour and self-employment business models mean many people effectively earn even less than the minimum wage.

Opposition to hunger, inequality and poverty is strongest in the peripheries of the British state. Scotland has reintroduced child benefit payments for third and subsequent children, in response to Westminster cutting them in 2017. In 2021, the Scottish child payment was introduced, and in 2022 it was extended so that all families on Universal Credit receive an extra £25 a week for each and every child up to age sixteen. Wales now strives to achieve well-being goals, which include concrete measures to create a more equal Wales. The Lancashire town of Preston has introduced a new economic model to build community wealth by trying to source goods and services locally. None of these national and local initiatives, however, are able to make much of a dent in the overall high-inequality programme of the London-based government. Britain did not become the most unequal country in Europe, apart from Bulgaria, by chance.

British Conservatives have tried many different policies to preserve the high inequality they have worked for and won. A large part of the reason they did not scrap Labour's minimum wage – and later even rebranded it as the National Living Wage, one which many people find they cannot live on – was in order not to have to address inequalities more widely. As just mentioned, in 2022 the minimum wage was £9.50 an hour for workers over age twenty-three (and just £6.83 for those aged eighteen to twenty, and £4.81 for sixteen- and seventeen-year-olds). The Trades Union Congress called for the minimum wage to be raised to £15 an hour for all workers, with a target of 75 per cent of median hourly pay. But that 2022 call was ignored by the Labour Party, which worried what potential voters might think about such a radical proposal, since so many people had been persuaded for so long to accept high inequality and poverty wages as normal.

Conservatives constantly come up with ways of trying to divert people's attention from the unfairness of inequality. In September 2021 they renamed one ministry the Department for Levelling Up, Housing and Communities. In 2022 we learnt that this department was only trying to 'level up' the pride people had in their areas – rather than their life chances and access to food, warmth and housing. This was similar to the diversion six years earlier, in 2016, when David Cameron introduced his Happiness Index for England, at the tail-end of his original Big Society joke. The cost-of-living crisis in the UK is, in reality, mostly a cost-of-living-with-high-inequality crisis. Those with less have so much less and so price rises affect them much more than people elsewhere in Europe, and more than people were affected in the UK when prices rose in the 1970s but wages were much more equitable.

The British welfare system has been re-engineered in recent years: instead of a welfare system, it has become a system of minimum pay-outs and frequent penalties (in the form of sanctions). This system of monitoring people and humiliating them is extremely expensive to administrate. The purpose is not to save money but to maintain control and a steep social hierarchy. There are now more and more groups that will suffer greatly when any new shock hits. Even with government mitigation, the rise in fuel prices in the winter of 2022/23 greatly increased destitution. But the underlying implication of policy is that government has tried to help, control and cajole, and so if someone is suffering, it is ultimately their own fault.

As that winter approached, in my home city of Oxford I heard a story of a baby being washed and cleaned in cold water because the parents could not afford the cost of regular warm water. In recent years there has always been some new story that shocks you. Fortunately, you now hear fewer people trying to claim that such things are not happening. However, people often still find it very hard to see how statistics about hundreds of thousands of families are the aggregation of so many individual stories of this kind.

Taking a closer look at the welfare penalties applied to the poorest, we see that in the first quarter of 2022 there were almost

50,000 sanctions, a big rise on the previous quarter and almost three times the number made in the last quarter before the pandemic began in early 2020. Sanctions result in the removal of a proportion of (or all) benefit income, almost always for 'failure to attend or participate in a Work-Focused Interview'.

Many of the people being sanctioned have in fact attended and participated in these interviews, but in the view of their 'work coach' they have not done sufficient work search or other activities. As the researcher who released these figures explained: 'The latest reported rate of sanctioning would produce 593,000 sanctions on all benefits in a full year. This would be the highest number since 2014, and higher than in any year under the previous Labour government, as far back as statistics are available in their present form.'[23]

The average length of a sanction is a month, but it can go on for much longer – deliberately and inevitably (in view of the inadequacy of benefits) causing immiseration and increasing the likelihood of mental and physical health problems, including anxiety, depression, hunger, fear, cold and occasionally starvation.

We could clearly choose not to return to the terrible levels of sanctions in 2014, when more money was clawed back from the poorest through sanctions than the sum total of all the fines paid in all the magistrates' and sheriffs' courts of England, Wales and Scotland for any crime committed that year.[24] But where do we draw the line in terms of what is possible? The public spending cuts of 2010 to 2015 resulted in the poorest fifth of people in England losing, on average, 11 per cent of their income as a result of austerity, compared with zero losses for the top fifth of households: 'There were a lot of choices, and the government chose to balance the budget on the backs of the poorest.'[25]

The debate in Britain over what could be afforded was dominated by less caring economists than most economists found worldwide. Economics in the UK and US has become an academic discipline that both attracts and retains people who tend to be less compassionate than most. It also makes them more callous the longer they stay in it, and it tends to eject those who are not part of this in-group.[26] In the UK, economics is also, incidentally, the social science that *most* attracts young people from the best-off families. Of all those undergraduates now studying economics at UK universities, nine grew up in the best-off fifth of households for every one student who grew up in the least-advantaged fifth.[27]

Out of eighty-six subjects studied at undergraduate level, the only ones more elitist than economics were dentistry and veterinary medicine – both pre-clinical courses that typically lead to lucrative careers – and classics (mostly studied at only a few elitist universities). As a result, when it is revealed, as it was in September 2022, that a quarter of households with children (and a fifth of all households) have had to cut back on the quantity and quality of food they buy in order to afford other essentials, economists are unlikely to be able to empathise from personal experience. Poverty is so far outside the lived experience of most of them. Some appear to believe that people must be exaggerating. In response to this news, a government spokesperson disingenuously commented: 'Our priority will always be to support the most vulnerable and we recognise that people are struggling with rising prices, which is why we are protecting millions of those most in need.'[28]

What economists believe reflects not only who they are, but also the culture of the country they practise their economics in. Child benefit in the UK is no longer the universal provision it once was. Since 2017, if you have a third or subsequent child you do not receive child benefit for them (as noted above, Scotland is the exception here). Everywhere, if your income is over a certain threshold, you no longer receive child benefit at all. The sanctions regime that plunges so many welfare claimants into misery was set up by an economist.

If you have never experienced or seen hunger, because you grew up in a well-fed, more equal society, or in a highly polarised society in which you were well off and none of your friends were ever hungry as children, then you may associate hunger with that feeling you have when you're a bit peckish. You may not realise quite how terrible and debilitating it is. Because of the huge social inequalities in who gets to study subjects such as economics at university in the UK, policy analysts will likely never have known anyone who has experienced hunger, and will be more likely to see people they might have spotted sleeping rough as being less like them, as less fully human.

Fairness

What is presented as normal and reasonable by policy analysts in the UK often appears abhorrent to other policy-makers in more equitable European countries. It is not just that those countries' analysts grew up in more equal societies, and attended university with fellow students from a much wider cross-section of society. It is also that so much else is now so different in those societies. For example, elsewhere in Europe, railways are much more of a public good, and are almost always far cheaper for everyone, by design, than they are in the UK. They are less often owned by companies trying to make a large profit. The same is true of European universities, was true of universities in the UK in the past, and is still true of universities in Scotland. In almost all of the rest of Europe, university education is a public good, to which you are entitled and for which you pay very little or nothing at all.

The argument for making some provision public is to ration it not by price, but in a fairer way, such as through university entrance qualifications. However, there are people who believe that as many things as possible should be rationed by price. In the UK this has even extended to government policy over having children. However, few people will decide not to have a larger family because they will not receive child benefit for a third child. Five years after that policy was introduced, researchers found that the numbers of third children born into poorer families had not fallen; the only change was that those families were now even poorer.[29] But suppose that the policy had been found to reduce the number of children born into poor families – would it then have been welcomed? It is not as if the UK has too many children. The numbers of babies being born has fallen hugely everywhere and continues to fall. In the next sixty years, world population will start to decline, which will bring with it a whole new set of concerns. There is no need to try to ration how many children people have.

So how do you distribute what actually needs to be shared in a fair way? With fuel, as with everything we use, we need to ration its use in some way. We need to reduce the profligacy of the affluent when it comes to heating their stables, swimming pools and multiple homes as much as they want. We need to encourage people to insulate their homes with free or subsidised home energy-efficiency improvements, but we need not do any of this by threatening the poor with cold.

In England in 2022, some privatised water companies rationed water when they introduced hosepipe bans. That was rationing brought about through incompetence and lack of planning, not because of long-term scarcity. The UK is not getting less rainfall overall. We already have rationing where we could plan to avoid it, and we don't have it where it is needed. The price mechanism, our main means of distributing resources, will only succeed in reducing the profligacy of the affluent to squander so many of our resources when they no longer have such high disposable incomes that they don't care about these costs.

The price mechanism works best when people have more equal incomes, and where there is actual competition between suppliers of goods, rather than monopolies like England's water companies. Millions of people have clicked on videos of sewage being discharged onto public beaches with captions such as: 'Private water companies, guided by the hidden hand of marketisation and competition, have determined, in all their wisdom, that we must swim in faeces.' The highest water quality and lowest sewage discharge in the UK is in Scotland, where the national water company is state owned.[30]

The price mechanism works quite well for goods such as clothes because there are few monopoly suppliers and people become quite expert at buying clothes as they do it often. People rarely become expert at buying a university education or a heart operation.

Economists have a clinical-sounding term for this: information asymmetry. What it means in practice is that there is no possible way for most of us to have the expertise needed to make an informed decision. Nevertheless, even with items that we do know enough about, such as clothes, the school uniforms most children are required to wear can be too expensive for many families today, and the unfettered market left to itself produces a wasteful abundance of cheap clothes. In more equitable countries, people tend to buy higher-quality clothes that last longer. Greater equality produces its own forms of more sensible rationing, such as not insisting children wear school uniforms (in Europe only the UK and its former colonies of Ireland and Malta have school uniforms). It is also now well known that people are also much less susceptible to advertising in more equal countries and are less bombarded by it.

When we don't ration scarce resources fairly, or ensure that income inequality is lowered, the most complicated, inefficient and bizarre systems of support have to be introduced. In summer 2022, when UK average real incomes first dropped by 3 per cent due to the rise in prices, the *Sun* newspaper explained to its readers: 'When inflation is rising at a rate faster than wages, it means that your money doesn't stretch as far.'[31] The *Sun* (owned by a billionaire) was trying to soften the blow. It didn't say that your money, including any savings you might have, was suddenly worth less. It just said that it would not stretch as far.

The newspaper went on to try to explain a part of the UK's incredibly complex and miserly means-tested benefit system (with its rule changes so frequent that it's almost impossible for anyone to keep up, resulting in many going without what they are entitled to). Having first told its readers that their fuel bills might rise by as much as £5,000 within a year, the article then explained that a proportion of them might be eligible for what it termed a 'giant' cost-of-living support package worth as much as £1,200. It mentioned that they might also qualify for a £150 disability payment, a £400 energy bill discount, a £300 pensioner cost-of-living payment and a £150 council tax rebate (the one that 3 million households previously missed out on). Furthermore, it pointed out, there was a Household Support Fund (although eligibility for that varies at the whim of your local council and there are now different rules in every local area). At most that fund could give a family in very straitened circumstances up to an extra £500. No family would be eligible for all of these payments, but even if they were, and they knew how to claim for them all, the figures above, excluding the arbitrary Support Fund, only sum up to £2,200, less than half of the then-predicted fuel price rise. That rise may not now be so large, but the *Sun* did not point out that the cost of almost all other essentials was rising too, which would more than outweigh any fuel bill price cap. The whole purpose of its report was not to advise people how to get these benefits, but to tell those who were managing not to worry about the poor, because there was supposedly plenty of help for them.

The UK benefit system is becoming more and more like the system ushered in by what was called the 'new Poor Law' when it was introduced in 1834. That law mandated 'outdoor and indoor' relief for the destitute. Indoor relief meant having to go into the workhouse. Outdoor relief was a series of paltry sums that only those deemed 'deserving' might be given. In summer 2022, UK politicians debated whether it might be better to try to reach freezing pensioners by increasing some pension credit payments (which went to the poorest), or by using the winter fuel payments allowance (which goes to everyone receiving a state pension). They had constructed a system so complex that almost no one understood it, and often their interventions were scattergun, with pensioners being told to go online to 'check your account in November and December to make sure you have been paid'.[32] The outcome, if not the intention, is that countless people struggling to cope do not actually get all the benefits they are entitled to.

The alternative to this mess is to aim for what other countries in Europe have already achieved, namely a redistribution of income for all households that is far more equal because pay is more equal and state pensions and welfare benefits are more generous. In the UK we tend to be unaware of how much progress nearby countries have made in moving towards this goal. As I write, France and Germany sit side by side in the OECD table of income inequality, separated by only four other European countries from the highly equitable Finland, and increasingly both are becoming more similar to that 'happiest country in the world'.[33]

Sometimes the opaque term 'pre-distribution' is used, meaning encouraging firms to pay higher earners less and lower earners more, before income tax is used to redistribute further. This is not some mystical utopian dream. It is what happens already almost everywhere else in Europe. However, the most important element in the mix of policies to achieve further increases in equality is progressive income taxation, but underlying that is support for more equal pay in the first place. There has to be an understanding that there are neither people who are worth dramatically more than the rest of us, nor people who are effectively worthless. It is this understanding that is the basis of the alternative.

When a country becomes as unequal as the UK, people are less and less able to understand how others live. I estimate that if you divide families with children in the UK into seven equal-sized groups by income (each group containing about 2 million children), then each group has at least 18 per cent more income than the group below it. However, the seventh (best-off) group has 35 per cent more than the sixth group.[34] The many people across the UK who found the initial real income fall of 3 per cent in 2022 shocking can presumably barely imagine living on an income 18 per cent or 35 per cent below what they live on now – and yet that is what the people most like them, but just a little worse off than them, already have to endure. The income gaps between us are far greater than the falls in real income due to the price rises we are experiencing.

Instead of addressing the huge divides that have grown up between us, we have tried to patch up the welfare system so that the very poorest don't actually starve or freeze to death. Despite that, every year in the UK, malnutrition contributes to hundreds of deaths, and thousands die due to living in a cold house or flat. This is why the UK sees much higher rises in mortality during the winter months than do other European countries. No matter what we do, further patches are always needed and a growing number of people, including what may soon be a majority of families with children, end up living on, very near or even below the minimum income necessary to survive. We talk of providing people with universal basic services as some kind of remedy, but many services that should be universal, such as dentistry, currently are not. Improving services alone, however, will not end hunger and want.

After the 1940s many countries in Europe looked to the UK as a model on which to base their own postwar welfare states, and their education, housing and health systems. Most did not dismantle what they had, but instead extended and improved on their achievements. In most European countries there are active and heated debates over what can be afforded and what should be done. This has happened much less in Britain, at least until very recently. The Conservatives have managed to subdue these debates in recent decades just by claiming that anything better is unaffordable. They now suggest that what used to be affordable no longer is, following more than a decade of austerity measures and 'efficiency savings' that have crippled most public services. However, the Tory government's response to the Covid-19 pandemic showed that a huge amount of public spending was suddenly affordable when there was a crisis that most affected their own voters.

The British must now look at Europe to see what is possible, what works and why no other large European society tolerates anything even slightly resembling the UK's regional and local economic and geographical divides.[35] Although some of the more damaging British ideas of the 1980s, 1990s and 2000s were imported to some parts of the continent, most notably in the east, there is also a growing awareness of how unusual the UK had become in Europe. Just before the UK left the EU, the European Statistical Agency produced a graph that showed how exceptional the country had become in terms of its economic geography. West Inner London recorded a GDP per capita almost ten times higher than that recorded in the north-east of England, in Lancashire, Yorkshire and Devon, across all of Wales, and in southern Scotland. But the divides were just as high within London itself – a tenfold variation! This helps to explain why serious alternatives are so little discussed. Because so many of the people who dominate public discussion live in the most affluent areas and tend to mix only with the best-off families within the best-off areas, their understanding of the less well-off is severely limited – and the higher inequality rises, the more blinkered they become.

Potential

> Our vision is for a society in which disabled people and those with long-term health conditions are able, where possible, to fulfil their potential and to work.[36]

This sentence is taken from the end of a letter that was forwarded to me, written by a senior civil servant in the Department for Work and Pensions (DWP). This was her reply to the welfare rights campaigner Mo Stewart, who wrote to point out how the department was using fear to try to force people who should not be working into work.[37] Stewart then replied, quoting the following research findings about the department's Work Capabilities Assessment (WCA):

What is constantly overlooked is the fact that the disabled community's experience of this DWP 'help and support' is via the politics of
fear using the WCA. The assessment is conducted by an unaccount-
able American corporate giant, with the fatally flawed WCA using a
discredited BPS [biopsychosocial] model which failed all academic
scrutiny. Every clinical lead in the UK demanded that the WCA should
be abolished, including the Royal College of Psychiatrists, the Royal
College of General Practitioners, the British Medical Association,
and the British Psychological Society, who all identified the WCA as
being unfit for purpose. They were all disregarded by the DWP, as is
the growing mental health crisis directly linked to the fear of the next
WCA, and the constant DWP threat of sanctions. To date, the DWP
have disregarded all published, independent academic research which
identifies the ongoing and inevitable public health crisis created by
social policies adopted since 2010.[38]

As I write, no DWP official has yet replied to Stewart. The DWP's
vision of society appears to be one in which people with disabilities
are either patronised or ignored. The model the department has
adopted amounts to victim-blaming, claiming that the inability to
do a paid job is very often not due specifically to a disability, but to
the person's mental attitude. The concerns of doctors are ignored.
Anyone who can be made to work, often irrespective of their
actual health condition or disability, will be made to work.[39] Over
a century ago the policy was similar, and out-of-work paupers
deemed fit to work, and so not 'deserving', were consigned to the
workhouse where they could 'realise their potential'. Of course,
those words – which imply that people differ greatly in inherent
potential and, consequently, worth – were not used then, as they
had not yet seeped into the vernacular of the British elite.

The first sociological graph to appear in an academic journal was a geographical chart of Poor Law areas showing variation in the incidence of paupers. It was published by the eugenicist Karl Pearson in 1895, suggesting a statistical normal distribution. In 2010 I looked at his data again and argued that Pearson had rigged his data to try to suggest that pauperism was a natural phenomenon and that the poor would not only always be with us but would grow in number if they were supported through welfare.[40] Those at the time who saw Pearson for what he was continued to argue for unemployment benefit and eventually won that battle. The battle today is all too similar in the shattered nation that the UK has become.

It was in 2015 that George Osborne, as chancellor of the Exchequer, announced that he was removing universal child benefit, including any benefit for a family's third or subsequent child. He never fully explained why. Was his thinking similar to that of Karl Pearson – that he wanted to discourage the 'wrong kind' of people from having more than two children? Not all third children, it should be noted: if you can show that 'the child is likely to have been conceived as a result of sexual intercourse to which the claimant did not agree by choice, or did not have the freedom and capacity to agree by choice',[41] you might still get a payment for the child. The term anti-poverty campaigners use for this 'deserving child' exemption is the 'rape clause'.

What have we become?

We have stepped backwards. Other parts of Europe are now so much more progressive. Some are on the way to introducing something quite like a basic income for everyone. This is the obvious next step forward. In the UK that step would begin with the restoration of a decent universal child benefit – hardly a radical demand – and with policies aimed at reducing childhood malnutrition.

The Trussell Trust story with which this chapter began described how those who started a charitable endeavour to assist Bulgarian children in 1997 ended up realising that it was just as needed within the UK, and just a few miles from the charity's offices. The Trust was founded in the year when it was said that 'things can only get better' – the theme song of the Labour Party that won power the same year, and that later introduced the current benefit-sanctions regime. Many things got worse in the years after 1997, rising hunger among them, although Gordon Brown's drive to reduce child poverty held that back for children, at least for a short time. But there was also a rise in awareness of what had been driving things to get worse. A quarter of a century after it was created, the Trussell Trust ends its description of itself with these words: 'So we bring together the experiences of food banks in our network, and their communities, to challenge the structural economic issues that lock people in poverty, and campaign for change to end hunger and poverty in the UK so that food banks can be resigned to the history books.'[42]

Some charities understand that they should not have to exist, that no one should be a pauper, and that it is possible for change to happen. They have come to realise that their existence does not alleviate the underlying issues, just as Joseph Rowntree realised that the soup kitchen introduced by his father in York in the 1850s was not solving the fundamental problem. Joseph's son, Seebohm Rowntree, would go on to survey the city of York repeatedly and show that by 1951, in his third study, food insecurity had all but disappeared.[43] Hunger has been eliminated before. It could be again. But as the UK shattered, those willing to use hunger to control others gained more power, and fewer people saw them for what they were – which is why they got away with it for so long.

4.

Precarity

In times of national crisis or emergency, the Scottish government activates the Scottish Government Resilience Room – the equivalent of the UK's Cabinet Office Briefing Room A (COBRA) or the US Situation Room in Washington, DC. In the past it has been activated in response to a terrorist attack or to deal with new unexpected diseases, but on 11 August 2022 the first minister of Scotland began to convene weekly meetings of the emergencies group over how to deal with the cost-of-living crisis and its many wider effects. The situation was deemed a national emergency. The first minister explained: 'This emergency may be of a different nature to the COVID-19 pandemic, but it is on a similar scale.'[1] At the same time, the UK's prime minister, Boris Johnson, was on holiday.

Precarity is the new squalor. Squalor was the name that Beveridge gave to the social evil of people having to live in slum conditions. Today, mainly because of the progress made between the 1940s and the 1970s, we have homes built to far higher standards than those most people were living in when Beveridge published his report in 1942, and older housing stock has also been improved. Yet we now have a housing crisis despite suffering no physical catastrophe on the scale of the Second World War bombings that so increased the housing shortage in the 1940s.

We have, however, managed to engineer our society to make it much less resilient. Housing that people can barely afford is precarious. The slightest misfortune can result in you becoming homeless. Tens of thousands of people are currently homeless, and millions more do not know how they will be able to pay their heating bills, rent or mortgage in the near future. One of the first decisions reached in the Scottish Government Resilience Room was to act to try to ensure rents would not rise and people would not be evicted.

From the far north of Scotland down to the heart of London, huge numbers are now living on a knife edge. Reports are starting to multiply of people borrowing from relatives to pay their rent, despite being in paid employment and often earning an average wage. These reports increased during the spread of Covid-19. But even as the pandemic abated, many other crises arose.

The term 'precarity' has most often been used to refer to insecurity in employment, but increasingly it is also about housing insecurity. If your rent or mortgage is too high then that also increases your overall financial precarity – your ability to pay for healthy food, to pay your debts, to do more than just survive. Redistribution of income is only part of what needs to be done if we are to become more equal. It is quite possible for there to be an increase in the incomes of the poor but for that group to still become worse off if their housing and other costs rise faster than their incomes. As the cost-of-living crisis deepens, landlords increase rents partly because of the rising costs of their mortgages, but also to maintain their own higher standards of living. The crisis – left to play out without effective government intervention – becomes a fight between social groups, and, for the poorest of all, increasingly a fight for survival.

Interest rates are increased by the Bank of England as it tries to quell inflation, but raising those rates also increases mortgages and consequently rents. Another reason for increasing the bank rate is the concern that there might be a run on the pound if investors try to pull their money out of a failing state. Higher interest rates attract money from abroad, including from people who are willing to lend to the UK government. But if the external impression is of a state that is itself becoming more precarious and less well governed, then raising interest rates may not be enough.

If you look online for maps of the distribution of deprivation, you will see that British cities are now the most divided in Europe. Within the UK, Edinburgh and Glasgow are as socially splintered as London.[2] The first minister of Scotland has very limited powers to change that, and no influence over what the Bank of England does. She (or he) can convene her emergency committee to meet weekly to consider what can be done with the resources they have; she (or he) can introduce slightly more progressive income tax regimes but cannot alter the fundamental decisions being taken by others on how the UK is run and the way it has been changing.

Housing

Many people suffer very little precarity in terms of how they are housed. Around 8.8 million British households own their home (or homes) outright and only have to worry about council tax payments and upkeep. The majority of these households are retired people. But 17.8 million have a mortgage that they must keep paying to retain their home, and 14.8 million households are paying rent, mostly in the private sector.[3]

Housing precarity has been allowed to become so bad in the UK because it is in the interests of a small but very powerful minority of people. Those who own several homes benefit from their properties' rising value, while people who own just one home may benefit in the long run by downsizing, but they cannot realise much of that benefit in the short term.

The largest privatisation in British history was the introduction of the 'right to buy' by Margaret Thatcher. That policy, introduced in the 1980s, had the unspoken aim of reducing the size of the social rented sector. That is why local councils were not allowed to use the money from the sales of council houses to build more council housing. Initially this was also one of the greatest apparent transfers of wealth to the poorest, as it allowed many council house tenants to buy their properties at a large discount. However, that transfer was short-lived, as many sold their properties on, often to landlords who then made the greatest gains. The policy also meant that the shortage of social housing quickly became more and more acute, as there were fewer and fewer homes to offer to those in most need. Most of all, the right-to-buy policy was a boon to poorly regulated private landlords.

As more council properties passed into private hands, a process called residualisation began – the leaving behind of those with the fewest resources. This was especially acute in council housing, where the dwindling resource became increasingly occupied only by the poorest. But as precarity moved up the hierarchy, that process ended in the 1990s. Researchers found that it had ended because of the 're-residualisation of private renting'.[4] The private rented sector had been slowly reverting to what it had been before most council housing was built. Today, it is once again the sector with the lowest-quality housing and the most expensive tenure.

In the short term, people who own multiple homes benefit by renting them out at exorbitant prices. In the long term, they make the most profit when they do the fewest repairs and do not insulate their properties. Rental prices in the private sector are only as high as they are because the social housing sector has been shrunk in the wake of right-to-buy policies with no equivalent effective 'right to sell' – a policy which would allow people with mortgages to become social tenants but still stay in their home when they have trouble with maintenance or making their mortgage payments. Rising interest rates and falling house prices would make this proposed policy more popular. The right to sell is just one policy a future UK government could introduce to begin to eliminate the new social evil of precarity, but there are many others.

If rental prices were lower, and tenancy agreements were changed by law to become more secure (as happened in Scotland in 2017) and permit rent not to be paid if repairs are not made, then more people might be happier renting, and the demand to buy a home would also reduce. Demand would also fall if fewer people purchased second homes. A major reason for buying a second or holiday home is as an investment – to profit just from its owner-ship. Who really needs a second home, or wants to holiday in the same place for years and years, or the bother of looking after an extra property, unless it is also to make a profit? If it were made more costly to own second homes, many would be sold, more housing would once again become available for family homes, and housing overall would become cheaper and thence less precarious.

The fact that arguments such as these usually get such short shrift when they are occasionally made is not because they are foolish. Across much of the European continent housing is much less precarious because the systems governing it are better. As the UK became increasingly unequal, a strong lobby built up which now ensures that little is done to reduce inequality in wealth and income. Housing is central to that. For this lobby, owning an underused property increases scarcity, which increases property prices, which increases owners' wealth; and increasing rents increases their income.

Had house prices only risen in line with inflation over the past seventy years, the average home in 2022 would have cost £63,300, or just over twice the median full-time UK salary of about £31,000.[5] Money is siphoned from the less well-off to the already wealthy when the former pay excessive rents, when they buy an overpriced house, and even when they keep up with their large mortgage payments.

So how do those who support the status quo attempt to justify it? They can hardly suggest that it works well! What they do – and what they have done since I first began working as a housing researcher in the early 1990s – is argue that we 'just need to build more homes'. They say that housing is a problem of 'supply and demand'. They might go on to blame building companies that hoard some of the land they buy, or the current planning laws. They might say people should complain less because the government (which they support) has spent a lot of money supporting 'help to buy' schemes (which, in fact, just increase house prices). Or they might even suggest that buyers consider the possibility of part-ownership, where you forever rent a portion of your home but can buy a part of it too, to 'get you on the ladder' (although this can turn out to be even more expensive than renting). All of these phrases are so overused that they have become part of the common language of housing. What is never acknowledged, however, is that we already have enough homes, almost (but not quite) everywhere.

In the short term we could very rapidly improve the housing situation in the UK by encouraging people who own more than one home to revert to owning just a single property. Only a small proportion would have to choose to do that for it to have a domino effect. We could also find ways of helping people who now live alone in large multi-bedroomed houses to downsize. The 2021 census (when the housing figures were released in 2023) reported another rise in empty bedrooms due to the number of new homes built being greater than the number of homes demolished, extensions being built, and the growth of the population being slower than in previous decades.[6] (The numbers for Scotland will not be released until later in 2023 or even 2024, as the census there was held a year later. Incidentally, this split in the UK census was another symptom of the UK further dividing.)[7]

The 2011 census revealed that of the 66 million bedrooms in England and Wales that year 22 million were unoccupied on any given night (assuming that only married couples ever shared a bedroom). Even in London, there were 92,000 more bedrooms than people to sleep in them, even if no one shared a bedroom! This count of bedrooms does not include all the potential and former bedrooms, the studies and 'dens', playrooms, walk-in room-sized wardrobes and the like. We have known for decades that there is a growing (and now remarkable) number of empty rooms in Britain.[8]

In the long term we do need to build more and better, but we don't need to build more to solve most of the immediate crisis. We need to build more in the long term because homes do not last forever, because we need more housing that is suitable for an ageing population, and because in a few parts of the country there are simply not enough homes and bedrooms any more. But we do not need to build in order to make housing less precarious or less expensive. The legislation required both to make tenancy agreements more secure and to tax multiple-property owners justly could be passed in months. We could also help reduce house prices by introducing much more effective wealth taxes on housing than just stamp duty.

People always find various ways to avoid paying wealth taxes. One useful thing about housing is that we can have taxes where if you do not pay the tax, you might no longer own the home. The well-off are remarkably keen to pay their taxes when not doing so would mean forfeiting their ownership of property. This would also be the case if a wealth tax on housing were introduced. Such a policy has been resisted by successive British administrations as being impossible, but it exists in neighbouring Ireland, where it is 0.1029 per cent of the value of property a year, rising progressively to 0.3 per cent on any property worth above €1.75 million.[9] Until we begin to tax wealth progressively, people will continue to say (as they have said for my entire life) that we can simply build our way out of the housing crisis. But most of those extra homes always end up being owned by the well-off, even if some of them are rented to the worse-off.

Until we change how we view housing, we will continue to see stories every Christmas about how roughly 100,000 children in the UK are homeless and housed in temporary accommodation. We will continue to top the European league tables of adult homeless deaths and poor-quality housing, with cramped housing for so many, and so many people living in properties that are officially deemed 'unfit for human habitation'.

Very poor housing conditions are now mostly found in the private rental sector, but they are also becoming more common in officially not-for-profit housing associations. In 2022, MPs called for housing-association tenants to be awarded compensation of up to £25,000 when forced to live in properties identified as being 'unfit for human habitation'.[10] It was a pity that they thought that the market mechanism of fines was the best way to deal with the problem, as the more exploitative of the large-housing-association landlords would pay the fines simply by increasing overall rents.

During the worst of the pandemic, we told ourselves we were going to change. There were countless stories in the press about what it was like to be homeless: three children living with their parents in a single room in B&B accommodation when the restrictions meant people were not allowed out for more than an hour a day; children kept indoors for weeks on end because schools were shut, with their parents 'trying to keep noise levels down all the time in case managers want you out. It's just unbearable.'[11]

A poor family often must spend the majority of its income on housing. Often much of that income is provided by the state and goes directly to private landlords in the form of housing benefit payments. In most parts of Britain, an average young family cannot now imagine being able to save a deposit large enough to get a mortgage to buy a home, but there is still – only just still – always 'somewhere they could go'. However, these are places with mostly only very low-paid jobs. A rich family, in contrast, can become ever richer by speculating in property, and can always opt to live where work is much more valued and better paid.

Here the solutions are known. So, the question is: why are they never applied?

The answer is partly NIMBYism. Property owners have been taught to defend their locality from the homeless, from immigrants, Gypsies, Roma and Travellers, from 'benefit scroungers', from the council that might want to build social housing near them, from any policy that might reduce their property prices. The worse the situation has become, the greater grows the fear.

Those living in any area other than the very poorest are the survivors; the people who can still pay the rent or mortgage in those places. Reducing the cost of housing and taxing wealth to ensure fewer rooms are empty would benefit everyone. However, in the short term this is presented as a threat to the housing-as-pension plans of millions who supposedly plan to downsize in old age to avoid poverty. Not a threat to current pensioners, therefore, but to future would-be pensioners! Housing policy must be part of a much wider set of policies, including on pensions. Rent regulation and wealth taxes alone are not enough.

We used to hear a lot more about social housing waiting lists – until they became so long that living in social housing became just a pipe dream for most people. In 2022, the *Big Issue* magazine compiled data showing that the longest wait for a social home could now be more than fifty years. The longest waits were in London (in the borough of Newham) and in the Yorkshire cities of Sheffield and Leeds. As a consequence, people are increasingly forced into private renting and often out of the areas in which they were born and where their family networks might be.

To avoid us seeing children sleeping rough on the streets, families with children deemed homeless are given higher priority. Nevertheless, in some London authorities, two-year waits for these families are now standard, with them being put up in temporary accommodation, often in a single room, while they wait. The *Big Issue* found that this was the case for nine out of ten people on the waiting lists in Tower Hamlets, and eight out of ten of those waiting in Greenwich, Lambeth and Brent. For them, the minimum time on waiting lists was two years.[12]

A decade ago in London, court summonses for not paying the rent doubled from 7,283 in 2013–14 to 15,509 in 2014–15, and there was a 50 per cent increase in the use of bailiffs. In the UK you pay for your own eviction: £125 in court costs and £400 in bailiffs' fees.[13] The number of evictions fell only with the onset of the pandemic of 2020. But once the temporary restrictions on evictions had been lifted, they surged again, to 4,704 in London in just the first three months of 2022, with a rate of acceleration suggesting that the record highs of the previous decade would very soon be exceeded. The number of repossession orders being made against mortgage-holders for non-payment was vastly lower, at just seventy-three over the same three months. But a year earlier that number for mortgage-holders had been just two families over the same three months in all of London.[14]

Austerity and the crisis in housing were part of the reason for the election of Jeremy Corbyn as leader of the Labour Party in 2015. Younger adults, who mostly rented privately, were drawn to support his policies on rent regulation – first those who were already Labour Party members, then the much larger number who joined the party during his leadership, and then the huge numbers who voted for Labour in the 2017 general election. Understandably, well-connected landlords and others who benefit from growing inequality fought back. They could not win the public argument on housing and so found other ways to discredit Labour, which lost badly in 2019 despite attracting over 10,270,000 votes nationally (other than in 2017, the 2019 total was the highest number of votes for Labour since 2001, but it was far from being enough). Renters lost out the most when the Conservatives won the 2019 election.

The temporary ban on no-fault evictions ended in October 2021, when the pandemic was deemed to have sufficiently abated. In 2022, as the eviction orders increased again, it was trade union leaders, more than Labour politicians, who came to prominence as they challenged official narratives around the current crisis, and both the government's and business's roles in creating and exacerbating it. Strikes became widespread, and there was a rise in resistance to evictions and to accepting what was happening without question. Tenants' organisations grew in size, in a process sometimes referred to as 'Corbynism from Below'.[15] The huge rises in mortgage rates that came in late 2022, which landlords quickly passed on in rent rises, added fuel to the fire.

Try to imagine that at some point the resistance to greed is successful and that a more progressive government, most probably a coalition, is formed. What if that future government's attempt to make housing more affordable causes speculators to no longer see the housing market as a good investment, so that property prices in future stop rising faster than wages? Falling house prices are already the case as I write (in February 2023). House prices might well fall more, regardless of government intervention, as confidence in the shattered state wanes more quickly. Investors would then have to look elsewhere to secure the kinds of returns they need. Some properties would fall even further in value, especially homes in poor condition.

Local authorities could then be allowed and funded to buy up property at auction, at the bottom of the market. That might stabilise housing markets in the future, and would also help rebuild the social housing stock far more quickly than actually building new council houses. Government would need to ensure that large asset-management firms could not outbid local authorities. We could, if we chose, end up with such a mix of housing that no one would know what is public housing and what is private – which would improve social mixing, create greater equality, and help in the long term to ensure prices do not rise so high again. This suggestion may appear to be utopian, but it is possible to imagine it becoming practical in a situation where falling house prices are undermining economic confidence more widely. A fairly random selection of what had been private housing would become state-owned homes.

Utilities

Housing costs are most people's biggest expense, and one that no one can escape. But there are other costs that are also unavoidable. Food and clothes have been discussed above. Other essentials include utilities – water, sewerage, phone, internet and fuel bills – as well as transport costs, and basic items such as soap, toothpaste and medicines.

The shattering of the UK has led to a growing number of people finding it harder and harder to pay for the basics. Others with higher incomes cannot see why it has become so difficult for so many. 'Surely people can afford toothpaste if they budget well?', a few of the wealthy who have no experience of destitution claim.[16] One reason people have to go without is that most of these costs have been rising while the real-terms incomes of millions have not. Many of those with meagre savings have depleted them as they have tried both to save face and to get by. This does not just shatter so many people, it also contributes to how shattered the nation as a whole has become. The UK is a state in which people live parallel and very different lives.

Utility costs have risen so much over time across most of the UK largely because so many utilities are now privatised. When I was a child, telecommunications and postal services were supplied by a state monopoly. Today, almost 10,000 businesses compete to make deliveries, with perhaps 100,000 vans criss-crossing each other's routes to deliver parcels and packages every day.[17] This is not only inefficient, and a contributing factor in the notoriously low rates of pay for ostensibly 'self-employed' van drivers, it is also highly polluting.

Access to the internet is provided to homes mostly through a single set of fibre-optic cables, and yet we have devised a market to make that delivery increasingly expensive. The wear and tear on cables should be minimal, so why is the price of this now essential service rising when the costs of installing the cables have mostly – though not yet everywhere – already been paid for? In some ridiculous situations there are now competing cables running under our streets. The UK is one of the most densely populated and most urban states of Europe, so why does it not have some of the lowest internet costs?

Countries on the European mainland benefit from the EU's aspiration for universal provision: 'Speaking to the European Parliament in October [2020] European Commission President Ursula von der Leyen emphasized that no one should be deprived of broadband for economic or social reasons.'[18] But more is needed than just a universal service obligation. There is a geographical incoherence in trying to split up natural monopolies and pretending that the information in the fibre-optic cables – or the gas and water that flows through larger pipes, or the electricity in power lines – is somehow actually being supplied by a series of different companies that manage to share this infrastructure. This is nonsense. But it creates new ways of extracting profit, especially from the least well-off.

On 6 July 2022 the French government announced that it would fully renationalise the energy giant EDF, after it had initially forced EDF shareholders to accept lower dividends to prevent fuel prices from becoming unaffordable. Privatised natural monopolies will increasingly find it hard to justify their existence as folk become less and less able to pay their bills. People would complain more if they understood just how much extra expense is added by introducing fake competition into a natural monopoly. We know that competition in the British gas market has been incredibly costly, but we often fail to acknowledge that the competition should never have been introduced in the first place. Attempts to make it palatable, for instance by capping fuel prices, resulted in bankruptcies. When the large majority (thirty-one)[19] of private gas providers ceased trading in 2021, the costs of their failures were added to everyone's bills.

If it is too expensive, then a monopoly needs to be nationalised or localised. Geography explains why you cannot have competing train services. There is a limited amount of space. You cannot have different companies with different trains running on parallel train lines, although when rail was first invented that was attempted. It is the same with fibre-optic cables today, even though they take up so much less space. When you are in the business of connecting buildings to services – whether postal services, electricity, water or gas – space constraints mean that the most efficient model is to share, not compete. No one would suggest introducing private pavements, even though some would like to see more gated-off communities.

The balance between public and private has become so skewed in Britain that we now have the lowest spending on public services of any large country in Europe, and lower per capita than almost all the smaller countries on the continent too. What is being argued here is that the British should become less American: less like the US, the only other rich Western nation to spend so little on the common good and to maintain the ridiculous pretence of competition being beneficial at all levels. The US also has the most roads built with no pavements for pedestrians, or lanes for cyclists, in the world.

It is often claimed that nationalisation is too expensive to be possible, but its cost depends on how much the companies being nationalised are actually worth and on what governments are willing to do. Once a water company is required to stop exploiting its captive market, then the profit its shareholders can make becomes so small that continuing to own shares in the company can even become a liability for them. This includes being properly regulated to stop wasting huge amounts of water. You might think that they have nothing to lose, because they have some innate right to always have limited liability. But in a democracy that can be decided by the government.

In just five years, between 1986 and 1991, a single private firm (Rothschild) was either lead advisor or heavily involved in the creation of twenty-five massive new private firms: 'the privatisation of British Steel (1988), the ten UK Water Authorities (1989), the twelve electricity distribution boards (1990), British Coal, British Telecom (1991)'.[20] There was not a great deal of competition involved in the organisation of the privatisations, and they did not take many years to achieve. If all that could be done in five years, then unravelling the mess could be done just as quickly because it is no more complex.

Utility services can be made very cheap, even free. In June 2022, Germany introduced a €9 public transport ticket. You could travel for a month on just the one ticket. Internal air travel within Germany fell by 49 per cent in the first month![21] This improved the lives and well-being of poorer Germans especially.[22] Spain went one better than Germany and introduced free train travel within that country from September 2022 until the end of that year, and then extended this to all of 2023.[23] What prompted both countries to act was the need to mitigate the rising cost-of-living crises. Europe's richest country, Luxembourg, has had free public transport for some time, as have the capital city of Estonia and fifty other large towns and cities in Europe.[24] In 2022, Italy joined the trend by providing very cheap public transport for anyone on a low income, as did Austria, while in France it was already affordable.[25]

This all makes sense. Private transport is very expensive. The whole country saves money by more people using public transport because so much less fuel is used to move people around compared to using private cars.

A well-integrated and affordable set of utilities, such as good public transport, helps to hold a nation together. It has wider benefits as well. There have now been thousands of studies showing how much more efficient public transport is in terms of carbon emissions in comparison to private transport. Way back in 2008, one study of people in the UK demonstrated that 10 per cent of those surveyed emitted 43 per cent of all greenhouse gases from transport use. It compared these to the least polluting tenth, whose emissions amounted to just 1 per cent of the total, or 43 times less per person. That study probably missed out the highest emitters of all, that small group among the top 1 per cent who use private planes. In 2018 there were 128,000 flights between UK and EU airports using private jets, and a further 14,000 trips to destinations outside Europe.[26]

Perhaps the most interesting aspect of the 2008 study is that although it made a number of policy recommendations, it did not include reducing the income inequality that underlies the high use of carbon-polluting forms of travel by the wealthier. Again and again in the UK, people tend not to see inequality as the underlying problem because they have become so used to it; they take it as given. Instead, carbon pricing and trading are presented as spanning the breadth of the debate: 'carbon pricing (technocentric) and cap-and-trading (ecocentric) of carbon emissions are two of the main policies to tackle CO_2 emissions and believed to have great potential to meet reduction targets cost-effectively'.[27] Countries with much lower income inequality invest more in public transport and have lower emissions overall. They do this without the need for any of these proposed 'technocentric' or 'ecocentric' policies.

Countries with high income inequality store up problems for later. It is not just that they insulate their homes less, but much else is neglected as well. In summer 2022, Mary Shepperson, an archaeologist and lecturer at the University of Liverpool, published a graph she had made using data collected during lockdown. She had looked at the details of around 500 UK reservoirs, searching for any that had been built recently. An average of one a year had been built in the decades up to 1869; nearer two a year from then until the First World War; slightly fewer each year between the wars; but more than two and often nearer to three a year until 1979. Then building plummeted. She could not find any major new reservoir completed since Carsington Water in the Peak District in 1991. She commented: 'The correlation between stopping reservoir construction and privatisation in 1989 is stark. I assume the money that should have been invested in reservoir capacity has gone into shareholder pockets, just as with infrastructure to stop sewage over-flows into rivers.'[28]

Privatised utilities need to be properly regulated. The UK national electricity grid is practically the only fully privatised grid in Europe and eye-wateringly profitable for its owners while being very expensive for consumers and not necessarily reliable.[29] Similarly, a properly regulated water utility would have an awful lot of reservoir-building to do to get up to scratch. The company would have the responsibility. However, it might end up having little or no money left to pay dividends if it did try to store more water (albeit on this very rainy island). Shares that pay no dividends rapidly lose value – eventually becoming extremely cheap for the government to buy. Fines could be calculated based on previous dividend pay-outs. Unfair, or just the chickens coming home to roost after all those years of negligence? Alternatively, a service as essential as water could be nationalised more quickly, rather than slowly, to be owned by society, as it is such an important foundation of life. It has been argued that this could be done quite cheaply and legally if shareholders were compensated for the amount they invested in improving the service in the past, rather than the amount of profit they might be able to extract in future.[30]

Inequality

There are a great many extraordinarily rich people in the UK. Not many in absolute number, but a lot compared to some other affluent countries. They also often have greater riches than the very rich elsewhere. It is hard to be sure, as they tend to be much better at hiding their money than those living elsewhere in Europe. They live in a country where the authorities are far less interested in what they might have than authorities are in other jurisdictions.

Tax avoidance is one reason why so many very rich people come here and stay here. The UK has had a non-domicile tax status since the French Revolution, which allows very wealthy people not born in the UK (or who had a parent from another country) to avoid paying UK tax on much of their income. In the tax year ending in 2021, 68,300 people considered it worthwhile to opt for non-dom status. Some public figures have rescinded this due to it being seen as a very blatant form of tax avoidance – most notably Akshata Murty, the wife of Rishi Sunak. She may have avoided up to £20 million in UK tax thanks to her non-dom status. However, there is still no publicly available list of all non-doms and what they do not pay.

The concentration of a particular group of extraordinarily rich people within the UK is one of the reasons why the state is so shattered. The very wealthy own almost all the newspapers that repeatedly suggest that doing anything to remedy the gross levels of inequality in the country would be foolhardy. It was not surprising that initially the *Daily Mail*, *Sunday Telegraph* and *Daily Express*, as well as the Institute of Economic Affairs, all lauded Liz Truss and Kwasi Kwarteng's ill-fated 'mini-budget' in September 2022. The super-rich also own the UK's most successful political party, because they fund it; and at times they also own large parts of the other parties – especially when it looks as if the opposition might gain power. Ever since the late 1970s the rich have been key funders of any party in government.

The fall and rise of the very rich in the UK since 1913 is a V-shaped graph.[31] The data is remarkably precise. The pre-tax take of the best-off 0.1 per cent (excluding the top 0.01 per cent) reached a pre–First World War peak of seventy times the average (mean) income, and then steadily fell to ten times the average income by the late 1970s.[32] The take of the even richer 0.01 per cent fell from 425 times the average income in 1913 to a minimum of *just* (if that is the appropriate word) twenty-eight times the average income in the years 1977 and 1978. These income shares had been falling relentlessly for sixty-five years. Since 1978 inequality has risen back up as fast as it fell, although it faltered following the 2008 financial crash. By the time the pandemic hit, the take of the 0.01 per cent was back up to 130 times the average income, the share it had last been around the time the Beveridge Report was published in 1942. It may well falter again in 2023. Currently it does not look as if it will manage to keep on climbing for as long as it fell.

The UK is becoming rapidly poorer, now mostly as a consequence of having become so unequal once again. Internationally, it fell below India for the first time in early 2022, to become the state with 'only' the sixth-highest GDP worldwide, or the eighth highest using the better measure of purchasing power parity. That, though, is still very high – especially when GDP per capita is considered. However, that measure masks the fact that only a small minority of people in Britain have an income similar to (or higher than) our GDP per capita. An even smaller proportion have a lot of wealth – in 2019/20 only 3.8 per cent of all deaths in the UK resulted in heirs having to pay any inheritance tax, due to so few people being wealthy enough to meet the threshold. Of that tax, 47 per cent was collected from deaths in London and the south-east, with hardly any resulting from people dying in the north-east of England, Northern Ireland or Wales.

Moreover, almost half of all adults in Britain receive too low an income to pay any income tax at all! This includes many pensioners, the unemployed and students, but also a very large number of people in work too. At the same time, the people who should be paying a high amount of income tax are often very adept at reducing their tax liabilities, not necessarily through illegal tax evasion, but frequently by legal tax avoidance. There is a profession devoted to facilitating this, and it makes up a large part of UK accountancy work that often dabbles on the edge of legality. Strangely, accountants rarely seem to be struck off or brought to court for facilitating tax evasion.

The very rich hoard property, money and services. They use Britain's self-employed builders, plumbers and electricians to constantly refurbish their many homes; their children use the time of far more teachers and teaching assistants per child than are available to the rest. Per head, they have access to far more nurses, care workers, private doctors, waiters, shop assistants and a myriad of other people in work than anyone else.

It is our labour that we have most power over redistributing.

Taxing wealth means redirecting where that labour goes. Taxation is primarily a means of redistributing human resources rather than money. The raising of wealth taxes would increase the time electricians have to fix the dangerous wiring in a poor family's home, instead of installing more underwater lights in a luxury swimming pool. It would also ensure that there is more time to repair dilapidated housing stock, insulate homes properly, repair public roads and adequately care for the sick and needy. But before such progress is possible, we need to curtail the excess of the rich in Britain just to begin to alleviate the hunger of the poorest, just to deal with the immediate effects of precarity and to readjust our priorities.

The very rich are not just good at avoiding paying tax, they are also good at avoiding being investigated over their tax affairs. Inland Revenue – part of HM Revenue and Customs (HMRC) – do not release detailed data on the number of investigations undertaken per taxpayer in each area. In the United States, however, such data is released. There you are most likely to be investigated over your tax return if you live in Humphreys County, Mississippi, where the majority of people are black and over a third live under the very miserly US poverty line.[33] People who live in more affluent US counties are audited far less often.

An overhaul of the HMRC is required so that at the very least we know the extent to which the same trend occurs here. We suspect this is the trend, but we do not have sufficient detail to pinpoint it. In the UK between 2010 and 2021, twenty-three times more people were prosecuted for benefit fraud than for tax fraud.[34] HMRC says that the figures for the latter are so low because criminal prosecution is only used in the most serious cases and that civil measures are preferred. However, you can't prosecute crimes that aren't discovered, or if the regulations are so complex that there are many loopholes. The 'big four' accountancy firms (Deloitte, Ernst & Young, KPMG and PricewaterhouseCoopers) provide the government with expert accountants to help draw up tax laws. Those firms then go on to advise multinationals and individuals on how to exploit loopholes in the legislation that they helped to write.

If you think it is a fantasy to believe that the rich can be reined back in, have a look at the data. In 2018 it became apparent that the take of the highest-paid company chief executives in the UK was no longer rising on the apparently ever upward trajectory it had been on since the late 1970s.[35] Income inequality at the extremes hit a peak in 2018, in both the UK and the US, and has been fluctuating in the years since then.[36] In 2022 the UK's High Pay Centre estimated that the chief executive to median pay ratio in 2020/21 was still lower than it had been in 2019 but warned that it could yet rise again.[37] It did.

By summer 2022 the FTSE 100 CEOs were earning 109 times the income of a median UK full-time worker, compared to seventy-nine times in 2020 (when there was a drop in CEO remuneration due to the pandemic) and 107 times in 2019. However, it would be remarkable if the biggest firms' chief executives were so lacking in awareness as to take a big pay rise in 2023. We are still in the territory of possible peak inequality today.[38] The take of the very rich is still teetering. We could be at the top, or this could just be a hiatus before inequality at the extremes rises yet again.

Those who examine the fortunes of the rich have numerous indicators they can follow for signs that they are either becoming richer or retrenching. One such indicator is the price and volume of exports of luxury Swiss watches. In the first half of 2022, exports of Swiss watches to China slumped by 65 per cent. They had rebounded overall, but that might simply have been because during the pandemic a great deal of production was halted and retailers closed their doors. As one source reported: 'Pricey timepieces valued at more than 3,000 francs [£2,650] continued to drive gains. Swiss watchmakers have been relying on selling fewer high-priced watches to fuel the recovery.'[39] Selling fewer, other than the most expensive, suggests more nervousness among the very rich but not among the most extremely rich buyers. Similarly, in recent years the wealth of the best-off 250 families in the UK has continued to rise, but since 2020 the next best-off 750 families have not done as well.[40]

When extreme inequality appeared to have peaked in the UK in March 2018, the prime minister, Theresa May, stated in her Integrated Communities Strategy green paper that she would 'build a country that works for everyone . . . in which everyone, whatever their background, can go as far as their hard work will take them'.[41] She herself thought she had finally made it to the top because of her 'hard work'. She was not there for long and was replaced by Boris Johnson, who famously did not work nearly as hard.

People tend to think they are in the economic group above the group they are really in – until it is too late. Writing about the wildfires in California in the summer of 2018, Ajay Singh Chaudhary pointed out that celebrities Kanye West and Kim Kardashian avoided losing one of their homes to the fires 'through the intervention of a private firefighting force'.[42] Chaudhary was not criticising them for their behaviour, but was simply reporting a trend, although he did point out that, by diverting resources, protecting private assets can be at odds with saving lives. The equivalent story in the UK might be the rapid rise in private hospitals and private medical treatment diverting scarce medical resources from those who need them the most.

Chaudhary's point was that when it comes to external threats, even ones as large as climate change, we are not all in it together

and even the rich are extremely divided. Some Californian celebrities who had not taken out elite private insurance saw their
homes burn, or at least parts of them (some of their homes are
very big). For the very rich, climate change need not be seen as
apocalyptic; they believe they will find ways to deal with even
its worst predicted outcomes. That is one reason why so little is
actually done to mitigate the risks by curtailing overall carbon
dioxide pollution.

Chaudhary also explained that squirrelling away funds offshore
began after the First World War, when income inequalities in
all rich nations began to plummet. It was then that the very rich
began to use the treasure islands. He estimated that, today, a tenth
of all global GDP sits in these offshore funds. Over that period,
the sum may have risen, dipped and then risen again, but because
of the secrecy around these tax havens, we simply do not know.
These islands remain mostly British protectorates, where money
is safe from the scrutiny of the US tax authorities. The British,
more than any other people on earth, could alter how the treasure
islands operate.

The rich have a huge fear of precarity, despite suffering from
it the least. Many of them are mortally afraid of ever being more
ordinary. Some of them know, far better than most of us do, just
how hard their agents work to extract profit from ordinary people.
But their huge wealth is not necessarily as protective as they might
believe. Those who know this become even more paranoid, or
else resign themselves to a disastrous outcome where all they can
do is try to extend the time they have to live in luxury as long as
they can, and increasingly rely on their own private security and
health services.

Tackling the excess wealth holdings of the very richest matters
most of all because it takes only a tiny number of very rich

individuals to run a huge disinformation campaign, one which is especially effective in those parts of the mainstream media that they own, and goes unchallenged by the politicians they fund. They know that the current system is unsustainable; they just want to sustain it for a few more decades so that life, for them, can continue as it is. Or at least until an alternative that they find acceptable is proposed.

Downsizing

> The next few months are going to be incredibly difficult: going through every single item I possess and condensing it by about 80% so that what I have left will fit into a one-bedroom flat. The bedroom will be for the growing teenage boy.[43]

Something similar could have been written by hundreds of thousands of people in 2022. This quotation happens to come from someone famous, which is why it was read by me and many others. The point of repeating it here is not just to illustrate yet again what is not working, but also to show that individuals cannot get themselves out of this mess. For people who run out of money, downsizing may not work out well.

Builders are not producing huge numbers of extra one-bedroom flats. As the costs of construction materials rise, they are building and converting less overall while continuing to build large luxury detached homes for the upper end of 'the market'. So how will all those whose fortunes have suddenly got worse downsize? They will have to squeeze into bedrooms in existing houses that are now increasingly being subdivided to accommodate two or three or more families, with often just one bedroom per family.

A vicious spiral results. Families downsize by sharing homes with other families, often families they do not know, as they vacate the more expensive property they were renting before. Landlords must lower the rent to attract new tenants or tempt back those they have lost, but they are unwilling to reduce the rent by enough to ensure this happens quickly. More properties remain vacant for longer. More landlords subdivide some of the flats and houses they own to allow them to rent them out at prices people can afford, overcrowding the property (possibly with a higher total rent income) but leaving other properties (for example, seasonal holiday lets) frequently vacant or underused.

Overcrowding at the bottom end of the rental market; under-occupation at the top. The spiral intensifies. We do not know how it ends because we have not been in this position before; but we do know that the market can produce incredible inefficiency. Already couples without children can often afford much more space than those with children. We know that Conservative governments will do whatever they can to keep house prices high in order to shore up the vote from their most loyal supporters and funders. Unsustainable, the market approaches a cliff-edge, with the cliff itself becoming higher and higher the longer house prices are artificially boosted.

In 2015 the Prudential Regulation Authority of the Bank of England produced guidance that the minimal deposit for residential mortgages should be no less than 20 per cent of what was being loaned. It may have been forced to do this because the government could not afford for people without such a deposit to buy homes, as it was providing so many guarantees against prices falling through its various 'help to buy' / 'first-time buyer' schemes. If prices rose quickly, and then fell, the help-to-buy liability would be huge. However, the effect of this limit was to make it easier for private landlords to buy yet more property, as they were competing with fewer potential homeowners. Interest rates then being very low, the landlords could often easily find the deposit from the profit they were making on the high rents they received from their other properties. The new regulation was a licence for landlords to extract money.[44]

The cliff has been rising rapidly in recent years, and as it rises new records are reached. In 2017 and 2018, households in the UK began for the first time to borrow more, in aggregate, than they were saving overall. The Office for National Statistics described the net borrowing position as unprecedented and explained that people were financing mostly from loans, but not new loans secured on dwellings, because too few had that as an option any more.[45] The pandemic briefly suspended that record, as affluent households could do little but save during lockdowns. However, figures released in 2020 showed that the net financial worth of all households fell even further as the estimated value of British private pensions also fell at that time.[46]

When it comes to balancing the books, the UK faces an uphill struggle. The answer that is almost always given is that in future we will dig our way out of our troubles through economic growth. We will then build more homes and somehow the market will ensure that they are shared out more fairly. This argument is wearing thin. Growth has been slowing everywhere for a long time, and more so in the UK than elsewhere.[47]

As times become even more desperate, new measures may be taken that were recently deemed impossible by those in power. We can afford to nationalise where nationalisation is needed. We can demand that natural monopolies act in certain ways, legislate that they must, and if they claim that they can no longer make a profit doing so, then we can take them back 'in house'. We need have no truck with claims that their shareholders will require great compensation. When you have bought into a business that starts failing, then you lose money. That is the risk that shareholders have purchased.

Only a small minority of pensioners in Britain have private pension schemes reliant on investments in monopoly businesses. In fact, only 6 per cent of UK listed shares are now owned by British pension funds.[48] Many pensioners will need a better state pension, because their private pensions will deliver less in future; but richer pensioners will have to get by with less if everyone is to have a decent standard of living. For goods such as oil, increasingly supplied from abroad, Britain will have to plan to use less. The old claim that economic growth will make a better future possible has not held since the 1960s. We should plan for less growth, and instead share better and use less.

Why are we told that pensioners will suffer if companies are not allowed to make vast profits? Because it used to be true. In 1990 one in every three of all UK shares was directly held by a UK pension fund. That proportion fell over the next twenty-eight years to less than one in twenty-five by 2018. Almost all UK shares are now owned by extremely well-off individuals (sometimes via hedge funds), not by pension funds for collective benefit. And the majority of those well-off individuals live overseas. They own 55 per cent of all UK shares, a tenfold increase since the 1970s.[49] How much control do people who live overseas actually have over the UK? We may be about to find out.

This chapter began with the news of Scotland convening its emergency disaster committee to try to find short-term solutions to the immediate cost-of-living crisis. The Scottish government has done a great deal, with the powers that it has, to try to soften various blows. It has tightened up regulation on private landlords, for example, but it does not have the power to do what a truly national government can do. In September 2022, however, it announced that 'emergency legislation will be introduced to bring in a freeze on rent increases and ban evictions in the private and social rented sector in response to the cost of living'.[50]

There is so much more we could do. For decades in Germany, the government has controlled how much rents can be increased by and ensured that tenants who pay their rent cannot be evicted. In Sweden, private-sector rent levels are set by national-level negotiation, not by individual bargaining. In the Netherlands, the quality of housing is ensured by government inspectors. In Denmark, there is rent regulation, as there is in France. Rent controls were revoked in the UK on 15 January 1989.[51]

A different world is not just possible, it already exists in Europe. Much of what appears impossible to us is already happening elsewhere. We simply have not looked. What is missing is the political will to change, and the understanding that change has happened elsewhere successfully.

5.
Waste

The old social evil of idleness – mass unemployment – has been revamped. Whereas William Beveridge was concerned with the waste of so many people's time and abilities because they had no work in the 1930s, today the unemployed are relentlessly criticised as skivers by politicians and very few people can be unemployed because they are forced to take low-paid work. Most importantly, countless people's time and abilities are now wasted while *at work*, rather than by the lack of work. So much of the labour we are employed to do involves filching off each other, casually stealing a penny here and a pound there. In the UK we spend more time than we used to persuading each other to buy things we do not need. And the UK public pays a premium for services that are not as costly in other countries.

The waste involved in so much of our working lives reduces our beneficial productivity and is one of the key reasons that our measured economic productivity is also lower than that of other countries. The growth and then dominance of financial industries in the UK has increased this waste and sustained the environment that encourages it to grow. Reducing this misuse requires us to better value our time and what we spend it doing. The route to prosperity for the majority of people is not the same route that leads to growing financial riches for a few.

Huge numbers of people are now employed in sales and marketing. Far more people than in the past now also work in finance and accounting, in all manner of jobs that appear to be focused on maximising profitability. An argument has been growing in strength and popularity that, in aggregate, these jobs contribute very little to overall well-being, actual efficiency or to making the UK a happier and more productive place to live and work.[1] This stance can appear to be quite judgemental depending on how it is put. Some people in some of these jobs enjoy their work, but many don't. Often, even when and where people do enjoy what they are doing, doing it well makes the lives of others more miserable.

Young adults worry far more than they used to about whether they will ever have a worthwhile career and whether, even if they do, it will pay them enough to live on. Some imagine that they might even enjoy their work, but it has become increasingly clear to them that the more their work involves actually helping others, the less they can expect to get paid. A state shatters when greed is put on a pedestal. Service, craft and care are all demeaned.

When looking at the increase in waste, it can help to focus on a particular place. The city of Birmingham was once the 'workshop of the world'. It became that workshop partly because Britain controlled so much of the rest of the world – a captive market, from which we bought cheap raw materials and to which we sold expensive manufactured goods. Britain made things that were needed within the four nations and elsewhere. We know that Britain has since deindustrialised, but we tend to be unaware of how much our residual manufacturing industry kept on collapsing long after deindustrialisation was supposed to have ended, and of what the consequence of that continuing industrial transformation has been.

Looking at contemporary maps of deprivation and affluence in Birmingham, it is clear that the city has developed a large core of poverty, surrounded by an increasingly narrow fringe of affluence. All of the UK's peripheral cities – those more than an hour's travel time from London – increasingly look alike, and in one way or another all of them look like Birmingham. Often, they also have a small affluent core, a miniature version of London's, but in none of the other cities is that core anything like as wealthy as in the metropolis. The Midlands, the North of England and the rest of the UK were abandoned to a particular 'managed decline', a phrase first used in 1981 by Chancellor Geoffrey Howe about Liverpool. In their 2019 manifesto, the Conservative Party recognised this and decided to reverse the process, promising to 'level up every part of the United Kingdom'. They even created a levelling-up secretary (the secretary of state for levelling up, housing and communities). Nothing useful has come of this so far.

Politicians talk endlessly of the need to increase productivity. However, they have helped to increase work in industries that on the face of it appear productive, but that don't produce much of substantial life-enhancing value. Car plants destined to make electric vehicles for a greener future close down. Consultancies that advise companies on how to project a better image of themselves multiply. Care homes become profit-driven and understaffed. Call centres proliferate.

Productivity

When looking at the statistics on what our economy actually does, and how most money is generated, the UK begins to look like a state that is consuming itself. What is more, this trend shows no sign of abating. All the statistics used in this chapter come from one source: the 2022 ONS estimates of how much each industry or business activity in every part of the UK has contributed to the economy each year. They are part of the 'Regional economic activity by GDP' dataset, and show 'Regional gross value added (balanced) by industry'. The figures are not easy to interpret. If access to what has been happening over the long term is required, it is necessary to download the ten-megabyte spreadsheet and make your own calculations.[2]

Since the last few years have been an economic disaster because of the Covid-19 pandemic (exacerbated by Brexit), only the period up until 2019 will be considered here. It is possible to compare how much money was being made (value added) twenty years earlier, in 1999, using the same classification of businesses and places. What has been happening can be clearly demonstrated by looking at how the share of each industry has either generally deteriorated or risen over the past two decades, rather than concentrating on short-term changes.

First, we will consider the UK economy as a whole. This is divided into over eighty areas of economic activity, so most areas account for only a small part of the total economy. But any small change in their share can mean a massive change for a particular sector.

The first eighteen sectors, in order of the size of their absolute decline since 1999 and as a share of the whole economy, are identified as: owner-occupiers' imputed rent (defined below); retail trade; food manufacturing; wholesale trades; the manufacture of coking coal used to produce steel, refined petroleum and chemicals; the manufacture of machinery and equipment; mining and quarrying; the manufacture of rubber and plastic products; land-transport industries including public transport; the manufacture of fabricated metal products; publishing activities; telecommunications; the manufacture of basic metals; the manufacture of computers, electronic and optical products; the manufacture of electrical equipment; printing; the reproduction of recorded media; and agriculture.

Altogether, this group of eighteen industries made up 15 per cent less of the UK economy in 2019 than it did in 1999. Some industries were not in the group in 2019 because they had already shrunk so much. Between 1979 and 1999 there was a 61 per cent fall in employment in clothes manufacturing in the UK, and that sector experienced a further 82 per cent fall between 1999 and 2019. An industry that had employed 365,000 people in 1979 employed only 26,000 by the end of 2019. Consideration may be given to the suggestion that we no longer need anyone in the UK making clothes. However, other European countries still have substantial garment industries, and when the pound falls in value the price of our clothes now rises directly in proportion to that fall.

The greatest change between 1999 and 2019 was a 2.7 per cent absolute fall in the share of what is confusingly called owner-occupiers' imputed rent. This is an estimate of the housing services consumed by households who are not actually renting their residence, but own their home, or part of it. As described by the ONS, this can be thought of as the amount that non-renters pay themselves for the housing services they consume.[3] Most people would think of it as how much you save by owning your own home. Imputed rent fell by so much because fewer people now own their home or have a mortgage.

To put it another way, when comparing 1999 with 2019, most people are worse off when it comes to the homes they live in than they were twenty years before. Fewer own their homes outright. Most of those who have a mortgage are paying more than people were in 1999, despite lower interest rates in 2019, because house prices have risen so much. Remember that following the introduction of the 'right to buy' scheme by the Thatcher administration in 1980, which sold social housing to tenants at reduced prices, the building of social housing came to an end and a new industry was created by the huge growth in private landlords. Many more people are now having to pay a private landlord just to have somewhere to live. Of course, there has been a benefit to some landlords, and this shows up elsewhere in these national accounts, but that benefit to those few is not large enough to outweigh the loss to the many.

The next largest fall in share of the total UK economy over these twenty years was a 1.1 per cent absolute drop in the retail trade. In 2019, its actual relative share was 18 per cent lower than it had been in 1999. And this was before the pandemic's dire economic effects. Think of all those shops that have closed down on the nation's high streets as compared to how many there were in 1999, and what replaced them, if they were replaced. This includes the independent stores that have closed and the charity shops that have opened. Many of the shops that existed in 1999, and which had disappeared twenty years later, did not just serve an economic purpose. They served a social purpose too. Many people who owned their own shop, or rented it long-term, were a part of a community fabric that was less threadbare than it is today. Today, buyers are more and more likely to use Amazon or a faceless supermarket chain to meet the needs that these shops used to serve.

Our 'nation of shopkeepers' has seen the share of the money that shopkeeping makes fall by almost a fifth in twenty years.[4] That may simply imply greater efficiency. Yet, the amount of goods purchased did not fall, nor did their value, just the overall relative take of the industry handling them. Retail employed more people overall in 2019 than in 1999,[5] but far more of those workers are now paid less than their predecessors and often have to work longer hours. These include the ever growing number of warehouse workers who are invisible to the public.

The next largest fall was in the share of money generated from food manufacture, which shrank to become 0.7 per cent less of the total economy (in absolute terms). That was because manufacture of food products suffered a huge 36 per cent relative fall in its share of the economy. Compared to 1999, the UK now imports far more manufactured food products from abroad. We make less of the bread we eat, with or without nowt taken out. The chocolate factories have been converted into flats to rent, and someone else somewhere else – often in far worse conditions than we used to have – monitors the conveyor belts along which our food is converted from raw materials into processed products. The reason this happened was that it was cheaper to import food products than to make them in the UK. However, as the pound has fallen, imported food has become more expensive and national food security is in greater jeopardy.

Businesses that sell to shops, who then sell on to us, are called wholesalers. Wholesale traders' share of the overall economy showed the next largest drop, although to one decimal point that absolute reduction was the same as in food manufacture: 0.7 per cent (a 14 per cent relative fall). Again, this could be interpreted as greater efficiency, but it only resulted in a very small fall in total employment in the sector, with 2 per cent fewer people working in wholesale despite that 14 per cent fall in its relative income. That fall without a similar workforce fall meant wholesale workers were on average being paid less than in 1999. Knowing facts like this, it is easier to understand why wages today are still lower than they were in 2008, despite more people being in work and it being harder to recruit workers.

When shops close, wholesalers can rationalise because they have fewer places to supply. This change is expected to produce an increase in productivity per person. So why didn't it? The economic activities that have seen the largest reductions in their share of the whole UK economy, being mostly manufacturing industries, may look as if they are sunset industries. However, their activities need to take place somewhere, and if they are not conducted in the UK then imports are expected to replace what these industries used to produce. Imports travel via wholesalers, so there is just as much work to be done and as many hands are needed, but margins are cut and wages fall.

Which fast-growing businesses have taken the slice of the economy that the above industries have lost? Often they have very obscure titles.[6] Note that even when these industries have grown in size in economic terms, that does not necessarily mean that they are employing more people. What is being counted here is the money being made, not the jobs created, although usually there are more jobs. The number of people working in real estate, for example as estate agents, doubled between 1979 and 1999 (a rise of 106 per cent) and then doubled again between 1999 and 2019 (by 108 per cent). We now have twenty-one people working in real estate in the UK for every person making clothes.

The following list of business activities that have grown the most in absolute money terms since 1999 includes examples in brackets when what might be included in the category is not obvious: other personal service activities (dry cleaning, hairdressing, funeral parlours); sports, amusement and recreation activities; accommodation (hotels); construction of buildings; office administration and business support activities; specialised construction activities (such as plastering); financial service activities; head offices and management consultancy; employment activities (temping agencies); social work activities (counselling); legal and accounting activities; education (universities); computer programming and consultancy; real-estate activities; human health activities (nursing homes); activities auxiliary to finance and insurance (stockbroking and investment advisory services).

The last six in the above list have risen the most as a share of the UK economy: legal and accounting by 0.7 per cent; education by 0.9 per cent; computer programming by 1.0 per cent; real estate by 1.1 per cent; nursing homes and the like by 1.4 per cent; and stockbroking and investment advisory services by 1.6 per cent.

What matters is that work in the UK has been shifting towards spending more time engaged in activities where more money is made from exploiting each other rather than helping each other. That is wasted money and time, but in the accounts it can appear as an increase in productivity.

Rather than consider the example of real estate, questioning how many estate agents are needed, how much money they extract and why that accounts for a growing proportion of the already overinflated property prices, we will next look at another less obvious sector.

Funeral directing is a service which is in the growth group, and one we will all eventually need. Funerals need not be expensive, but over at least eighteen of the last twenty years they rose in price faster than inflation.[7] When the price of a funeral rises, the funeral industry is then declared to have become more productive, provided that its employment and other costs do not rise as quickly. So, productivity in the funeral business is said to have risen, even though it was not burying and cremating many more people, or becoming otherwise more efficient, more kind or more caring. Instead, more staff time is spent sweet-talking the relatives of the recently deceased into purchasing more expensive funeral packages. More money is extracted from the deceased prior to their death in the form of funeral insurance, and the wealth of a few of the most successful funeral directors grows.

There are those things that one needs, which have mostly been made more expensive, and those things that one wants, or can be persuaded to want. The art of sales and advertising is to shift the boundary between what one wants and what one needs, and to discourage people from choosing – or even being aware of – the cheapest or most basic alternatives. What is needed in a particular society can be assessed by what most people consider to be necessities: adequate free or affordable health services, education, refuse collection and numerous other public services; access to utilities; and a sufficient income to afford everything else that is needed but is supplied by private enterprise. Charities have a small role in this, but what they provide is typically intended as a stopgap because adequate public provision is not yet, or is no longer, available. However, they do help highlight unmet need, as the rise in food banks in the UK has demonstrated.

It is unfair to single out particular service industries that have grown in size in order to point out this trend of money moving from the many to the few. And as profits have grown, there will have been some laudable improvements in provision, not just rising exploitation, and some sectors such as nursing homes will have grown because of people living longer. But, in both nursing and residential care homes, the main reason costs have risen is private finance taking an ever greater cut,[8] and, in at least one very prominent case, the managers of one of the largest care home companies wanting more too.[9]

There have been some big relative falls in the money being made by some economic activities. Forestry fell by a fifth between 1999 and 2019, while three-quarters of what was left of mining and

quarrying income was lost. We now import more wood and many
other basic products. In some cases there was no choice, as we had
exhausted what the UK once had. More people are working than
ever before despite some workforces having been partly replaced
by automation.[10] Because shareholder profit has been prioritised
over investment, some UK industries have simply shrunk due to
competition from more efficient companies abroad. Others have
shrunk because demand for their products has fallen.

We need not, however, have reduced ingenuity. Some 9 per cent
less was made from scientific research and development in 2019 as
compared to 1999.[11] The *Financial Times* reported that between
2010 and 2017 alone productivity in UK pharmaceuticals industries
fell by around 33 per cent. The total measure of goods and services
produced, less the production costs, had fallen back to 2001 levels
by 2017.[12] More and more was being spent on dividends, marketing
and advertising, than on research and development.

Most other economic activities have grown, but largely in areas
that exploit other people more, and they have grown least where we
make things for each other. The industry that has grown the most
in terms of employment – up by 209 per cent in the past twenty
years, with a threefold rise in its share of the UK economy – is
head offices and management consultancy. This sector had already
doubled in size by 1999, up by 107 per cent over the previous two
decades. Were this rate of increase to continue, then by 2059 almost
16 million of us would work as management consultants or in head
offices;[13] globally, 100 years from now, a majority of the world's
population would be similarly employed. That is obviously not
possible. These straight-line projections are included only to point
out that such a rate of rise must be coming to an end. However,
although the fastest relative rise has been in management consultancy and head offices, the largest absolute rise has been in finance.

Finance

The greatest shift in the British economy in the past twenty years has been towards office work. The industrial tables produced by the ONS are divided into many sectors, including financial service activities, legal and accounting activities, and the one that grew the most of all: activities auxiliary to finance and insurance (including stockbroking and investment advisory services). All these obscure labels hide a plethora of activities, each of which can be described as beneficial in some way, but when they all grow in terms of the amount of time spent doing them and the amount of money they generate as a share of the overall economy, then there are fewer people, with less and less time available, to do the essential non-finance work that really holds us together.

The gross value added (GVA) of people in Britain – a measure of goods and services produced minus the inputs – is reported to be highest in the financial heart of London. That is where we find the people who supposedly add the most value to the UK. They do things that the public is not expected to understand, because they are supposedly so very difficult and of such great significance. These activities are said to be immensely valuable for 'world markets', but they are actually of most value to the financiers in London and to a few people abroad who benefit from their involvement.

The government does have an economic plan: it is that our finance industry should become less regulated, and take ever greater risks, so that the trickle-down from that will sustain our future. This is why the financial services industry was so quiet during the Brexit debate and why one of the first acts of the Truss government in autumn 2022, and one of the very few not to be immediately reversed, was to lift the cap on bankers' bonuses to encourage them to gamble more. However, that economic plan relies on the rest of the world seeing the UK as a safe place to engage in financially. Although the brief Truss government greatly damaged that reputation in just its first few weeks in office, it was really an extension of Conservative policy and it has continued under Rishi Sunak's premiership.

It was George Osborne, who was then chancellor, who said in 2015 that if we followed his economic plan until 2030, the UK would become the richest large country as measured by GDP per capita. Osborne thought this was possible without Brexit; his successors did not agree. As the number of years to that 2030 deadline began to shrink, successive Conservative chancellors carried on peddling some version of Osborne's promise. In effect we were being told that the future profits which the finance industry would make from exploiting people abroad would more than make up for the burdens of living with a higher rate of exploitation within the UK, and that we would all eventually see the benefit. But patience is wearing thin.

Even if the UK were suddenly to become the offshore island of choice, and its GDP in 2030 (when divided by the population of the UK) were to be the highest among larger countries, that would *not* mean that most people in the UK would benefit. Before the financial crisis hit in 2008 we were told that finance provided 12 per cent of GDP from just 4 per cent of the workforce. But there was never a trickle-down effect that reduced inequalities or helped alleviate poverty – the money was not shared out.

If you think that the supposed financial wizardry involved is beyond you, it might help to know that 'working in finance' used to be one of the most favoured graduate destinations for geography students. While geography students are very capable, they are taught almost nothing in their undergraduate degrees about how financial industries work. A key reason for so many geography graduates ending up working in finance was that they were more likely to come from families with the highest incomes, who had connections with the City of London, sent their children to private schools (or lived in the catchment area of a top state school), and more often than not expected their children to go into jobs with very high incomes.

Finance was once thought to be the UK's panacea. It was credited with helping Britain regain what some saw as its rightful place after the Big Bang of 1986, when Margaret Thatcher deregulated many aspects of the financial markets, and the London Stock Exchange became more computerised. But that all ended with the crash of 2008, which hit the UK especially hard because of all the financial risk-taking the deregulation had facilitated. One group of economists and other key figures recently lamented how, while it had looked as if the UK was becoming more productive, it really was not:

> We caught up with more productive countries like France, Germany and the US during the 1990s and early 2000s. But that came to an end in the mid-2000s and our relative performance has been declining ever since. On the eve of the financial crisis, GDP per capita in the UK was just 6 per cent lower than in Germany, but this gap had risen to 11 per cent by 2019. Our GDP performance would have been even weaker were it not for strong employment growth, with hours worked having increased by more than two-and-a-half times the rate in France (11 per cent compared to 4 per cent).[14]

These words appeared in 'Stagnation Nation', the 2022 executive summary of the Resolution Foundation's interim *Economy 2030 Inquiry* report, directly beneath a curious headline: 'Britain's *huge strengths and talents* are not being harnessed: we are 15 years into a period of relative economic decline' (emphasis added). Quite what the UK's innate huge strengths and talents are is never made clear. Perhaps that was because the report's authors unconsciously realised that this was, when analysed more closely, twaddle.

It is also possible that this headline was inserted simply to break up the page. The second part of it is certainly true. The British have had to work longer and longer hours as they fall back economically. This is yet more time wasted. In 2019, workers in the UK worked longer hours, on average, than workers in any other mature EU economy.[15] Now that the UK has left the EU, there is even less control over how many hours people may be forced to work a week. Strong employment growth for such little gain is hardly worth celebrating.

Unlike in France and Germany, where people get to enjoy more of their own time (7.4 per cent and 4.5 per cent more than UK workers respectively), in Britain adults have had to work more and more hours as their wages fell compared to prices. That is not a good thing. The Resolution Foundation report (page 8) went on to suggest that GDP growth is essential for wage growth, neglecting to point out that it is the share of GDP that goes to wages that matters most. Over 100 pages later the report did suggest that reducing inequality matters, but then on page 138 revealed, 'The next step is to design the policies for us to achieve a richer and fairer Britain.' This suggests that its authors cannot see a way in which Britain can be fairer without first becoming richer.

There have been many similar reports over the past twenty years. All that changes, for the small group of us who read them, is that our collective sense of déjà vu becomes more pronounced. But these reports are increasingly running up against a counter-argument that says that the growth we saw in the past is less and less likely to be possible in the future, no matter what we do. What we do not hear enough about is how we could be happier and healthier, waste much less of our time, be better housed and educated and have far less acute poverty – all without great economic growth. If only we valued each other more, and possibly valued the better-off among us a little less, we could become better at sharing what we have, but this would take a fundamental change in the underlying culture of the UK and the politics of greed and indifference that is currently so dominant.

In a more equal society fewer of us would need to work servicing the whims of the very wealthy. Fewer of us would have to do jobs that are a waste of time. Fewer of us would need to work in finance. More of us could engage in more valuable activities. One tragic outcome of the shattering that has occurred is that we are less good at recognising what matters most. Everything is judged in financial terms or by tick-box targets that devalue what is truly worthwhile and what actually adds to the greater good.[16]

Valuing

How should people be valued, if not by how much money they make (or take)? I once talked to a doctor, a general practitioner, who told me how hard he believed he worked. He had been told all through school that he had worked *very* hard. He was told he was working hard when at university. During the long shifts at his first hospital posting he was told he had been working ever so hard, hardly getting any sleep, although if no patients needed urgent attention he was allowed to get some sleep while on duty. He believed he worked hard, and he did.

But when he started work as a young man in general practice he was shocked. Men of his age who worked in factory jobs looked so much older than him. It was physically hard work that had aged them. They were paid far less than him and had often been told they were lazy. But what they were doing was extremely hard work, and in comparison his life had been relatively easy. He had still worked hard, but he did not have to do so in a way that damaged and aged him prematurely.

When the UK was more equitable, status hierarchies still existed. They were often about the kind of work people did, and sometimes reflected inequalities in incomes from an earlier era, with vicars and doctors being ranked high by status despite not being paid so much more than others, 'only' twice as much as the average in the case of doctors in the 1970s. However, when people are increasingly valued by the amount of money they make, by definition they are not valued for their hard work or for their more socially useful contributions. The groups that are most devalued are those who do all the unpaid work, the caring for families, for children, for older parents, for partners who cannot do it for themselves and those who still choose not to do it for themselves. Care is possibly the hardest and most poorly paid work of all. We are still learning what hard work really is.

We should not value very hard work highly. There is no need to see work that is so arduous that it ages people as good. We could all work less and be better off. Reducing the working week could increase the hours actually worked by reducing sickness absences and idling at work. We should measure the value of a job by the amount of happiness it brings to others, not by the profit that can be made by the person employing the worker.

The relentless cry of the boss, and of the boss's political party, is that we are not working hard enough – even when it yet again becomes apparent that there is not enough money from work to go round, given the growing share that goes on dividends rather than on workers' salaries. Even as upper management take more, they continue to say, 'Let's all roll up our sleeves and get grafting', and then cut real pay and conditions. We need to better direct the time we spend working and waste less of it, rather than simply graft for profit's sake. This is how we can level across, rather than up, and all be better off as a result.

Six out of every seven companies that trialled a four-day week in Britain in October 2022 said that they were minded to adopt it as policy without loss of pay. Some 3,300 workers were involved in that trial alone.[17] There are many other options for how we could live better today. Similarly, more work needs to be directed by public hands for the public good, as already happens in almost every country in Europe and as happened in the UK in the past. It is not just that fewer people are then exploited as much, including all the captive customers of privatised monopolies, it is also that the work people do in a publicly owned and run enterprise can be better directed.

Work in the private sector needs to be better regulated. Funeral directors are now required by law to display a sign listing the cheapest funeral available through their business. That is a start. But to date there has been a tendency to regulate private business only after a public scandal, and only to mitigate the most extreme of the antisocial actions that some of the people searching for ever higher profits engage in. Look at how uncontrolled the private rental sector now is, and how reluctant the establishment is to do anything about it. The same is true of numerous other sections of the economy, especially those involved in finance.

Most people working in private business would dearly love to provide a more worthwhile service or a higher-quality product, but they cannot if in doing so they would be undercut by a more unscrupulous rival. Well-run private businesses need regulation to ensure they are not having to compete with less honest rivals. Such regulation can become over-bureaucratic, and that of course must be held in check. However, the thousands of pages of 'small print' that the private sector and its lawyers produce every year has put paid to the lie that the state is more bureaucratic than business. They hope customers and clients never read the small print, but they get them all to sign it for a reason.

The state can be a hindrance when it is used to promote policies that are nonsensical. The current government's levelling-up policy has at its heart a publicly proclaimed desire to raise the gross value added everywhere in Britain. So, what does the map of GVA look like and what does it really mean? You may be surprised to learn that the GVA figures (per hour worked) for the town of Blackpool and the city of Oxford are almost identical,[18] or that they are very high in the relatively poor Tower Hamlets but low in the picturesque and relatively affluent Torquay. In all of the UK, Torquay is only beaten in the low stakes by the borough of Ards and North Down in Northern Ireland.[19]

GVA is an awful measure of anything – not just of how hard people might work, which it has almost nothing to do with, but also even in terms of its own conventional definition of what it is supposed to be measuring. It is allocated to areas on the basis of the addresses of company headquarters. Even then it is just a measure of how much money they make. This is roughly the difference between the costs of raw materials plus running costs and how much the goods or services the company produces are sold for – hence gross value added. Areas with many pensioners or students, such as Torquay and Oxford, can appear to be very unproductive. Areas in which almost every working-age adult has to be in paid work because the rents are so high, such as Tower Hamlets, appear to be ever so productive.

Within England there has been no levelling up since the levelling-up policy was announced – quite the opposite. Despite the rhetoric of the levelling-up agenda it was recently reported that 'public spending on the North is lower, and has grown less since 2019, than in other parts of the country'.[20] Some people blame Brexit, and it undoubtedly had a detrimental effect, but it is now almost impossible to know by how much because Brexit did not actually start until 31 January 2020, one day after the World Health Organization (WHO) declared Covid-19 a public health emergency of international concern.

The pandemic caused many sectors of the economy to shrink. One way people can determine what effect Brexit has had is by comparing the changing size of different business activities in other European countries with those in the UK before and after it left the EU. However, before Brexit occurred, in fact even before the referendum on it was held, analysis was undertaken of what its possible effects might be on other European countries.

It was widely predicted (and belittled as 'Project Fear') that the UK might suffer because of Brexit. However, only a few small EU countries were thought likely to also be affected detrimentally: Ireland, Malta, Luxembourg and Cyprus.[21] In the event, Ireland did very well as the new alternative location for firms wishing to be based in an English-speaking country within the EU, and Malta has not fared badly despite being less easily accessible to British pensioners. Luxembourg has found new financial partners to replace the British, while the GDP of Cyprus was higher in 2021 than in 2019.

Even though the hours worked in Britain have increased, that does not mean that more people are working. As we'll see later when we turn to health, more people in the UK have been shattered physically and mentally than anywhere else in Europe. Fewer are fit to work, making the UK an international outlier in that measure. By April 2022, 600,000 fewer people were in the workforce than before the pandemic began. The prime minister, Boris Johnson, misled Parliament nine times in suggesting that there were many more people working in 2022, because he ignored the huge fall in the numbers of self-employed. The UK Statistics Authority repeatedly told him that this was misleading, but he never corrected the record.[22]

There is mounting evidence from around the world that people who have grown up in more equitable countries are more productive in their work. That is not just because they will have usually received a better and more useful education. They are also able to argue, innovate and improvise more at work. Jobs become less about appearing to perform, or trying to get the most out of your subordinates; they become a vocation to take pride in. This is what geographical analysis comparing countries reveals. There are many stereotypes of people from different nations being more or less industrious than others, but it turns out that when we enjoy our job and need not work as many hours in the week, we work better – we teach better, care better, produce better, waste less, think more and contribute more constructively.

High inequality does not necessarily mean that higher-income families have more to rely on when a shock hits. One further remarkable fact about the UK today is that 45 per cent of families in the top 10 per cent income bracket have less than one month's income saved. This is a higher proportion than the 41 per cent in the lowest income bracket! Overall, 47 per cent of all households in the UK have almost no savings, with the highest proportion with no savings (53 per cent) in the third highest of the ten income groups![23] So the high-inequality, high-insecurity society that the UK has become is not even helping make life more secure for those very near the top, with so many people living from one pay cheque to the next.

The Conservative Party favours lowering taxes for the better-off. Ostensibly this is because they claim (falsely) that this will stimulate growth and make the country richer. Could it be that part of the reason is that the better-off themselves are struggling financially? Boris Johnson is reported to have said that he could not live on his prime-ministerial salary of £157,372 a year plus extremely generous expenses (including two homes) paid for by the public purse.[24] The expenses scandal revealed by British newspapers in 2009 suggested that many MPs were either extraordinarily greedy or struggling to cope financially, as they were trying to claim every penny they could. High inequality makes so many people attempt to live beyond their means – keeping up with the Joneses – that it even makes many of the better-off functionally poorer.

Although people quite near to the top may not have benefited in recent times, those nearer the bottom have done far worse. While it is true that having less than one month's income in savings is evenly spread across the income distribution, the consequences for low-income families of any fall are far greater than for high-income families.[25] People on higher incomes can cut back immediately on many items, despite having many 'commitments'. They can eat out less, take fewer holidays, delay projects, and they can gain easier and cheaper access to credit should they need it. Some can even sell some of their property. But the lack of savings does suggest that wealthier people in the UK view a great deal of their current spending – on private school fees for example – as essential.

People at the bottom have none of the options of those at the top. Any unexpected increase in the cost of living leaves them with growing, and increasingly expensive, debt, or going hungry in a cold, poorly insulated property from which they risk being evicted because of rent arrears. A shattered and divided society becomes a very expensive society for rich and poor alike.

Prosperity

Boris Johnson resigned as leader of the Tory party on 7 July 2022. In his resignation speech he repeated George Osborne's 2015 promise, although he downgraded the claim from 'the world' to 'Europe', saying that if only we keep on doing what he wanted us to do, then soon 'we will be the most prosperous in Europe'.[26] Clearly, we will not. Before thanking his audience, he ended his speech promising that 'even if things can sometimes seem dark now, our future together is golden'.[27]

And then, before ceasing to be prime minister, Johnson went on a series of holidays, including at least two overseas. The promise that we will all one day get to visit the fabled sunlit uplands is a regular favourite of those who so frequently holiday in sunlit lands. We will become more prosperous, we are told, and then (and only then) can more of us have any kind of holiday at all.

It is through the holidays we take and don't take that we are now most clearly socially divided in this shattered nation. In the years before the shattering, taking an annual summer holiday had become the norm. For most people it was within the UK, but it was time off nevertheless. Now, each year, over a third of all children and their parents have no holiday that involves going away for a week or more and not staying with family or friends.

In October 1977, the Sex Pistols released the single 'Holidays in the Sun'. The lyric most remembered and commented upon was 'A cheap holiday in other people's misery'. This was a reworking of a slogan about Club Med that appeared on walls in Paris during the May 1968 protests.[28] By 1968, Club Med, a French package holiday company founded in 1950, was still a relatively small endeavour, but it had just expanded into the Pacific and the Caribbean, to islands where extreme poverty was the norm. By the 1980s, holidays with Club Med would become less cheap and more exclusive. However, very few people in Britain could afford to fly abroad for a holiday even then. It was only the more affluent who began to visit cheap destinations within Europe more frequently. Many more British people had no annual holidays at all.

Today, the key reason more people in the UK have no holiday, and a few have many each year, has been rising inequality. We increasingly waste people's lives by making them toil in drudgery, with no significant time off and no money to enjoy themselves. In contrast, those who have worked so hard to ensure inequality has grown reward themselves with more and more holidays.

In November 2020, long before Johnson resigned, his newly installed chancellor, Rishi Sunak, announced that there would be a real-terms pay cut for most public sector workers. He said that he 'could not justify an across-the-board increase when many in the private sector had seen their pay and hours cut in the [Covid-19] crisis'.[29] This was an odd line of argument because, in the years when average private sector pay was rising in Britain, neither Sunak nor any of his Conservative predecessors had ever said that the public sector should also see a commensurate rise.

After its housing costs are paid, the average household in Britain is already less prosperous than the median in every other large European country – worse off than in Germany, France, Italy or Spain.[30] We have been moving down the ranks for decades, and the fall has accelerated recently. We are going to have to consume less in future. However, we could also aim to be more normal and fail less, with fewer crises in the NHS, in elderly social care, in children's social care, in education at every level, in housing, in transport, in the number of potholes in the roads, and in being prepared to deal with snowy weather or droughts. Even while consuming less, we could aim to have as much leisure time as other Europeans have. And we could aim to be less polluting. The majority of our carbon emissions are made by the richest people.[31]

We should also aim to reduce the growing social immobility that blights so many people's lives, constricting their options from birth. People's futures in the UK are increasingly being determined by what their parents earned. In *all* other European countries for which there is comparable data, social mobility by age forty is higher than in the UK and income is less dependent on how well off your parents were when you were a child. In contrast to the UK, social mobility has been rising for all countries measured other than Denmark, although it has risen there as well if income is measured after taxes (which are very progressive in Denmark). Even in the United States – the only country in the most recent study to do worse than the UK – there has finally been a rise in that measure in the past few years.[32]

And what of Birmingham, the former workshop of the world mentioned at the start of this chapter? It is the largest local authority in the UK and so has the most comprehensive economic statistics of any local authority. Using the same source and analysis as was used above for the UK, Birmingham and places like it can be seen to have taken the brunt of the shattering. Between 1999 and 2019 the value of Birmingham's manufacturing sector, as a share of the national economy, fell by twice as much as the service sector grew there. The city shrank economically, with the biggest losses being in manufacturing.

In its place, the most growth was in social work activities. These include the category 'eligibility determination in connection with welfare aid, rent supplements or food stamps'. Remarkably, that is now a specific business activity in Britain and has been classified as such since 2009.[33] The data is not disaggregated enough to know how much of the rise in social services work in Birmingham came from that subsection of the industry.

After the growth in social work and related human health activities, the next largest rise in the share of the national economy in Birmingham was in education – mostly as a result of the privatising of Birmingham's universities. Economically, education was said to have been 'worth' £44 billion to the UK in 1999. That had risen to £120 billion by 2019. Education was one of the few industries that did not contract during the pandemic, being 'worth' £126 billion in 2020 UK-wide. In Birmingham, its 'value' rose from £0.9 billion in 1999 to £2.6 billion in 2020. Most of this increase was achieved by creating enormous student debts. How valuable was that?

6.
Exploitation

Snobbery is so very British. William Makepeace Thackeray's *Book of Snobs* was published in 1848, the same year as Marx and Engels's *The Communist Manifesto*, and while much of the rest of Europe was engaged in revolution. Thackeray noted that snobbery in England was pervasive. He lamented: 'How are you ever to get rid of Snobbishness when society does so much for its education?'[1] It had become ingrained in what it meant to be English and in customs that had recently been developed but were starting to be presented as if they had always been there. Born in Calcutta, Thackeray was a child of the empire – his father worked for the East India Company. The riches that the empire brought home to England allowed the wealthy to become the very wealthiest in the world, and with that wealth came increased inequality and the snobbery needed to justify it – which continues to this day.

Snobbery rose when inequality in the UK climbed towards its highest peak. In British English publications, it accelerated upwards in the years before the First World War. Even as inequalities began to fall, use of the word continued to rocket upwards until it suddenly peaked in 1942 and then began to fall.[2] It was often suggested that this reduction was due to men of higher social classes actually conversing with poorer men during the Second World War and realising that they were not that different, especially on the battlefield. The women at home also had to get on with each other better than before in order to get through the war. In England in 1913, when the acceleration in the use of the word was greatest, the most common job for a woman was that of domestic servant. In 1978, use of the word hit a minimum, as did the number of servants. In March 2022, the ONS estimated that the number of people in the UK employed as servants was about 20,000, of which about 9,000 were full-time.[3]

There is no national statistic on snobbery other than counting the frequency of the use of the word in publications. Undoubtedly, it would be hard to measure it more meaningfully than that. But as we pull apart as a nation we have once more become more conscious of snobbery.[4] This is not just because it has increased again, but also because we have become more sensitive to its implications. Inequality affects us all, intimately.[5] Once you look for it, you begin to see it everywhere. Two decades ago, discussing the new phenomenon of book clubs, a writer in the *Guardian* announced: 'There's something so insanely *Daily Mail* about the whole enterprise.'[6] Either the *Guardian* was being snobby about book clubs, or the book clubs were snobby, as it was implying, or both. I suspect we are beginning to rail against snobbery again, and so remarks as disparaging as the book club one are becoming less commonplace. This change is a repeat of the past, but happening faster than before.

Snobbery is still, however, very much alive and kicking under the surface of British culture. The terms 'reverse snobbery' and 'inverted snobbery' first appeared in the 1870s. The latter was increasingly used until the 1960s, after which reverse snobbery became more popular. Combined, their use peaked around 2013.[7]

Joking about the trappings of respectability appears to be on the decline now too. Perhaps affecting effortless superiority is harder today, as even the supposedly 'best' of British people begin to see themselves as not good enough and not quite as rich as they would like to be. Attempting to maintain status (often by showing off) has become more of a necessity for those who can manage it. One of the key ways in which snobbery has arisen again in the UK has been through educational achievements being increasingly presented as if they make some people better than others.

Education was seen as the remedy for the old social evil of ignorance, and at first it was. However, when economic inequalities began to rise in the late 1970s, this was accompanied by the beginnings of a shift in the purpose of education. Across the UK, educational priorities have moved away from trying to eliminate illiteracy and innumeracy, although there is still plenty of that. Instead, education has been turned into a competition. Young people compete against each other; there must be winners in order to have losers. Schools compete against each other to create the good and the bad: an official hierarchy built on phoney league tables. Education businesses profit greatly as a result, while education itself suffers.

Schools and universities have been sucked into a competitive maelstrom. The extent to which this occurs varies greatly geographically. Towns and cities in the UK are now much more segregated than they used to be. The expensive neighbourhoods now tend to be within the catchment areas of what are considered good state schools. The least expensive areas are now around the supposedly dud schools, effectively making parents pay to get their children into the schools of their choice – a decision, in other words, reserved for the affluent, those who have a choice of where to buy or rent. The large majority of private schools are clustered in the south-east of England, along with a number in Edinburgh and a few other large cities outside of the south-east.

For Scots, Scotland's university education is free at the point of use.[8] But the direction of travel in the rest of Britain has been largely one way: towards an education system that exploits people while teaching them less that is of practical use or that encourages imagination. Education becomes a programme to train pupils to pass exams. Of all the countries internationally surveyed by the OECD, England's education system encourages the flourishing of students' imagination the least.[9] Instead, pupils and students are increasingly being exploited as a source of income by educational establishments that are forced to do this in order to survive, as they turn into businesses instead of being public services.

The ramifications of this rise in exploitation within the education system are far-reaching. There is a tendency for people to think that students are better educated in the UK, when they are unaware of the actual international comparisons. If those comparisons were known, it would not be so easy to be lulled into believing that the status quo is near to the best that can be achieved. People would not fall for the story that the UK is a remarkable country stocked full of world-leading universities and schools. In recent decades these claims have been repeated so often that most folk have come to believe them.

The alternative interpretation is that the most exclusive private schools and some courses at UK universities are extremely expensive, rather than extremely good at helping people to think more openly or skilfully. England has the highest university fees in the world. Average UK undergraduate fees are 33.8 per cent higher than the next most expensive country, the US, and those are just the fees for tuition, not accommodation. England's tuition fees are also 138 per cent higher than Japan's, 144 per cent higher than

Canada's and 157 per cent higher than those of the very unequal South Korea. They are six times as high as Italy's, seven times higher than Spain's, fifty-three times higher than those of France, eighty-three times higher than Germany's and infinitely higher than Sweden's (where university tuition is free). As the source of this data (the German company Statista) points out: 'England's tuition fees weren't always so high. However, since the beginning of the 2000s, annual costs have increased by 700 per cent.'[10] But there is no evidence of an improvement in actual achievement. The British are not more clever because they have the highest university fees and numerous expensive private schools.

One particular type of private school aims to draw in a more international cohort of affluent students. 'International schools' tend to offer a similar curriculum and frequently have no state sponsorship at all. According to the International Schools Database, just four countries feature in the top ten most expensive: the United States, China, Switzerland and the UK. In London, the most expensive international schools in 2021 cost £28,264 a year in fees alone.[11] England's top private schools that also include boarding (seen as an essential part of the education) cost much more. Eton, Harrow, Winchester, Cheltenham Ladies' College and Roedean are all in the mid-£40,000s a year range, while Oxford International College, Queen Ethelburga's College and Brighton College (all pre-university crammers or sixth forms) all have combined tutorial and boarding fees of over £50,000 a year.

The headline prices are shocking. But, rather like the top prices paid for property in London, the costs to overseas buyers of a UK school or university education are so high that they falsely make the high cost of domestic university education or private school places look reasonable. It is often overlooked that between 1962 and the 1990s, higher education in Britain was effectively free, as the state paid students' tuition fees and also offered maintenance (accommodation and food) grants to many. The wider ramification of the rise in exploitation in education is the growth of a new form of ignorance. People in the UK, some much more than others, have been increasingly exploited. They may not believe that what they are living with is always the best, but they do believe that our top schools and universities are unsurpassed. However, if our elite establishments create such great minds – and so many of our politicians have gone to them – then why is the country in such a mess? The dilapidation of what is left of free state education appears inevitable.

International comparisons, though often contentious and not at all easy to make, show that the UK is almost always outside the top dozen countries in educational attainment when students are tested.[12] This is quite remarkable, given how much British education now concentrates on trying to teach children to do well at tests, rather than learning more widely.

It is, admittedly, unfair to pick out any one place, but I will. When I first drafted this chapter, rather than begin with the international comparisons above, it started with a story about Manchester and its schools and universities, because the financial profit from education had grown so much there. What other industry or business could have expanded so much to take up the space, provide the jobs and prop up the communities and housing market of a city that had been so shattered by deindustrialisation? I could have chosen one of many other university cities as my example; Oxford, for instance, where it is often not realised that the two universities there expanded due to deindustrialisation as well. The numbers of students and university staff were able to grow as much as they did because the homes of former car workers were there for them to move into when those houses were sold off.

There is an historical irony in using Manchester as our example. The heart of this new exploitation of hope in the city lies in the former slum area that Friedrich Engels mapped in 1844 in his first book, *The Condition of the Working Class in England*. Engels was mapping a particular geography of exploitation where mill workers toiled for very little, while the huge profits from their labours went straight to their bosses. Today, many of the sites of those former mills have new student blocks built upon them, places where students pay a fortune for the privilege of toiling for a degree. They do so in conditions not of their making, but usually with an en-suite toilet in their room. No comparison with the slums of the past is ever made. However, the British students will spend most of the rest of their working lives paying back their tuition fee debt, and very often the debt from another loan for the rent, including access to the most expensive toilet they will ever use.

The same story could be told of many other northern English cities too, where education is now the main income earner. In today's Sheffield the two universities bring in more in export earnings from overseas students than the exports of the entire South Yorkshire metals trade. No other state makes as much money from education as the UK. Even Scotland has a large number of private schools, and although it has kept the profit motive largely out of its university sector, many of its universities still rely on the very high fees paid by the English and overseas students who study there. The highest fees quoted on the internet for the University of Edinburgh are (in US dollars) $36,330 a year for an undergraduate degree, $58,173 for a master's degree and $61,342 a year for a doctorate.[13]

At the University of Manchester, the largest single-site university in the UK, the highest annual tuition fees listed for undergraduate students from abroad in 2022/23 were £32,900.[14]

However, some postgraduate courses cost as much as £46,000 a year. British students pay £9,250 a year for an undergraduate degree, and often more for a postgraduate course. A small number of students may be awarded a state- or charity-funded postgraduate place. But overall there is a clear incentive for every university to take more higher-paying students in future. Annual fees for 2022/23 for international students studying at Manchester Metropolitan University were between £16,500 and £26,500.[15] The British Council estimated a few years ago that there were 41,000 international students in Manchester.[16] It is possible that overseas student fees alone will soon bring £1 billion a year into the city. On top of that is the income from rents and other spending. Much the same is happening in many other parts of the UK.

You could paint this as a great success story, especially as the pound falls in value and it becomes possible to increase the fees even further without them appearing to rise in foreign currency terms. Who could ever have imagined that cotton mills would be replaced with degree factories? The fact that this achievement is not celebrated more, however, might suggest a little unease over whether this is the flowering of a great new export industry, akin to the original industrialisation of Manchester, or something that might be much more short-lived – another symptom of the shattering rather than a solution to it.

Flowering

By 2012, UK universities had effectively been privatised, so that today they increasingly exploit the hopes of students from home and abroad. Less well understood is how academy schools have become businesses and how a majority of England's secondary schools have also been privatised.[17]

An academy trust is a charitable company limited by guarantee, also called 'an exempt charity'. It may be funded as a standalone company, or as part of a multi-academy trust, which is itself a single legal entity. Most of the funding comes from government in the form of student premiums and other grants. The total sums these trusts deal in are often staggering. Because of their charitable status, they (and the academies they own) cannot legally make a profit, which is one reason why corruption occurs so often. Nepotism, fraud, waste and cheating have become widespread. Furthermore, the corruption is not well hidden; it is now just accepted as part of the cost of running things this way. In 2020, one academic published research that listed 3,800 examples of corruption of this kind, often involving Private Finance Initiative deals, and mainly, but not exclusively, occurring in academy schools in England.[18]

This was privatisation by stealth as, officially, these schools were still described as state schools. But by 2012, a majority of state secondary schools (3,261) were no longer accountable to local government. Instead, they simply had to report to central government via an obscure regional arrangement. Each school could vary teachers' pay and conditions, and they were often part-funded by businesses or 'philanthropy'. In the ten years since then, there have been many reports of corruption in academy schools, thanks in no small part to their being outside local government oversight, ethos and control.

In that ten-year period, a further 1,092 state secondary schools were privatised, bringing the total up to nearly 80 per cent.[19] By 2022, only 726 state secondary schools had not been academised. Roughly 6,500 primary schools had been academised by 2022.

That will soon be the case for the majority of primaries. There are also 2,500 traditional private schools in England, according to the British Educational Suppliers Association (BESA), a private body that is 'accountable to an Executive Council elected by member companies'.[20] According to BESA's website, by 2015 the turnover of its member companies exceeded £2 billion a year.

Why has the UK education system become so shattered, with so many people now taking a slice of the ever rising cost of running it? The roots of this shattering can be traced back to the late 1970s, when a rearguard action was launched that attempted to reverse the progress that had been made since the 1940s. The intention was to stop the remaining state selective grammar schools from becoming comprehensive schools. There are still 163 grammar schools in England, out of roughly 3,000 state secondaries in total. Pupils get in through the eleven-plus exam, often after having had private tuition or attending a (private) prep school. The remaining grammar schools were preserved because the Labour Party wavered in the late 1970s. As the Labour prime minister James Callaghan put it in his famous 'Ruskin speech' in 1976: 'There is now widespread recognition of the need to cater for a child's personality to let it flower in its fullest possible way.'[21]

Those words appear so innocuous now, and 'flowering' sounds like a good thing, but in hindsight this statement marked a turning-away from providing a decent education for all, as the majority of other European countries have continued to do, and towards catering more and more for apparent difference, but instead creating rising segregation.

Margaret Thatcher took up Callaghan's theme, and with it the flower metaphor. She talked of the need to look after the 'tall poppies', her name for what she saw as unusually able students that she believed included people like her. But children are not born with special abilities, not even the children of wealthy parents. Ability is the norm. We all have a variety of disabilities, many of which (like dyslexia) are not immediately obvious. Education should be about identifying these problems and difficulties and finding ways to overcome and circumvent them. Would that it were so. However, the biggest disabilities are staring us in the face, and they are social: deprived backgrounds, poverty and inadequate local provision, especially for those who can't pay their way out.

Ruskin, the trade union college in the city of Oxford where Callaghan gave that speech, is no longer associated with trade unions. It has become 'A Private Company Limited by Guarantee', with its board of trustees chaired at the time of writing by a member of the board of governors of the University of West London.[22] It is now 'part of the University of West London Group', which was once the Polytechnic of West London. Nearby Oxford Polytechnic, which used to take mostly local children, became Oxford Brookes University in 1992. In 2020 it admitted just 68 per cent of its UK undergraduates from state schools.[23] The figure for state school students attending the University of Oxford was higher, at 68.8 per cent.[24] Both universities took very few students from their home city.

In the years after 1976, the 'need to cater for a child's personality to let it flower in its fullest possible way' slowly morphed into the mantra 'realising their potential', a phrase that is heard so often today. This became the underlying excuse for promoting more and more diversity of provision in what had once been a far more unified and inclusive state system. Under the cover of letting a thousand flowers bloom, our school and university systems were shattered into a million pieces.

Flowering 'in its fullest possible way' implies that some people will flower much less than others. Those who flower more, and who have been helped to do so by the increasingly privatised and diversified education system, are to be rewarded by higher pay later in life. That is the carrot that attracts so many young adults into the world's most expensive higher education system. The sales pitch implies: don't worry about the costs you are accruing; you will be more than rewarded later in life for the investment that you (or your parents) are making now.

When the Institute for Fiscal Studies produced its 2022 report on educational inequality, it suggested that 'today's education inequalities are tomorrow's income inequalities' – but of course this need not be the case. Segregated patterns of schooling do build segregated communities, driving a wedge between the haves and the have-nots, right at the start of life. But they can be reversed. Countries with far lower income inequalities than the UK has today have usually had wide educational inequalities in the past. Today's educational inequalities need not be tomorrow's income inequalities. In fact, they are very unlikely to be, as it becomes less and less possible to reward the majority of young people (the 57 per cent) who go to universities in the UK with sufficiently high salaries to make the 'investment' worthwhile. This is numerically impossible, unless there is both a further huge rise in income inequality and incredibly low social mobility in future – even lower than we have today.

Under that headline, 'Today's education inequalities are tomorrow's income inequalities', the IFS researchers also pointed out: 'Strikingly, the most common annual salary for low-educated forty-five- to fifty-year-olds (i.e. those with qualifications at or below GCSE or equivalent) is between £15,000 and £20,000 – the same as for twenty-five- to thirty-year-olds with those qualifications.'[25]

They are suggesting that if only those forty-five- to fifty-year-olds in the past had attended university, or done better at school, then they would not be so lowly paid today. But if that cohort had grown up in almost any other country in Western Europe they would be better paid today, while their peers who did go to university would not be paid so much more than them. This is because income inequalities have not been allowed to rise as high in any of those countries as they have in the UK.

As the exploitation rises, the myths the establishment tries to peddle become less and less believable. We then see people begin to tell a fabricated story of the past. Comprehensive schools under local authority control are talked about as if they were something terrible. Liz Truss, before briefly becoming prime minister, said: 'Many of the children I was at school with were let down by low expectations, poor educational standards and a lack of opportunity.' In fact, she attended the premier comprehensive school in one of the wealthiest areas of Leeds. She was found out, and criticised by the mainstream press, including right-wing tabloids and *The Times*.[26]

As yet, few people have claimed that university was terrible when you could go for free, but many do suggest that university expansion would simply have been unaffordable without fees and hence privatisation. That is patently untrue. By 2021, a similar number of young people were going to university in many EU countries as in the UK. Proportions vary from over 60 per cent in Ireland to around 30 per cent in Italy.[27] The UK proportion is now near the top of that range and may well rise further up the ranking within Europe in the coming years,[28] but our great concern in the future will be whether this rise is about a larger cohort of young people receiving a good education, or institutions covering their rising costs by squeezing in a few more bums on seats. Once you start charging for it, and making money out of it, seeing a rise in students going to university as a good thing could well be largely delusional.

Privilege

Private schools are not the greatest problem faced by shattered Britain when education is considered. But the preservation of the private education sector after the Second World War was one of the reasons why it was so easy to subsequently shatter the state school system. In recent decades it has been usual for a majority of Cabinet ministers to have been privately educated, but in September 2022 that proportion rose to 68 per cent, making it the least diverse Cabinet by education seen since the 1990s.[29]

The UK system of education is not only unusual. It is now the most expensive such system in the world, because so much of both secondary and primary state education has been shattered and transformed into privatised or semi-privatised charities and business ventures over the course of the past two decades. It is also unusual because, unlike any other country in Europe, the UK has retained a very large number of private schools from the time before the state became involved in education, and it maintains an environment in which it is relatively easy to open up new entirely private schools.

Among all the thirty-eight current members of the Organisation for Economic Co-operation and Development, only Chile (and only before the uprising of 2019–22) spent more on the private education of a few children than is spent in Britain today. Those with the greatest financial advantages have had the most spent on their schooling. Nowhere else in the affluent world is like this. We do not understand that private schools are not actually good schools – just as private healthcare is not good healthcare, but is simply queue jumping.

Private education can be brought into the fold by ensuring fewer people have the excess income and unnecessary wealth needed to pay for it, and by ensuring that private schools pay taxes like any other business, instead of being treated as charities. The tax concessions given to private schools, and the tax loopholes that allow parents to reduce the cost of sending their children to such schools, need to be stopped. If this were done, private schools would begin to opt to become state-controlled to remain viable. They would not shut. Furthermore, state provision needs to be better funded, and if less money were being siphoned off to support the iniquitous private school system, more could be forthcoming. In England, schools in deprived areas have seen the largest cuts in spending per child in recent years. The most deprived secondary schools saw a 14 per cent real-terms fall between 2009–10 and 2019–20, compared with a 9 per cent drop for the least deprived schools.[30] That could easily be reversed if the tax concessions and loopholes to private schools were removed and the savings used to make up the money needed.

The British idea of private education being a privilege that should, where possible, be offered to a few more who might have the potential to benefit from it, reeks of both snobbery and ignorance. To be a snob is to think you are better than other people. Likewise, to think that your expensive education made you better educated. But it is understandably very difficult to even consider that this may not be the case if you have been indoctrinated throughout your childhood.

The illusion then crystallises when private school exam grades are, on average, so much higher than those received by most pupils who have attended state schools. The certificates apparently confirm the superiority. Subsequent entry into an elite university that collects together people with almost identical exam grades, and disproportionately from similar schools, helps to cement a lifelong bias through like-minded confirmation.

A new crisis in Britain's 'top universities' emerged in 2022. Children from the most affluent families in the UK were securing fewer places, apparently because they were being displaced by even more affluent students from overseas. Within the home 'market', affluent children make the most applications to this group of universities. That has always been the case. But in 2022, for the first time, individually they became the least likely home group to be offered a university place. The top fifth had become a squeezed middle, in the weird jargon of UK inequality. This is how the *Telegraph* put it:

> If your child isn't being discriminated against because you were stupid enough to have a successful career and go to a private school or buy a family home in a leafy postcode (NB: remember to purchase flat on sink estate next time), then the few remaining stellar university places they might have had a shot at will be snaffled by a Chinese or Indian student.

This was dissected online by some of those who knew a bit more about the subject than the *Telegraph*'s writer. They pointed out that there was obviously no discrimination against those in the top fifth, but that in the past too many of them had felt entitled to a place at a 'top' university.[31] There was no shortage of university places generally, despite the increase in overseas applicants.

A few days later, the *Sunday Times* ran a story on its front page suggesting that the solution to this problem was to increase university fees for home students towards £24,000 a year rather than the current £9,250, explicitly to stop affluent British students losing their places to foreigners.[32] The idea being presented was that 'top' British universities would admit more UK-resident students if the universities made more money by doing so. When the vicious circle of rising inequality starts to reduce the opportunities of the very best-off, there may be some hope.

Snobbery eventually comes back to bite you. Those proud to be 'ever so privileged' end up contemplating paying £24,000 a year in student fees to try to secure places for their own children at elite universities – probably like the ones that helped them 'realise their own potential', or, to put it another way, provided them with a stepping stone to an extraordinarily overpaid job. Inequality is completely out of control when the most well-off openly consider bribery to be a respectable way to get what they want.

Many arguments can be made as to why the most privileged people in the UK are not a terribly well-educated elite, but perhaps the most compelling evidence comes simply from looking at what it is they have created – the shattered state of the UK. In countries where children are educated together, rather than segregated by school and parents' income, they achieve so much more as adults. A divided education system is one of the best ways to ensure that social divisions are perpetuated, by creating fear, distrust and myths about others. This is the case whether the divisions are by religion, ethnicity, wealth or sex. Despite that, every gain in equality made in the UK in the past, and across the rest of Europe, began to be made when educational inequalities were high and before they fell. We can have hope.

Disorder

So what can be done to address the huge disorder that has allowed so few to exploit so many financially, in the name of education? Things are so bad now that we have to address the basics first.

The first imperative is simply to ensure that children are not hungry. They need to be fed at school and during the holidays, as a matter of course rather than on an ad hoc or highly means-tested basis. Finland first introduced universal school meals after the Second World War, and daily holiday lunches in Helsinki, too. This is now simply a part of education there; school lunch is as everyday in Finland as school furniture and lighting.

Emergency measures will be needed to ensure that schools can heat their buildings in winter and fix the boilers when they break. The current system is crumbling, and this repeatedly throws up issues requiring government intervention. In the summer of 2022, the examination board Edexcel (owned by the massive multinational education provider Pearson plc) faced criticism over failing to even mark exams on time.[33]

The day-to-day disorder in our schools and universities creates hundreds of immediate problems that consume time and energy and divert attention from the serious underlying issues that in turn help create and recreate the continuous short-term chaos. Educational provision for children in private schools during the Covid-19 pandemic was adequate, but in deprived areas and especially for state school children without adequate internet access at home, it was a disaster. The system had no way of coping.

In the medium term it makes no sense for schools to be arranged in academy chains akin to car dealerships. In particular, it makes no geographical sense. If you want to group schools so that staff can move between them without moving home, or to offer a more specialist subject in one school so that pupils from neighbouring schools can also study it, then you need to group schools geographically so as to make it easier to move between them. Academy chains encourage no enthusiasm for such cooperation, despite knowing that it would help reduce disparity between schools and increase standards overall.

Looking back, it is clear that so much of the legislation introduced in the long 2010–12 parliamentary session was carefully designed to make it impossible to easily reverse. This scheming had probably happened in the thirteen years when the Conservatives were out of office, and it was barely modified by the Liberal Democrats with whom they had to form a coalition in 2010. University tuition fees in England were tripled to £9,000 in 2012, despite Liberal Democrat MPs having been elected on a manifesto promising to abolish them entirely.

Large sums of money are lost through the inefficiency of academy-chain schools being scattered geographically. This is in addition to the money siphoned off to cover the excessively high salaries of academy trust 'leaders'. Chain competes against chain. Real standards fall. Rejuvenation will require reorganising the chains geographically, to make it possible to share teachers and other staff resources between sites. It also requires democratic oversight and ownership. Schools are not businesses. Neither are universities – and yet there are now university chains with a university in one part of the country operating buildings, hiring people and recruiting 'customers' in another.

We have demonstrated to the world that the British way is no way to run an education sector. Now that the majority of young people go to university, universities should be seen as part of local education for local people. That this is so hard to imagine demonstrates just how strange higher education in the UK has become, how disordered and how shattered the system now is. The fact that most students go away from home to attend university is one of the things that makes the British way so extravagantly expensive.

Unravelling the mess may take decades rather than years, but the direction of travel can be altered more quickly. Professional and accurate audits of academy chains should be adopted, in place of the audits they currently organise themselves. Truly independent audits would deter them from committing the worst offences and resorting to financial chicanery. Board members should include people nominated by democratically elected local councils. They should be incentivised to cluster better geographically, ideally within the boundary of a local authority. But achieving any of this will require political power – a party or parties in charge at Westminster that believe that unravelling the mess is the right thing to do. The largest obstacle here is what the main opposition party believes is the right thing to do.

What would a second New Labour government achieve if it behaved like the first? It would not reduce divisions. It would maintain them, suggesting this was all that was now possible. Between 1997 and 2010, Labour did increase funding per head for pupils in state schools, but at the same rate that funding per head was increasing in private schools. The two moved in near perfect lockstep, meaning that the absolute gap in funding per head widened each year Labour was in power.[34] After Labour lost power, funding per child in state schools fell, while that in private schools continued to rise. By 2021 the average gap had risen to an extra £6,500 being spent per year on every private school child, up from an extra £3,100 in 2010.[35]

If a future Labour government behaved like the last one, it might maintain these levels of educational inequality, but would probably decide that it could not afford to do even that. Opposition parties are going to be forced to rethink their policies if they want to offer a transformative agenda. Labour also maintained the level of income inequality in the UK throughout the entire 1997–2010 period at almost exactly the level it had inherited. It was that income inequality, more than anything else, that allowed the private education sector to grow. Only a few of the most economically unequal countries in the world have as large a private education sector as the UK (although the rest of this cohort are poorer than the UK and none of them are members of the OECD).

Bringing order back into the chaos is not a call to return to the past, to the world that James Callaghan so foolishly derided in 1976. We could have moved on in a different direction back then, more like most of our European neighbours, and if we had we would be in a very different place today. We would see, for example, hardly any children being excluded from school each year, as that is not normal on the continent (or now in Scotland).

The most sensible way to reorganise education in future is geographically. If academy trusts will not do so when incentivised, then local authorities could be offered the option of bringing the educational resources of their areas under one local chain that they control. Those resources could range from nursery provision through to universities. Some parts might remain private, but they would struggle to survive privately if income inequalities were to shrink in future. Whenever a private provider folded, it could be taken into the public provision.

Such a process has worked in the past. It was applied to state-funded secondary schools when, in the 1960s and 1970s, county after county opted to become comprehensive and abandon the old eleven-plus exam that had so divided family from family and children within families. The difference in future is that the remit would be wider, including further education colleges, all tertiary education and any form of education to which the state directly or indirectly contributes funding. It would be a battle, but the end result would be a system that is far cheaper, more efficient and less divisive. It would be part of a wider war on inequality, a necessary war against greed and indifference.

The longer that war is put off, the worse hunger, precarity, waste, exploitation and fear will become. The rich will live in growing fear of the battles to come, and of their day of reckoning. Their preferred route, instead of such overt actions, is covert. It is to ensure that their opponents – a more progressive government, for example – cannot undo their work. To achieve that, they need the public to believe that there is no alternative to being nasty, other than being slightly less nasty. However, when too few people benefit, the disorder becomes much harder to tolerate. Ask why the schools in your area don't work together better. Ask why your local university tries so hard to sit aloof from the area it is in.

Motivation

A good education system does not charge university students to study. It does not encourage schools or universities to compete for pupils or students. Its curriculum is broader and more up to date. Systems like this already exist elsewhere. No country's education system is perfect, but nowhere in Europe has education become as shattered as it now is in the UK, where parents are fearful of what schools their children might go to, of the costs of feeding them or paying for totally unnecessary school uniforms, or of the huge debts their children are likely to incur if they go to university.

It is fine to argue for free university tuition, proper maintenance allowances, free school meals for all, and decent apprenticeships for many, but someone has to pay. Other countries can afford all this by *not* running their economies in such a way that those who go to university expect to be paid two or three times as much as those who do not. They also ensure that people who do not have a degree are much better paid than they are today in the UK, so there is far less resentment about the state funding of universities.

Surveys find that British university graduates are in favour of greater equality in everything but their future pay.[36] On average they tend to believe what they have been taught – that they will be worth a lot more after they graduate than before, and that they have a right to much higher salaries. This is both untrue and unjustified, but hearing this might be difficult. University graduates tend to be socially progressive, but economically regressive. This is not just the case in Britain, but to a lesser extent across Europe and very much more strongly in the United States. The author of the British study that demonstrated this also quoted a European study from 2022 that concluded: 'university education fosters norms of inclusion, while eroding norms of solidarity'.[37]

A group of economists who looked at data from many affluent countries over many decades found that in recent decades 'left-wing parties have gradually developed a more elitist approach to education policy, in the sense that they have increasingly been viewed by less well-off voters as primarily defending the winners of the higher education competition'.[38] This framing may be partly because it is in the direct interest of right-wing parties to paint the left as having done this. Right-wing parties benefit greatly when some less well-off voters believe that the right has created an alternative ladder to success and fortunes, a route which their obviously wealthy leaders try to epitomise. They also benefit by portraying left-wing supporters as being overpaid young university graduates. But, of course, the American dream of social mobility and economic 'success' has always been just a dream for most people, whether in the US or the UK, including the large majority of graduates.

The right can only win through divide and rule, by telling a series of very different stories to different groups of people and hoping they don't notice the growing inconsistencies. The right tells university students that they have a bright future ahead, one in which, if they work hard, they will prosper financially. It tells older people that these same students are a drain on society and should not be supported other than in minimal ways. It tells people who do not go to university that it cares more about them and their futures, and about 'levelling up', than about the futures of graduates. It derides any proposals that government should behave differently as either unworkable or somehow unfair.

At this point you might well ask: where are the detailed proposals for real change? Why, in books like this one, are there only hints about how we could better organise our schools and universities? But before you can plan for a better future, you have to question the belief system that has been constructed, concerning what different people are worth, how much inequality can be justified, and what education is actually for. This questioning becomes easier to sustain as the existing arrangements begin to fall apart, as schools and universities get into financial difficulties, as the pension arrangements of even the most secure academics falter, and as the excessive salaries, the chauffeurs and other perks enjoyed by those at the top of educational institutions become ever more galling and clearly indicate the exploitative mindset at the heart of how our society has been organised.

Education is about more than schools and universities, or at least it used to be. We used to worry about education in prisons, in the workplace, pre-school, and about lifelong learning – including into retirement. Today, we fill our prisons with people who should not be there, and the provision of educational opportunities is minimal. It is minimal because we have been taught to believe that prisoners are neither capable nor deserving and because prisons have also become so disordered.[39]

Education for those aged over twenty-four has collapsed since fees were introduced in universities. Those who wish to extend their education often have neither the time nor the money to do so. So many have to work long hours to earn enough money to just about get by. What little education remains is increasingly provided by for-profit companies and quasi-charitable bodies. And it is often a sham.

There is a great deal of unravelling to do. The underlying motivation behind a good education system must not be to exploit people for profit. Rebuilding an ethos of care cannot happen overnight, but it can happen. The last time it happened we were very divided, but we slowly came together.

The Workers' Educational Association was founded in 1903, at a time when public lectures were becoming common. Vocational education and lifelong learning were seen as a normal part of life. Community and further education colleges allowed anyone over sixteen to enrol in a course with few or no prior 'qualifications'. In 1969, the Open University was created. In terms of early learning, the Pre-school Playgroups Association, also created in the 1960s, supported parents and their young children, giving parents confidence in their new roles.[40] Often the parents were then able to become playgroup leaders themselves, in an environment where children explored a brave new world. It was an example of what education should be at every level – exploratory, not prescriptive. Campaigns for comprehensive education in most areas got rid of the evil of the secondary modern schools to which most children, deemed academic failures, were consigned.

Nowadays, however, there are schools everywhere that are seen as being just for failures. Thousands of children are excluded from school altogether. Excluded pupils can end up in Pupil Referral Units, or what is called 'alternative provision'. They are twice as likely to be from deprived backgrounds and eligible for free school meals, and also twice as likely to be boys. Extraordinary profits are made from providing alternative provision, with little proven benefit to the children. There are teachers and others in these systems who genuinely care, but so many of them have had their collective agency shattered by the imposition of a for-profit model in the sector. It need not remain this way forever. When a model has been debunked in the past, and the establishment has owned up to its mistake, people have changed how they behave and what they believe remarkably quickly.[41]

So much is often said about just how important a child's first few years are – yet so little intervention to improve learning in those years takes place. The number of children being born in the UK is still falling rapidly, but the government has told the privatised nursery industry that it will increase the ratio of children to staff in what it obviously sees as the warehousing of babies and toddlers. In 2022, however, the for-profit model of nursery provision fell apart as private nurseries could not find enough staff due to the low wages they paid, and parents increasingly could not afford the high rates they charged.[42]

It may well take the post-pandemic cost-of-living crisis to make the situation so bad that change has to begin. As the autumn term of 2022 loomed, parents began to notice advertisements for school uniforms with 'buy now pay later' finance schemes. These adverts frequently appear on brightly illuminated electronic hoardings that consume, per day, three times the amount of energy the average household needs to survive. The irony of being asked to buy your children's school uniforms on credit, by a company that makes so much profit it can pay for such environmentally polluting energy-intensive advertising, has not been lost on parents.[43]

The rising hunger, poverty and inequality, the increased precarity of housing, the waste of our time through so much counterproductive work, and the increasingly obvious exploitative nature of the education system all increase anxiety and depression. We become more fearful as we have more to fear.

So next we turn to the last of the old five evils, which in 1942 was termed disease, but which is now more often mental than physical, and is better labelled as fear. How ill and frightened have we become as we have been shattered? What can be done differently to confront this? Our education system currently worsens our mental health and pushes us into economic divisions that only exacerbate other inequalities – all these new giants of social evil are connected.

7.

Fear

When the five social evils were first named by William Beveridge in 1942, disease was the one that was most feared, especially disease among children. It was common for parents to experience the death of a child, with one in seventeen babies dying before they were a year old.[1] Physical health improved greatly in the decades following the establishment of the National Health Service in 1948, and mental health too (as fear fell). However, when economic inequalities rose in the UK from the late 1970s, people's mental health again began to suffer and then also their physical health.

Since 2012 there has been a dramatic worsening of physical health in the UK. Life expectancy has fallen in some areas and for some social groups, and it has been rising much less than had been predicted for everyone else. It fell overall for both men and women between 2014 and 2018. This decline in life expectancy gains was far greater in magnitude than the initial toll on life expectancy caused by the Covid-19 pandemic in its first three years.[2] The upper estimate for the number of premature deaths in Great Britain attributed to austerity between 2012 and 2019 was 335,000, much greater than all the deaths attributed to the pandemic in 2020–22.[3]

'The essence of a satisfactory health service is that the rich and the poor are treated alike, that poverty is not a disability, and wealth is not advantaged.'[4] So wrote Aneurin Bevan in 1952, in his book *In Place of Fear*. From 1929 to 1960 Bevan was the MP for Ebbw Vale, a constituency in South Wales, and minister of health when the National Health Service was created. Health improved markedly then and became much less variable across the UK. However, beginning with the service cuts of the 1980s and the growth in economic inequality since the late 1970s, the divisions between areas have grown again. Rich and poor are now treated very differently, wealth is once more a great advantage in terms of access to healthcare, and in the local authority district that included Bevan's constituency, residents can now expect to have, on average, 16.4 fewer years of good health than those in the best-off places. They once again have the worst health of anyone in England and Wales. The life expectancy gap within Britain has become greater than that between the UK and Sudan.[5]

It is no surprise that the fifth of Beveridge's great evils was disease. Using Google Ngram surveys we can see that in printed publications in the English language, the incidence of the words 'illness' and 'disease' peaked during Beveridge's and Bevan's childhood. Use of those words fell to their lowest levels in the twentieth century in the year 1966, but has risen steadily since the late 1970s.[6] Now we are once again living with the fear of infectious diseases, and the unexpected return of some of the diseases of Beveridge's day: rickets, polio and tuberculosis.[7]

The UK's health service is failing in terms of its growing waiting lists, and even in how long it takes to be treated in an emergency. By 2022, in the richest parts of the UK, a quarter of all NHS care was being delivered by private hospitals and private providers. Even in the most deprived areas, the proportion is more than a tenth. The researchers who revealed this, however, chose to use a different term for private health, referring to it as the independent sector. They raised what they saw as the key question: 'If the independent sector further increases the share of NHS-funded care it delivers, these findings raise questions about whether different areas of the country will have equal access to care.'[8] In the last decade, 40 per cent of new NHS contracts have been bid for and won by private firms, 41 per cent by NHS bodies, and the remainder by other charitable, non-profit or so-called social enterprise entities.[9] Between 2015 and 2019 the value of private sector NHS contracts increased by 89 per cent.[10]

In 1960, aged sixty-two, Aneurin Bevan died of stomach cancer, which is now known to be much more likely later in life if you grew up in poverty as a child. Four of Bevan's brothers and sisters died in infancy and a fifth at age eight.[11] Today, thanks to the reduction of poverty that the welfare state made possible, death caused by childhood poverty is much rarer. Instead, we have seen the greatest rises in what are termed 'diseases of despair', among both younger adults and older people. These include deaths from suicide and from alcohol-related and drug-related causes. The rises in mortality from diseases of despair have been greatest among people born between 1965 and 1984, a generation that grew up when the shattering started. The rates are highest in Scotland but also very high among many people in the poorest groups found throughout Britain.[12]

Deaths from diseases of despair are just the tip of the iceberg of huge rises in poor mental health. Mental health practitioners are beginning to change how they talk about the symptoms and causes of despair in Britain: 'In traditional mental health practice, threat responses are sometimes called "symptoms". The [new] framework instead looks at how we make sense of these experiences and how messages from wider society can increase our feelings of shame, self-blame, isolation, fear and guilt.'[13] The story of health today is increasingly a story of fear. The fear is well founded and will not subside until its causes are reduced.

No amount of levelling-up boosterism, trying to make people feel proud of where they live, can alleviate the suffering when people and places are becoming more divided, locally and nationally. To reduce the fear, it is necessary to reduce the reasons for its growth. On any given day in 2022, some 1.6 million people in the UK were waiting to see someone about their mental health. For every one of them, another five could not even get on the waiting lists, which continue to grow. The psychologist who revealed these figures wrote: 'The most effective therapy would be transforming the oppressive aspects of society causing our pain.'[14] Better health requires far more than just a better-funded health service.

Health

By 2017 it had become apparent that austerity was the main reason for the slowdown in rising life expectancy in Britain. Nevertheless, a few people at the time, especially people in opaquely funded right-wing think-tanks, continued to contest this fact.[15] At first it was thought that there had been about 120,000 additional premature deaths in the UK between 2010 and 2017 due to austerity, but that figure was later revised upwards by other researchers.[16] More than two years before the pandemic, on 26 October 2017, the Office for National Statistics announced that it now projected that people in the UK will, on average, live shorter lives for many decades to come.[17]

By 2017, after just seven years of cutbacks, it was becoming clear that life expectancy for women in the UK was now lower than for women in Austria, Belgium, Cyprus, Finland, France, Germany, Greece, Iceland, Ireland, Italy, Liechtenstein, Luxembourg, Malta, the Netherlands, Norway, Portugal, Slovenia, Spain, Sweden and Switzerland. Often it was significantly lower. The costs of austerity have fallen disproportionately upon poorer people, women, racial and ethnic minorities, children, single parents and people with disabilities.[18] Government spending in England on adult social care was lower in 2019 than in 2010, despite the rising need.[19] Older women were more likely to be living alone, and poorer older women suffered the most because they also had the lowest pensions.

By 2018 there were growing calls for a public enquiry into the rise in mortality in some groups, and a review of the data was announced by the Department for Health and Social Care (DHSC).[20] It was carried out by Public Health England, then an executive agency of the DHSC. In hindsight, the review could be interpreted as trying to cover up or underplay the significance of the mortality data. It is now part of the historical evidence of why we did so little to address the shattering of health and social care.[21]

Not long after the NHS was established, the UK achieved some of the best records in health internationally. By 1950 people in only six countries in the world had higher life expectancy. The UK had a larger population than all of those six combined.[22] As other countries caught up, the UK very slowly slipped down the ranks by a place or so every year, until, by the late 1970s, it was twenty-first worldwide. It more or less held that ranking until 2015, when it was still placed twenty-first.[23] Then it suddenly dropped down the ranks to thirty-seventh in the six years to 2021.[24] This disturbing and sudden fall was not due to the pandemic; it was due to austerity. All countries had been affected by the pandemic, although the UK's austerity measures may have made it more vulnerable when it hit.

The post-2022 health crisis is largely a continuation of the previous pre-pandemic austerity crisis. In August 2022, the *Financial Times* linked data on the approximately 100,000 people each month who had waited over twelve hours to be seen in A&E with estimates made in earlier years of how many deaths occur when people are not seen. Their journalist concluded: 'The total number of additional A&E linked deaths since waiting times rocketed is an almost perfect match for the missing 12,000 [excess non-Covid deaths].'[25] The story was accompanied by a graph showing how, by 2022, dying as a result of being unable to access hospital care had overtaken the pandemic as the main cause of excess (above expected) deaths in the UK.

From being above all other large European countries for life expectancy in the 1950s, the UK had dropped below all of the rest of Western Europe by 2021.[26] From being nearly first worldwide for child health in the 1960s, when measured by neonatal mortality rate, the UK had dropped to seventh place among twenty-eight European countries by 1990, and nineteenth by 2015.[27] According to the latest data, by 2020 the UK had fallen further, to twenty-third place out of the same twenty-eight countries. Only Slovakia, Bulgaria, Croatia, Romania and Malta had worse neonatal mortality rates.[28] In terms of child death rates up to age five, the UK fell from ninth place in 1990 to twentieth in 2020 out of these same twenty-eight countries.[29]

Our relative fall down the health league tables has been speeding up in recent years. It affects people of all ages, from shortly after birth through to old age – from the cradle to the grave. In a 2022 article published in the *British Medical Journal*, a colleague and I charted the remarkable fall since 2012 in the UK's projected life expectancy. The effect of the pandemic was large, but not as large as that of austerity.[30] In July 2022 a headline in the *Telegraph* also noted: 'Excess deaths are on the rise – but not because of Covid'.[31] The UK is now in a continual health crisis, just as it is suffering continual crises in housing, education, poverty and, since 2016, politics.

Without a hint of irony, a doctor quoted in the *Telegraph* article was the chief executive of a private healthcare company that supplies private GPs. Dr Charles Levinson said: 'If anything, the situation seems to be worsening. Considering the relentless focus on one virus for more than two years, requesting answers from Government on thousands and thousands of non-Covid excess deaths is entirely reasonable.' The more the UK's doctors are directed towards working in private practices, looking after a much fitter section of the population (the well-off), the harder it is to recruit GPs into the NHS and provide the best care for those who most need it. As with private education, as with housing affordability, the growth in unequal access to healthcare is a problem that is most directly addressed by lowering overall income inequality. These are all problems which are made much harder to address without that initiative.

The data on adult health before old age is just as bad as the data for children and the very elderly, and the international comparisons are worsening.[32] Within the UK, adult health inequality is shocking. For statistical purposes, England is divided into small areas (LSOAs) which each contain on average 1,500 people or 650 households. Sixty-year-old women living in the poorest tenth of these now suffer from the same levels of ill health as seventy-six-year-old women living in the wealthiest areas. The gap for men is less: sixty-year-old men in the poorest areas have the health profile of seventy-year-old men in the best-off areas.

The Health Foundation, which released these results (based on a very detailed analysis of individual patient records), did not note that they represent a fundamental injustice or compare such health inequalities in the UK to those in other European countries. Instead, it drew conclusions such as: 'This has a big economic impact, with many older workers now leaving the labour market due to ill-health.'[33] Were they implying that if we just spent a little more on the health of the worst-off, more of them could continue in work, hopefully till they were just about eligible for their state pension, in their mostly very low-paying jobs, to the greater benefit of their employers and the better-off who gain most from their labour?

The UK's leading health think-tanks are mostly based in London. They present a public image of being greatly concerned over trends such as these. However, their implicit messages downplay and often sow seeds of doubt over the known causes of the UK's decline in the international rankings. For example, when the Health Foundation published a report in 2019, one of the headline claims in the press release was: 'There is no single cause of the slowdown, and no single solution: instead, actions must be taken on the wider factors that shape the conditions in which people are born, grow, live, work and age.'[34]

In their main report, under the heading 'What is driving these changes?', the authors cast doubt on austerity being a significant factor, claiming that the evidence is 'limited and inconclusive'. They concluded that

> there is no single driver of the current slowdown in mortality rate improvements. This means there will be no single solution. As most deaths are among the 80-plus population, variations in mortality rates among the oldest can have a big effect on life expectancy estimates. This has led to inconclusive debate focusing on the impact of flu or austerity through constraints in social care or NHS budgets.

Another London-based health think-tank, the King's Fund, went further in casting doubt as to why the UK was slipping down the ranks. In 2022 it suggested that:

> While a slowdown in improvements in life expectancy between 2010 and 2019 was seen in many European countries, it was greatest in the UK. It's likely that there were several reasons for these trends, some specific to the UK (such as widening inequalities) and some common to the UK and other European countries (such as the swings in flu-related mortality and slowdown in [cardiovascular disease] mortality improvements in some countries).[35]

But if a cause is common to many countries, then it does not explain the UK's fall down the ranks.

General austerity and the specific cuts to state-funded services were not mentioned as the key possible causes. Inequality was mentioned. However, although income inequality in the UK was almost the highest in all of Europe in these years, it did not rise much in this period, whereas the cuts to services were sudden, severe and frequent. State-funded social care support was decimated many times over between 2010 and 2019.

In 2014, towards the end of an appendix that few people are likely to have read, the King's Fund Commission on the Future of Health and Social Care in England pointed out that very few children, young adults and elderly people were served by private healthcare in the UK: 'The numbers who benefit from private medical insurance are thus concentrated in the 30- to 64-year age group – an area where NHS spending is relatively low, with relatively few people covered past retirement age where the volume of need is greatest.'[36]

Private medical insurance inevitably becomes much more

expensive once you are out of a company scheme and as you get older – with individual premiums being increased annually by unspecified amounts. Health think-tanks' reports often imply that the significance of state spending cuts has been overstated. They often mention private medical insurance positively (as a 'benefit'). They sometimes appear to lament the fact that private medical insurance cannot be applied more widely. They hardly ever suggest that it would be good if the private sector were less involved.

The Health Foundation was created in 1998 from a one-off charitable donation of £560 million. This was one of the largest in UK history and came from a private health insurance organisation. The donation had become possible because of the sale of the PPP Healthcare group, which had been a mutual fund. By 2018 the endowment had grown to over £1 billion.[37] A century earlier, the King's Fund had been established in 1897 to fund voluntary hospitals. In 1907, it 'took on responsibility for an emergency beds service and encouraged hospitals to open pay beds as a means of raising extra income'.[38] It, and its money, was not incorporated into the NHS in 1948, but instead it continued to act as a charity with an interest in health. Both of these two key charitable institutions were established in times of very high inequality – not with the explicit remit to address that inequality, but to suggest ways in which we could live with it and somehow still preserve or improve health.

A large part of the shattering of the state in the UK has been a shattering of the post–Second World War consensus about what matters and why. It muddies the waters if the leading commentators on health constantly imply that the UK's worsening position is due to a series of complex factors, including not enough use being made of private healthcare, and individual behaviours leading to higher mortality.[39] This all promotes the not too subliminal message that people need to do more for themselves. That is hardly likely to reduce fear.

Government needs to fund and organise the UK's health services properly without privatisation, and to reduce the income inequality that is intrinsic to the reasons for our worsening record. There is a lot that can be done, but first we need to be clear about where we are now and why. As stated above, but well worth repeating: between 1950 and 1955 the UK had the highest life expectancy in the world of any large country. Only six smaller countries, with a combined population smaller than the UK's, ranked higher: Norway, Iceland, the Netherlands, Sweden, Denmark and New Zealand.[40] Today the list of countries where people live longer than they do in the UK is too long to print here.

Care

Social care is just as important as healthcare in influencing health outcomes. Hospitals cannot discharge patients needing support if there is inadequate social care, no family able to help and nowhere else to discharge them to. If the hospitals are full, ambulances cannot unload patients and must queue outside. When the capacity of the state to provide social and personal care decreases, the shattering is magnified. In the UK, the vast majority of care for people with long-term illness or disability, especially the elderly, is provided by families and friends.[41] But our private capacity to care for others begins to fail if we need to work longer hours just to manage, and more often when the public services and support that so many rely on also falters.

The list of failing health and care services is long and growing longer. In recent decades, only half of UK adults have been registered with an NHS dentist at any one time. In August 2022 we learnt that in a third of areas in the UK there is no longer any provision at all for new adult NHS dental patients, and four out of five NHS dental practices are not even accepting children. An increasing number of NHS practices said 'they would take on a child under the NHS only if a parent signed up as a private patient'.[42]

Too few new dentists are being trained. Brexit and dentists' dissatisfaction with NHS contracts have further contributed to the shortage. In 2021 the total number of NHS dentists fell by almost 10 per cent. If this trend, which has been worsening for many years, is allowed to continue, we will soon have almost entirely private dental provision in the UK – only for those who can afford to pay and only then if what they need doing is within their budget. NHS dental care is shattered, but that surprises no one because shattering in health services is now the norm.

In July 2022 it became clear that the UK's largest care home chain was in trouble.[43] It had made losses of £83 million, up from £68 million a year earlier, despite charging the average resident £41,000 a year. In most cases that bill, or most of it, was paid for by local government from public money. The short-term reason for the losses was the pandemic, which had probably killed 867 of its residents and three staff by May 2020;[44] but the long-term reason was profit-taking.

Despite all this, the chief executive of the company was paid around £600,000 a year in 2022. The previous director had been paid even more, over £800,000, in 2019, which was almost double what he'd been paid the year before. In 1980 even the chief executive officers of FTSE 100 companies were paid only eleven times the salary of a median worker.[45] It is because their take was allowed to rise so high, to well over 111 times the median salary now, that salaries of nearly £1 million a year in other parts of the private sector are tolerated at all.

Between 1970 and 1981, state spending on the NHS rose from 3.4 per cent of GDP to 4.7 per cent, in line with the ageing population. However, it took the Conservative government elected in 1979 only two years to turn that trend around. Health spending then fell, not returning to its 1981 level until the run-up to the 1992 general election, and then falling back again through to 1997. The election of a Labour government that year saw the share rise once again from 5.1 per cent of GDP in 1997 to 8.1 per cent in 2009. The election of the Conservatives in 2010 again saw it drop, a fall not reversed until 2020 when the pandemic forced the government to spend more on health.[46]

A great deal of the argument about the NHS and social care has been about the amount of money that is spent and how that usually falls (as a proportion of GDP) when Conservative governments are in power. However, it is not just how much is spent but how well it is spent that matters. In 1970, after six years of progressive Labour government, only 3.4 per cent of UK GDP was spent on healthcare. Eight of the sixteen OECD countries for which there was data spent more than that. Despite being cheaper than average, the NHS was then highly effective because it was so efficient.

By 1980, twelve countries in the OECD were spending more per head than the UK on public health services, but by 1990 that figure had risen to sixteen. Because the number of countries for which there was data was also rising, the UK's slide down the ranks was not quite as fast when measured as a proportion of all OECD countries. By 1980, 57 per cent of OECD countries were spending more than the UK on public health, and by 1990, 64 per cent. The Labour government elected in 1997 began to reverse that trend, increasing healthcare spending considerably, but that growth in public spending no longer had as much effect on improving overall health. One reason was the increased privatisation within the NHS – supposedly 'to help inject plurality into the system' – which made it much more expensive to run.[47] Another reason was that increased economic inequality had such a detrimental effect on health (especially for the poorest) that it increased illness and made the job of the health and social care services harder in the UK than in other countries. However, growing inequality also had many other, more indirect effects on health.

The rise in economic inequality in the UK has hugely increased health costs, in particular the costs of skilled staff. Once the top 10 per cent are paid much more than everyone else, it costs a lot more to employ doctors, even if they slip down the rankings slightly compared to other highly paid professionals. Inefficiencies also rose because of the market that had been introduced in the NHS in the form of internal privatisation. In health, the market is the epitome of inefficiency. Labour's increased spending on health after 1997 was less effective, both because of increasing income inequality nationally and within the NHS, and because more of the money was diverted through the NHS to private services.

By 2010, public health spending in the UK was higher than in all but five of the twenty-five OECD countries with continuous data records since 1990. By 2019 it had slipped to tenth out of twenty-five. A year later, with the pandemic, UK public health spending per person had risen to become the fourth highest in the world. However, in 2020 that spending included huge frauds related to the pandemic,[48] the most commented-on being the government's funding, via referrals and a 'VIP lane',[49] of their friends' companies to supply personal protective equipment (PPE) that often did not work. But mostly the extra spending went on front-line services – services that became less effective when treating a population that had become more divided, hungrier, older and more precarious.

More equitable countries such as Finland spend much less money per person on their public health services, to far greater effect and with minimal waiting times – often no more than a few days in Finland, rather than the months, or even years, that are now common in the UK.

There is one way in which inequality almost always adversely affects healthcare. The inverse care law is the principle that the availability of good medical or social care tends to vary inversely with the need of the population served. This perverse relationship was proposed by a UK general practitioner in 1971 at the time it probably least applied, but it is obviously true almost everywhere and is exacerbated by increased inequality. For example, GP practices and hospitals in areas with the greatest need (usually generally deprived areas) find it hardest to fill vacancies. Then, because they become so seriously understaffed, they are less able to offer the best service.

Having to wait for care is a great incentive to try to jump the queue. In 1980 the British public spent less than half of 1 per cent of GDP a year on out-of-pocket private health expenses. These include everything from prescriptions to paying for a private operation. By 2021, those out-of-pocket expenses had more than tripled, to 1.5 per cent of GDP. Furthermore, the story of private health insurance is even more damning than that of out-of-pocket expenses. In 1970, 0.54 per cent of UK GDP was spent on private health insurance; by 1980 that figure had dropped slightly to 0.53 per cent, but by 2021 it was over 2 per cent.[50]

Private medicine is inefficient. It is more expensive than the NHS for the same procedures. It is less productive if you think in terms of staffing and how many patients get treated. It also does not train new health professionals, especially doctors. Although the proportion of those who can afford and are willing to go private is still only a tenth of all adults (each year), that tenth uses up far more resources per head than anyone else. When the *Guardian* reported in 2022 that one in ten adults had turned to the private sector, it did so with great sympathy for those who can afford to jump the queue.[51] The tone of the health debate changes as private provision begins to be presented as normal.

A large proportion of doctors and nurses in the UK are now working part-time or full-time in the private sector. By 2020 there were 515 private hospitals offering healthcare services in the UK, a mixture of for-profit and non-profit (but high-salaried) enterprises. By July 2022, partly because of the failures in healthcare, the UK moved to a new and unique position within the OECD league tables. An analysis in the *Financial Times* summed the situation up as pithily as is possible, while still including all the relevant details:

> In the EU, there were 5.8 million missing workers by summer 2020, but by late 2021 inactivity rates were back on the pre-pandemic trend. All but one of the 38 OECD member countries had either completed their labour force rebound or were well on the way there by the first quarter of 2022. Not in the UK. As 37 countries saw an ascent and descent in inactivity rates, Britain's line kept climbing. Uniquely among developed countries, the number of working-age Britons who are neither employed nor seeking work has risen in almost every quarter since the end of 2019, and was higher in the first quarter of 2022 than at any time since the pandemic hit. Chronic illness is the main driver of this stalled labour recovery. Of the roughly half a million Britons aged 15–64 missing from the workforce, two in three cite long-term illness as their reason for not holding or seeking a job. It would be easy to point the finger of blame at Britain's handling of the virus, but the data suggest otherwise.

The article concluded that:

> Covid is undoubtedly a factor in the NHS's ongoing crisis, through staff absences, additional pressure on hospitals and limiting the capacity to work through backlogs. But where other countries' healthcare systems are proving resilient, the UK's is on its knees. The virus may be the proximate cause of economic inactivity, but it's not the ultimate one, and the latter must be addressed to heal Britain's workforce.[52]

By 2014, a fifth of government MPs had financial links with private healthcare firms.[53] So how do you turn around a health and social care service that might have been deliberately run down with the intention of encouraging people to seek private healthcare instead? And what happens when those who thought they had saved enough to afford their own private hip replacement or cataract operation see their savings diminish by around a tenth each year due to inflation, at the same time as the charges for these operations rise 'due to inflation'?

You can't turn this around overnight, but you can begin to change the direction of travel. The number of local authority carers for old people in their homes has more than halved since 2010. Most of that fall had already occurred by 2014.[54] The crisis of care in the UK did not just happen. It was made.

Pandemic

If a national public health and care service is significantly reduced, then when disaster strikes, the country will be badly prepared, even if the disaster had been deemed the one most likely to occur according to the national risk register. In January 2020 the UK had five times fewer ventilators per person than did Germany.[55] By February the new disease was spreading rapidly across Britain, although largely undetected. By the start of March people began to modify their own behaviour due to fear of the disease, weeks before lockdown was imposed. As I wrote at the time: 'This disease will be brought under control despite the actions of central government, not because of them; although it may turn out to have been national policy (or lack of it) which led to so many patients being discharged into care homes with the disease.'[56] It was later revealed that the discharge of patients was the result of a government directive; but where else could they have gone?[57]

Government interventions during the pandemic had not been planned in advance, and so were not well thought out. Some 140,000 low-paid workers who lost their jobs when the pandemic hit were not protected by the furlough scheme that was introduced. There was also widespread fraud by employers. In one survey, a third of people supposed to have been furloughed reported that they had been asked by their employer to work unpaid. The first arrest for fraud was made on 8 July 2020; a fifty-seven-year-old man was accused of falsely claiming £495,000.[58]

Analysis of government data at the time showed that some rich people were doing very well and the poor were losing out, despite the Treasury claiming the opposite. The Treasury claim was that it had supported the poorest working households the most, in terms of help given as a proportion of income. However, they ignored what had happened to households in which people were not working, or were no longer working, or were on furlough. The Treasury also assumed, without evidence, that their self-employment support scheme would most help the poorest two deciles of households. Looking in more detail at the Treasury data it was clear that households in the bottom decile received less than half that which households in the middle received from government, and four times less than the very generous £330 a week the best-off tenth of households received.[59]

For those of working age, the highest death rates from the disease were among men working in the lowest-paid 'elementary' occupations, and in care and leisure services. Case rates and mortality in the second wave of the disease were highest in the very poorest parts of each city. A disease that had first arrived in the country carried by businesspeople and tourists very quickly moved from being most common in places like Westminster (at the time when Dominic Cummings fled Downing Street for County Durham) to becoming endemic and deadliest in the poorest of housing estates, where people were most crowded. Many of them could not work from home.[60]

Infection rates rose and fell in waves, with the waves rising highest in places that had previously been least affected, where acquired immunity was lower. The legacy of the first half-dozen waves of the pandemic has changed much about how we live, and especially about how we work. Many people are still working mostly from home. This may have benefits in the long term, but in the short term it reduces the flow of money to businesses that rely on commuters.

The Covid-19 pandemic did not end. In England in 2022 there were at least four peaks of the disease. Eventually it is thought that it will become more seasonal.[61] In the very long term, as levels of immunity rise through repeated infection and vaccination, it is hoped that Covid will have an effect more like that of the four common cold viruses it is so closely related to, possibly once a milder variant or a new less harmful coronavirus out-competes it. However, in the medium term it is now becoming accepted that it is causing heart disease and strokes to rise.[62]

The enduring austerity-related health problems from before the pandemic also show no signs of diminishing. Thousands of international researchers are currently following up millions of patients who have had Covid-19. Roughly half the UK population tested positive at some point before 2022, and most of the rest will have had the disease without knowing it. Arguably, the most traumatic event since the Second World War required a better response than simply trying to get back to normal as fast as possible. Especially as normal was so dire.

Internationally, between 2019 and 2021 life expectancy fell the most in those countries where health and social care systems were already not performing well. In Oman and Russia life expectancy fell by five years.[63] It fell by four years across all of southern Africa, much of South America and in places ranging from tiny Lebanon to massive India. Nearer to the UK, between those two years, life expectancy fell by three years in North Macedonia, Armenia and Bulgaria. This is not a complete list of those places that fared worse, including for children who, though not affected directly by the disease, were affected in how they were cared for. This included not being vaccinated against other diseases.

In contrast, life expectancy fell in the UK by one year between 2019 and 2021, mostly due to deaths directly from the disease. The UK may be failing, its health and care services may be greatly depleted, but we still managed to avert a catastrophe of the kind that occurred elsewhere in the world at this time. However, the UK could have done better. Compared to most other European countries, our pandemic record was not good.

Twenty of the thirty countries initially least affected by the pandemic were islands, the largest of which was Australia. These thirty were those in which life expectancy rose the most between 2019 and 2021. They were affected not just by not being impacted by the disease until much later, but also in being able to control it enough when it arrived to keep health and social care systems functioning. Others among that thirty which were not islands but were relatively self-containable included Canada, Norway and Western Sahara; or were able to almost entirely close their borders, like China, where life expectancy rose by a quarter of a year over those two years.

The UK, so reliant on its links with Europe and its people's ties to the rest of the world, could not have shut itself off like that, even if it had wanted to and even though it is physically an island too. However, the UK could have sheltered its frailest people better, which would have been far more effective than simply being able to vaccinate a few weeks earlier than other European countries.

How traumatic was the pandemic? The use of antidepressants across the UK rose by 6 per cent in the year to 2022, with 8.3 million NHS patients being prescribed the medication annually by then. That was 22 per cent higher than six years earlier. The most likely person to be prescribed these medicines is a woman in her fifties, but their use is also increasing in children and teenagers.[64]

Lockdowns were also traumatic, as was not being able to visit loved ones in hospital. Preventing school and university students from attending classes may not only have harmed their education but may also have made it more likely for them to spread the disease to older relatives. In hindsight it might have been better to shelter those at highest risk, while not requiring those least at risk to isolate. Since parents who could not work from home often had to ask grandparents to care for their younger children, a policy aimed at increasing isolation and reducing infection could have inadvertently increased the transmission risk to grandparents in poorer families.

What longer-term effect did the pandemic have on inequality and poverty? The temporary increase in Universal Credit social security benefit of £20 a week during the first year of the pandemic, coupled with the overall fall of 1.7 per cent in the median disposable household income in the year to April 2021, made poverty (as officially measured) appear to fall for a short time, and the Gini index of income inequality also fell from 35 to 34.[65] In a crisis, a little like in a war, inequalities can fall and there is the potential for that to be carried forward into the future.[66]

However, these changes due to the pandemic were only temporary, and the authors of the report on the change in the Gini measure of inequality expected them to be reversed within a year. Furthermore, affluent households were more likely to save money, owing to the reduction in the most accessible ways to spend their disposable income, whereas poorer households' debts increased and many had to borrow from friends and relatives to get through, even if they had been lucky enough to be furloughed (which still meant living on only 80 per cent of their basic income).

Similar one-year falls of the Gini coefficient have occurred before, in the years 2000, 2005, 2012, 2014 and 2018, for the very same measure (calculated after housing costs).[67] It had always rebounded the year after. You have to go back to the period from 1961 to 1979 to find this measure to be much lower in the UK, where it was then among the lowest in Europe. Even with a one-point fall in 2021, the UK would still be the most unequal country in Europe apart from Bulgaria, and it is very possible that the out-of-date Bulgarian figure, when updated, may turn out to be lower than in the UK now. It is also possible that the UK in 2022 became even more unequal after housing costs are included. Rents rose even more than mortgages, and the multiple cost-of-living crises deepened.[68]

If we look a little more closely at the timing of the changes, rather than simply comparing whole financial years, then it becomes clear that all that was achieved by the temporary uplift of Universal Credit in 2020 was a *partial* mitigation of the huge rise in inequality that had occurred in just four months in early 2020. The median household earnings of people living in the poorest fifth of households in the UK fell from £287 a week in February 2020 to £228 a week by May. This fall of over 20 per cent was larger than for any other quintile group and resulted in a huge and sudden widening of the gap between the best-off and worst-off quintiles. For the best-off fifth, the fall was 11 per cent, down to an average of £765 a week by May 2020. Income inequality actually rose with the Covid-19 crisis and then possibly rose again in late 2022 as the pandemic continued but with far fewer deaths per week. As that year came to an end the Autumn Statement introduced measures which, like every other government initiative, also failed to reduce income inequality.[69]

The economic effects of the UK's response to Covid – how it increased the wealth gap between rich and poor, how it led to lower real incomes for most people – may well have a greater long-term detrimental impact on health than the disease itself.

Exhausted

By 2022, people in the poorest parts of Britain were still three to four times more likely to die from Covid-19 than those in the richest. Long Covid is now most concentrated in these areas and among people aged thirty-five to sixty-nine. Its rates doubled between March 2021 and June 2022. Anxiety levels did reduce slightly in 2022, but remained especially high among women and those with least money. The already large academic attainment gap between children living in poorer areas and more affluent children grew even larger. The Health Foundation stated: 'Evidence to date suggests gaps between children from richer and poorer backgrounds that widened during the pandemic are likely to persist.'[70]

Although children may have been harmed in the long term, they tend to bounce back emotionally in the short term; but what of the emotional state of the wider population? To see how significant the pandemic was in this respect, it should be compared with past events. In the UK, after the economic crisis of 2008, and with the election of the coalition government in 2010, people's sense of well-being plummeted. It recovered only very slowly in the subsequent austerity years. We can only speculate as to what gave people more hope, but the degree to which respondents in the ONS survey of well-being said that 'things in life are worthwhile' eventually peaked in 2017 (with the unscheduled election year when Theresa May unexpectedly lost her parliamentary majority). Overall, the small rise in life-satisfaction measures peaked then too, as did national measures of happiness. Perhaps, then, in 2017, it was the idea that an alternative was becoming possible that began to cheer up enough people?

However, once Boris Johnson secured the Conservative Party leadership, and especially with his election victory in 2019, all these well-being measures plummeted. The onset of the pandemic brought them down further, but not by as much as the election of Johnson had. As the pandemic abated in the worst of its impact, all the UK's well-being measures rose again, but by the summer of 2021 they were still below the already low pre-pandemic levels of 2019.[71]

A further Covid-related factor that makes it very unlikely that overall income inequality actually fell briefly in 2020 or 2021 was the huge incomes received by the very small number of people involved in making money out of the pandemic. In March 2021 the

BBC reported: 'The government has . . . been accused of favouring firms with political connections to the Conservative Party with a "high-priority lane".'[72] The chance that anyone in that high-priority lane who received a huge boost to their income will have also been in the official government surveys of income is vanishingly small; the chance that they were included and then decided to honestly complete the voluntary survey about their sources of income is even smaller. The taking of monies from government by fraudsters may appear unrelated to everyday life, but it reduced the overall impact of government spending.

I am writing these words in the freezing winter of 2022/23 in the city of Oxford, which is home to one of the largest hospitals in Europe, the John Radcliffe. It can never fill all its job vacancies because the cost of housing in Oxford is so high and the wages of most hospital staff too low. People and patients cannot easily get to the site because the traffic backs up. There are not enough young doctors to staff the hospital properly, not enough skilled administrators, and not enough caterers for its kitchens to be run reliably. Every day the queues of people on trolleys in its A&E grow longer, as do the numbers of people dying at home in Oxfordshire. In December 2022, the Royal College of Nursing took its first strike action in the 106-year history of that union.

Across the UK, homeless people are sixty times more likely to go to A&E and five times more likely to be admitted.[73] Homelessness is now the most common cause of death for locals under the age of sixty-five in Oxford – and it has been like this for over twenty years. It is worse when it is cold.

Eventually, inequality grows so high that the whole edifice becomes unstable and begins to crumble. We first saw this occurring in the United States and in relation to health. In the early 2000s a health gap began to widen between counties that tended to vote

Democrat and those that voted Republican. Controlling for differences in age distribution, by 2019 an extra person a year was dying
in Republican counties for every thousand alive, as compared to
the mortality rate in Democrat counties. Had health in Republican
areas improved as it did in Democrat areas, then individual mortality rates in the former would have been 11 per cent lower by 2019.
There had been almost no gap between the two in the year 2000.
The gap has grown most clearly among white voters, whose health
stopped improving in Republican-voting counties after 2008.[74]

Traditionally, Republican areas had been the more affluent areas,
but now they were suffering more poor-health outcomes, partly
because they were no longer so affluent. However, the authors of
the study that identified these differences also cited many other
reasons as being of potential importance. In more conservative
(Republican) US states, increased restrictions on abortions had
already been linked to lower life expectancy for women. These
states also reduced gun controls. Furthermore, social welfare was
worse in the Republican states, with lower unemployment benefits,
and worse 'Temporary Assistance for Needy Families'. Democrat-
led areas of the US tended to have introduced more state healthcare
and better funded the provision already in place.

A similar divergence can be seen within the UK today. Before
2010, life expectancy was still rising in almost every neighbourhood, no matter how poor. By 2019 it had fallen in almost a fifth
of all neighbourhoods for women and in over a tenth for men.[75]

So, what is Britain good at? As we saw in Chapter 2, in 1979
Nicholas Henderson, Her Majesty's ambassador to France, had
complained that the French, when they tried diplomatically to find
something good to say about the UK, could only praise British
humour. Arguably British humour became even better after 1979.
The 1980s saw the rise of alternative comedy and a much more

satirical, less forelock-tugging form of humour than its more racist and sexist predecessor. What you find funny may well depend on your age and the times you have lived through, but what are the examples of great British humour today? We may be less able to laugh, and less able to produce material to laugh about, because we have become so exhausted and anxious. Rising fear is not funny.

Part III.
Mountains

8.

A Failing State

Growing prosperity and deepening knowledge inspired an atmosphere of unprecedented optimism throughout the Western world. Now that optimism has received a rude shock. The last war and subsequent crisis, producing even in the midst of horrible poverty an apparent surplus of goods, have undermined its economic foundations. Doubts as to the reality of 'progress' are widely entertained.[1]

These words were not written after the Russian war in Ukraine began in 2022, or after the American war in Iraq two decades earlier, but in 1936 at the height of the Great Depression. They were the thoughts of V. Gordon Childe, an archaeologist and social observer based at the University of Edinburgh. The 'last war' he was referring to was the First World War. Within a year, the German Luftwaffe bombed the town of Guernica in Spain, to aid the fascists in the Spanish Civil War. Two years later, the whole world was once again at war.

We are not living in times as bad as 1936, despite all the horrors we see now. However, doubts about the reality of progress are just as widely entertained today as they were then. We still live amid horrible poverty, both at home and abroad. We still see our

economic system produce a surplus of goods that go mostly to
those who need them least. We still worry about war, world war,
and politicians who might favour war over peace.

Today, unlike in 1936, it is widely known that through producing and consuming so many goods we have also now irreparably
polluted the planet. Nevertheless, between the late 1940s and the
early 1970s, there was a great deal of optimism. Most things did
get better. That optimism was so strong in the UK that on 20 July
1957, the prime minister, Harold Macmillan, could tell the population that 'most of our people have never had it so good'. What was
even more remarkable is that he could say this during the start of
the deadliest influenza pandemic since 1919.[2] When you have never
had it so good, a pandemic is easier to deal with.

The optimism grew greater still in the 1960s, but faltered in the
1970s and was crushed during the 1980s. It was regained temporarily in the 1990s, but then dashed further in the 2000s with another
war (in Iraq) and the unthinking acceptance of high inequality (as
long as the rich paid their taxes). Hope was broken again by the
austerity of the 2010s. And so, in the 2020s, battered by both the
pandemic and the general economic malaise, we find ourselves
struggling to be optimistic. Nowadays, few people apart from
the super-rich think that we have never had it so good. And yet
not enough of us ask why Britain in particular is so shattered as
compared to nearby countries.

The UK is not a failed state, but it is failing in more and more
ways. The Fund for Peace has published its Fragile States Index
every year since 2006.[3] The index is the sum of twelve separate
indices. It is intended as a tool to highlight which countries in the
poorer parts of the world are becoming more fragile, including
many countries that are widely considered to be failed states, such
as Yemen, Somalia and Syria (the three countries heading the list

in 2022). Countries can also be ranked by the separate indices and much other data. The index covers 179 countries and includes annual monitoring of the UK.

The UK's Fragile States Index ranking improved slightly each year between 2006 and 2010. By 2010, it was ranked 161st – 160 countries were more fragile. But after that year the UK ranking worsened in most years. By 2022, only 149 countries were *more fragile*. The components of the index that led to this change for the worse were the following: increasing 'group grievances' after 2010; 'factionalized elites' after 2016; and the 'worsening overall economic situation' after 2018 – all in comparison with these same measures in other countries. How each of the components was measured and then combined may be questioned, but the index was certainly not designed to make the UK look bad.

Finland was deemed to be the least fragile state in 2022. Of the twenty-nine states *more stable* than the UK, twenty were in Europe. By 2022 the UK was a fraction more fragile than the Czech Republic in Eastern Europe, and a fraction less fragile than Costa Rica in Central America. The UK was still deemed to be less fragile than many Eastern European countries because the index tends to award greater weight to overall prosperity. Among those doing worse in Europe was Bulgaria, although its position was better in 2022 than it had been in 2010. Like the UK, Bulgaria also does very badly in terms of its 'factionalized elites'.

The measures that the Fragile States Index uses to determine if elites are factionalised include – alongside wealth concentration and how redistributive the tax system is – an assessment of whether state institutions are fractured, including along class lines, and whether there is 'brinkmanship and gridlock between ruling elites'. The index also factors in xenophobia, the use of nationalistic political rhetoric and 'the absence of legitimate leadership widely accepted as representing the entire citizenry'.[4] It is an odd feeling to read these criteria and realise how many of them now apply so well to the UK.

Bulgaria is the only other state in Europe to suffer from as much inequality as Britain. Between 2021 and 2022 Bulgaria held four national elections, as its politicians tried hard to find solutions to the state they were in.[5] Britain now changes its prime ministers most frequently without elections. Edward Heath (1970–74) was the last UK prime minister to be not only voted into that position as a result of winning a general election but also ousted by a general election.

The UK's similarities with Bulgaria are many. In May 2022, annual inflation in Bulgaria surged to 15.6 per cent, a twenty-four-year high.[6] But the differences are obvious too. People are paid much less in Bulgaria. The median wage there is less than 40 per cent of Britain's. Bulgaria is the poorest country in the European Union.

Every unhappy state is unhappy in its own way. Former empires tend to collapse to an unequal core: Russia after the Soviet Union, Turkey after the Ottoman Empire, the UK after the British Empire, and the United States today – all are failing in different ways. In and on the edge of Europe, London is rivalled only by Moscow and Istanbul in terms of cities being outsized and over-powerful for the state they are in. But those other two dominating cities have been ruled by the same autocratic men who have been in power for a long time. In Britain, more like the US, more like Bulgaria, the people in charge keep changing.

Britain is not yet a failed state. Its currency has not yet collapsed, and its politicians (some of whom would like to be autocratic) no longer individually manage to hold on to power for very long, although their political parties tend to. Before turning to the politicians themselves, it is worth first considering the soup they swim in, the media. Shattered states tend to have a very distinct form of subservient media. In Britain, the subservience and role of the media became most clear during the state funeral of the Queen. It is usually less obvious because we have become used to it.

Media

There are now well-established rankings for most aspects of societies. Reporters without Borders ranks each country in the world according to various measures of press freedom. The Nordic countries are almost always at the top of the rankings.[7] The UK ranked twenty-fourth in the 2022 index, which is better than it did previously, but that is mainly because of recent changes to the way the index is calculated, rather than any change in the behaviour of the UK press.[8] Britain scores highest on economic indicators, meaning it is relatively easy to start a new newspaper or magazine in the UK. However, just one set of TV channels dominates British broadcasting: the BBC, with Sky and ITN coming a very distant second and third. Just a handful of newspapers report most of the news, often faithfully tweeted by readers on social media, one of the most faithfully retweeted being the *Guardian*, because it is still free to read online.

The majority of media sources cited in the notes to this book are open-access newspapers and websites. However, along with all British media, and England's main political parties, even the UK open-access press slowly moved to the political right as the state became more and more unequal. A more inequitable society does not develop a press that is more free, as the Reporters without Borders' international press freedom index demonstrates.

However, the situation can improve even in very unequal countries. As those who devised that press freedom index pointed out
in 2022: 'Moldova (40th) and Bulgaria (91st) stand out this year
thanks to a government change and the hope it has brought for
improvement in the situation for journalists even if oligarchs still
own or control the media.'⁹

The *Guardian*, unusually for a major newspaper in the UK, is
not owned by oligarchs, but that does not make it immune to the
conformist trend. The (Manchester) *Guardian* is now a London
paper. Those producing the paper, who consider themselves to
be the harbingers of change, increasingly support the status quo:
the Liberal Democrat Party, the right wing of the Labour Party,
and even occasionally the Conservative Party. This was seen in
2019 when the newspaper's main columnists gave succour to the
Conservatives' election campaign by fuelling divisions within
the Labour Party. Few people with significant jobs in Britain's
media would like to envisage having to pay more tax, because their
chosen lifestyles are expensive to maintain.

A decade ago, when he was secretary of state for education,
Michael Gove joked that he was looking forward to the day when
someone who had attended a state school could actually be the
editor of the *Guardian*.¹⁰ Newspapers are dominated by people who
attended private schools and also the University of Oxford. The
chairman of the company that owns the *Mirror*, purportedly the
workers' paper, was educated at the same Oxford college as Boris
Johnson. Though he did not attend a private school, the editor
of *The Times*, when he was editor of the *Sun*, went jogging with
Johnson.¹¹ Our media, and the lives of its most powerful members,
reflect our inequality.

Way back in 2006, the Sutton Trust, which champions social
mobility, found that 54 per cent of the top 100 newspaper editors,

columnists, broadcasters and executives were privately educated –
in 1986 it had been 49 per cent.[12] To blame the media for a shattered
state's woes is merely to blame one of the symptoms of that shattering. In a more equitable society the press is populated by a
more understanding group. Today, the Sutton Trust estimates that
Britain's most influential people are five times more likely than
average to have attended a fee-paying school. The media changes
when the state, as a whole, changes.

Until British society becomes less segregated, it is very likely
that people working in the higher-paid jobs at the BBC will continue to believe that they are impartial. In practice, however, they
have a narrow definition of impartiality that boils down to what
a few people, who are doing very well for themselves, think is
reasonable. In more equitable states, the media questions its own
impartiality and role far more thoroughly, and hence more effectively. From the *Guardian* to the BBC, what we see is a reflection of
our very unequal society. We see this in the views that are discussed
among those at the top. There is debate, but it is a debate between
those who have succeeded in an unfair race.

Sometimes people suggest that the mainstream media matters
less because so many people, especially younger people, are influenced by news reported via social media. However, the stories
that dominate social media are almost always stories that were first
broken in the mainstream media and were framed in a particular
way by those who write, edit, produce or direct their content.
A handful of popular political magazines, including the *New
Statesman* and the *Spectator*, also have a dominant role in shaping
opinions when they are referenced or copied on social media.
They too have all shifted to the right today, compared to how they
were placed when I was much younger. The same is true of their
equivalents in the US.

The academic Jonathan Haidt, writing in the *Atlantic* on the woes of the United States, has suggested that its current polarisation is a product of social media. He claims that 'a democracy depends on widely internalized acceptance of the legitimacy of rules, norms, and institutions'.[13] One obvious response to his claim is to point out that social media is universal but few other affluent countries are as politically polarised as the US has become. The US was splitting apart economically, socially and politically long before social media arrived on the scene, and it is this that made the country what it is today. Haidt describes most Americans as members of the 'exhausted majority', but they began to become exhausted before social media further fuelled the hate that grows when trust dies, and which has now become so vocal and public.

Another North American media commentator, Ezra Klein, writing in the *New York Times*, identified a trend where the middle classes are losing the ability to afford essentials. Fewer and fewer better-off-than-average Americans can afford healthcare, housing and the cost of education. Education, housing and healthcare are basics, but the American middle classes became deluded by their increased capacity to purchase expensive items that fed their understanding of financial success: advanced computers, amazing phones, upmarket clothes and sleek cars. Klein wrote: 'In the 1960s, it was possible to attend a four-year college debt-free, but impossible to purchase a flat-screen television. By the 2020s, the reality was close to the reverse.'[14] However, Klein's suggested solutions call for looking internally within the US. Americans should instead ask how most other affluent nations have housing that is so much more affordable, healthcare that is so much more accessible, and education that is usually free, or nearly free, up to and including university level.

Klein's article is typical of thousands of newspaper stories written in more unequal affluent countries – where comparisons with what occurs elsewhere are avoided. In contrast, newspapers published on most of the European continent often include stories about what is happening in other countries when discussing what could be done at home. Although many of these stories now usually express shock when the UK is mentioned, they allow people to draw comparisons and take stock. Only very rarely will a UK news outlet make comparisons such as these.

To give one example of when such a comparison was made, we can return to that 2012 *Guardian* article in which Michael Gove mentioned how nice it would be if the paper's future editor were to be chosen from among the 93 per cent who had attended a state school. Gove went on to say:

> More than almost any developed nation, ours is a country in which your parentage dictates your progress. Those who are born poor are more likely to stay poor and those who inherit privilege are more likely to pass on privilege in England than in any comparable country. For those of us who believe in social justice, this stratification and segregation are morally indefensible.

The point of quoting this is to point out how rare it is to hear such a statement. In his next ten years as a serving government minister, in increasingly rightward-moving administrations, Gove mentioned these issues less and less.

Gove is an unusual politician, sometimes prone to saying what he actually thinks; but his worldview is libertarian. Consequently, he fitted in well enough for his occasional outpourings about unfairness to be tolerated by his right-wing mostly privately educated colleagues. He did not question the general climate in which commercial interests trump other interests. He did not suggest new economic or social thinking that was too threatening. He was himself originally a journalist, rising to become a leader writer at *The Times* in 1996, then its comment editor, news editor, Saturday editor and assistant editor. Before that he had worked in television and for other newspapers.[15]

There is a revolving door between politics and the media in the UK. When listening to the debonair tones of BBC radio news, it is always worth thinking why the news is presented as it is and the reasons behind what has been chosen to be news. BBC Radio 4 in particular provides reassuring voices, spoken by people who are more affluent than the vast majority of their (better-off-than-average) listeners. When listening to Radio 4, assume that you are listening to a polite internal debate being held within the Conservative Party. It then all makes much more sense in terms of what is not said or ever discussed. The same can be claimed of much of the rest of the BBC. One example came after the local elections of May 2019, when the loss of eighty-four Labour seats and the loss of 1,330 Conservative seats were described as 'comparable' by BBC News on its website.[16]

Politicians

In an increasingly unequal society, as inequality rises, there are more and more examples of people being appointed to jobs they do not appear able to do. It can take some time to work out why. They may have had family connections, attended a particular school or university, and cultivated friendships that may have been crucial in why they ended up where they did. These are just individual microscopic parts of a much wider pattern of low, and in some cases declining, social mobility. Social mobility is almost always higher in more equitable societies. In those societies people end up in positions better suited to them, and are drawn from a much wider pool of potential candidates. In a highly unequal society, affluent parents try harder to place their children on trajectories to the top jobs, and have the resources and connections to achieve this. Friends and colleagues also tend to be drawn from similar backgrounds and look out for each other, often having a lower opinion of people less like themselves.

The tendency for the top jobs in the UK to be filled with people from an increasingly narrow range of social backgrounds is apparent in almost all 'top' professions. The Sutton Trust first revealed this many years ago and continues to update its analysis.[17] It is most strongly the case for high court judges (65 per cent privately schooled), and remarkably less among university vice-chancellors (16 per cent, but still more than twice what would be expected). Most professions are not subject to the same glare of publicity that politicians are, so the patterns in those fields are not examined in as much detail as they can be for MPs. As we become more unequal, we slowly get used to being governed by 'our betters' once again, and that too makes us less aware of how unusual UK politicians have become.

By 2022, only one in 100 Conservative MPs had entered Parliament from a job that was identified as being working class. The proportion had fallen over time for other parties too, but not by as much. Labour's share halved between the 1980s and 2022, to now stand at 13 per cent.[18] One reaction to these trends is to suggest that the UK is now being governed by a more able minority. But that is just the kind of view that is tolerated in an unequal shattered state, where the idea that a few people are especially able is more commonplace. In the past, when the UK became more equal, its MPs began to be drawn from a much wider range of backgrounds and some became extremely able ministers, in contrast to today.

The argument is not that politicians drawn from a wider pool will be better because those selected will have greater ability. Instead, it is that between them they will have a whole range of experiences and aptitudes that together make them better as a group. A more diverse group is less likely to cause harm, as there will hopefully be some among them able to point out the folly of taking a particular path, given their wider experiences. This is the very opposite of suggesting that greater competition produces better politicians because it promotes those with supposedly greater ability.

A group of MPs drawn from a very narrow social pool may result in them reinforcing and then amplifying each other's often very elitist attitudes. When Michael Gove was education secretary, his views on eugenics – that people's apparent cleverness was greatly influenced by their genetics – were not questioned within government. A fear grew that we were seeing a return to a time when different children were seen as having very different potential. In the words of one of Gove's advisors, this did not mean 'giving up on the less fortunate', it just meant spending less on their education.[19] The phrase 'the less fortunate' harks back to a time when it was common among the elite to view those below them as lacking in both fortune and ability.

British politicians, even the most well meaning, are increasingly drawn from a narrow stratum of society and have had less opportunity to interact with others from different backgrounds as children. That opportunity then falls even further when they go to university, as most of them do, even if they imagine they are meeting a wider range of people there. It falls again when they go into work. Meeting a few constituents on a Friday is not the same as interacting with a wide range of people.

Among people at the top, there is great sensitivity about having their backgrounds discussed. No one is responsible for who their parents were, and very few children are given any real choice about what school they attend. For those who go to university, their route there is usually more heavily steered by their parents and their schools than by themselves. So why the sensitivity? Hopefully because there is an underlying understanding of the unfairness of society among some in the elite, and they know they have mostly got where they are not solely because of their own personal ability. Some, though, do appear to harbour a special dislike of having their inherent advantages questioned.[20]

As Britain became more and more economically divided from the mid-1970s onwards, the people who became MPs changed. What they felt they needed to do to survive financially also changed. Some even said they could no longer afford to take up paid ministerial posts (which would entail giving up their second jobs) because their salaries were too low for them to maintain their lifestyle, despite the fact that they were being paid several times the average wage.

In 2021, 114 Conservative MPs, twenty Labour MPs and twelve others (mainly SNP) had second jobs, often as consultants to industries ranging from gambling to the arms trade. A fifth of MPs admitted to being landlords in receipt of rental income, with a few of them owning multiple properties; and we have our MPs to thank for the UK now having the largest gambling industry in the world.[21] In contrast, just 3 per cent of the general public are now landlords (not long ago it was 2 per cent), and there is little public enthusiasm for a gambling industry that operates without regulation. Many MPs also have vested interests in private healthcare. None of this ever prevents them from voting on issues in which they have a personal financial interest. A country that becomes very unequal creates an increasingly unrepresentative political class. A very small number of people also become incredibly wealthy and a subset of them begin to be relied upon to fund the main political parties. The possible influence of party funders on future policy choices is only rarely discussed.

It is not just the social backgrounds of politicians that matter but also those of their donors.[22] The geographies of these donors, and their backgrounds and lived experience, need to be better understood to comprehend how Britain changed from being nearly the most equitable large country in Europe in the mid-1970s to being the place where, today, huge divisions are presented as acceptable. A toxic influence has set in since then, slowly spreading outward from the most right-wing think-tanks and parties, and eventually affecting all of British politics.

Charting the rot within the Conservative Party is easy. But it can also be found in the Liberal Democrat and Labour parties, and in any party that accepts large donations from a few people.[23] However, there is more to this toxicity than just dodgy donations and individuals gaining lasting influence. For instance, in the early 2000s, a problem arose among the salaried people employed at the Labour Party's head offices.[24] In the words of the report that followed: 'A practice of officials recruiting in their own image (politically speaking) had, post-Blair [by 2008], ensured that the HQ's broad political alignment remained steadily on the Right of the Party even as the elected leadership (and membership) moved to the Left.'[25] The hostility of some officials was so high that they 'joked' to their colleagues that they would like to see their opponents within the party 'run over by a train' or 'die in a fire'. Hardly comradely.

The internecine conflict within both of Britain's two largest political parties has reached a level previously only seen when parties have actually split, such as when right-leaning Labour MPs left the party in the 1980s to form the Social Democratic Party. Politics in the mainstream parties is becoming more like the uncompromising politics that used to be associated with the fringes. On the far left and right of British politics, groups tend to be unwelcoming to new ideas and outsiders, so eventually people stop trying to join or influence them. Instead, they may drift from group to group or start their own group, which explains the fragmented nature of the British far left and right.

Occasionally there are signs of a counter-reaction. The prime ministers John Major (Conservative) and Gordon Brown (Labour) played similar roles in British politics, undoing a fraction of the damage done by their predecessors. The relentless rise in inequality stalled slightly when both Major and Brown were in power. Just occasionally there has been a willingness to halt the contamination at the top of British politics, and that is why we look back on some politicians as having been far more decent than others. But Britain has a long legacy of producing some of the most brutal politicians in world history. You cannot be the chief executive of a huge empire without being brutal as well.

This British legacy did not disappear when the empire collapsed. It was kept alive in the ethos of boarding schools and Mayfair clubs. It emerged again in a series of London think-tanks and in the ideology of a new post-empire generation of Conservative politicians who had been too young to feel the shame and reality of the Suez crisis in 1956. They were brought up on, or later came to be converted to, the myth that Britain was destined to have a special place in the world in future. This new jingoism ended in the tragedy of Liz Truss, holder of the record for the shortest premiership in British history.

There were low expectations when Truss took office. She had surrounded herself with people whose political opinions were on the fringe of what is normal in Europe today. She was not the first choice of Conservative MPs, and within weeks of her election as party leader (and, by default, prime minister) by 47 per cent of her party membership, many Tory MPs wanted rid of her. In early October 2022, the *Economist* magazine suggested she had the shelf life of a lettuce (about ten days), a comment that the *Daily Star* then gleefully took up and ran with. But the *Economist* had overestimated Truss's staying power. To understand how this all happened – and the mindset of those who promoted Truss and fed her so many untruths, and who now half-heartedly support her successor, Rishi Sunak – we have to turn to the far-right ideologues of the UK.

Ideologues

Increases in social segregation can encourage the creation of myths and beliefs that are perpetuated if most of your friends and colleagues are from a background similar to yours, and if you can live your life mostly among them. A good example comes from a single address in central London: 55 Tufton Street, Westminster. This is or has been the home of at least a dozen lobbying groups, including BrexitCentral, Leave Means Leave and the TaxPayers' Alliance.[26] These groups are not independent from each other, and they all have a shared goal, which is to help the wealthy to stay rich. The main funders of these organisations are not ordinary people, not even millionaires, but unnamed multimillionaires and billionaires and their businesses, all of whom would like to see a low-tax, deregulated society, and ideally one without trade unions.

There are undoubtedly some clever people working in Tufton

Street, and they are out to persuade the general public, but more so its elected representatives, that the policies they advocate are, or will be in their fantasy brave new world, beneficial to everyone. Many within their organisations believe this, and dismiss other views out of hand. They believe that while some people deserve a fantastic amount of money as a reward for their efforts, the majority of people are virtually worthless except as a source of labour and exploitation. Such views come from people separating themselves from society. Working among such people it would be difficult to believe anything else.

Internationally, the UK has become the central European hub for proponents of the idea that incredible extremes of inequality are beneficial and somehow natural. The main European think-tanks promoting inequality are almost all based in London, many at Tufton Street, but others in very nearby offices. The funding behind these think-tanks is opaque, but in the case of 55 Tufton Street it appears to be closely linked to the arms trade – a business-man involved in making 'defence equipment' apparently owns the building. But the web of connections and addresses is far more complex and obscure than that one relationship. It is not hard to link it all back to an ideology whose roots lie in the ashes of the British Empire, hosted now in iconic streets and houses built when that empire was first growing.[27]

It may at first glance appear odd that the main location in Europe for an extreme fringe ideology should be on the edge of that continent, but most other European countries have been much less welcoming environments for ideas from the far right. Until 2020, the UK provided the largest number of members of the European Parliament who were to the right of the main European Conservative group block. Now that there are no UK MEPs because Britain has left the EU, the country with the most far-right

MEPs is Poland. However, there are not, as yet, a great number of far-right think-tanks in Warsaw.[28]

The influence of the United States has also been crucial.[29] Calls to dismantle Britain's state housing system were first made from the US in the 1950s.[30] Mass provision of decent housing was seen as a dangerous precedent that other countries might choose to follow, and it is still hard to make the case for more state housing in the UK today as a result of those attacks.[31] The increasing privatisation of the school, university, social care and healthcare systems has also followed an American model, with encouragement from US policy-makers.[32]

In very recent years, key figures from the extreme right have been appointed to civil service posts or as government advisors. Several appointees were drawn from just one think-tank, the Tax-Payers' Alliance. Jonathan Isaby, its former chief executive, was appointed to a civil service position by Priti Patel, then the home secretary, in August 2021.[33] In August 2022, the chancellor, Nadhim Zahawi, appointed Duncan Simpson, a research director at the TaxPayers' Alliance, as a special advisor.[34] In September 2022, Prime Minister Liz Truss appointed Matthew Sinclair, former head of the TaxPayers' Alliance, as her chief economic advisor.[35] On the same day, she and her chancellor sacked Tom Scholar, the most senior civil servant in the Treasury, with a long and distinguished career, in a move that two former Cabinet secretaries said 'compromised civil service independence'.[36] However, they should have expected it, because in 2011 Truss founded the 'parliamentary wing' of the Institute of Economic Affairs, another London-based right-wing think-tank, and appointed its communications director as her deputy chief of staff in 2022.[37]

People like those appointed to key government positions in 2021 and 2022 come from a very particular orientation. Recently, the head of political economy at the Institute of Economic Affairs outlined what he and his colleagues thought of those who politically opposed him. He wrote:

> We often describe 'the typical Leftie' as someone who is overly emotional, prone to knee-jerk reactions, intellectually lazy, shallow, conformist, easily swayed by fads and fashions, unable or unwilling to think things through properly, and above all, preachy and sanctimonious. (For the record, I believe all of the above). But these are the attributes of an annoying person, not the attributes of a villain. They are the attributes of someone you'd rather avoid, not the attributes of someone you hate with a passion.[38]

The writer concluded his missive by stating: 'Thus, while plenty of her enemies celebrated the death of Margaret Thatcher, I struggle to imagine something like this happening in reverse.' Many people did not respond to the news of Thatcher's lonely death in the Ritz Hotel, without her family, with sadness. In life she had 'all that money could buy', but for her, at the end, there was no such thing as either family or society. I would not like to die that way.

Thatcher's death was both mourned and celebrated by some when she died. Most people ignored it. Her rise as the figurehead of a new and more extreme right wing in the UK had been very similar to that of her contemporary, Ronald Reagan, in the US. Both became totems for having helped usher in a golden age for conservatives. The beliefs of both lived on long after their deaths. If everything is not now as it should be, this, according to some on the right, is only because others have since strayed from the true path.

Truss in particular was said to have tried to model her image on Thatcher, in both ideology and dress. She was not alone in this. Penny Mordaunt, an early rival of Truss in the 2022 leadership race, harked back to 'the Falklands spirit', one of Thatcher's 'career highlights' when prime minister. Rishi Sunak also tries to peddle the message of a potential revival of past greatness. He has published three books: *A Portrait of Modern Britain* (2014), *A New Era for Retail Bonds* (2017) and *The Free Ports Opportunity: How Brexit Could Boost Trade, Manufacturing and the North* (in 2018). Two of the three were published by a Tufton Street think-tank, and the third by one located very nearby. As the days darken, and the ideologues continue to flail, we should expect to hear more retelling of a whitewashed past from those who were barely old enough to experience it. But these fictionalised tales will become harder to take as our present predicaments grow.

The UK's current cost-of-living crisis was soon recognised as being significantly worse than that of other European countries, such as Germany's – in spite of the latter's reliance on Russia for gas. During the early days of the Conservative leadership contest in 2022, one commentator observed that, instead of trying to address the crisis, 'all the potential successors scrabbling around their podiums for Johnson's crown have retreated to the safe space of Thatcherite dogma, promising to shrink the state just when the state's protective hand will be needed more than ever'.[39] Some commentaries did at times descend into hyperbole, with this observer continuing:

> How much state is even left to shrink? Try to get a GP appointment; try to get the police to attend an incident of crime, let alone provide justice. Crime is rampant, incomes are shrinking and education is worthless. Our external borders are now purely notional, and the union's survival is doubtful. We already pay Scandinavian taxes for Mediterranean public services, and all the candidates are offering is a further diminution

of state capacity. If Conservatives do not relearn how to run it, then the state will collapse, and deservedly so.

State collapse is unlikely. However, the conclusion to this tirade, that 'soon Britain will just be a gloomy Italy, halfway between museum and nursing home', was less wide of the mark. As the winter of 2022/23 approached, it was unclear whether there would be enough gas to heat people's homes, let alone whether most people would be able to afford enough of it if there were.

Italy and the UK are not that different. Italy is the most unequal large country in Europe after the UK, and in September 2022 it elected the most similar government.[40] Both states suffer from widespread tax evasion and avoidance, although the problem is sometimes tackled with more flamboyance in Italy. A decade ago, the number of Ferraris sold in Italy was higher than the number of people declaring the level of income one would expect someone able to afford those Ferraris to have. In 2012, Italian tax collectors uncovered $12 billion in unpaid taxes, partly through identifying more than 2,000 luxury-car owners and then investigating their tax affairs. The police were involved and, at one point, even the army and secret services.[41]

It is only an ideological belief that top earners should be left alone, apparently to protect the economy, that prevents the UK tax authorities from copying the Italian model and treating tax evaders as criminals. The fear is that businesses might desert the UK if their owners could not make a packet here, flout the law and avoid EU regulations that protect workers and consumers. Italy is far from being as gloomy as the UK has become; and by remaining a member of the EU, it may find it is better able to ensure access to basics, like heating in winter.

The old stereotypes about Britain, as a place with poor weather but good order and patient queuing, are taking on new meanings. We now fear the cold weather more and increasingly worry about how many people will jump the queue. In-person appointments with GPs are still possible, but less (easily) accessible than before. Petty crime is not necessarily skyrocketing, but only because there isn't a great resale value for stolen goods. Incomes are certainly shrinking. Education is not entirely worthless but is now usually considered to be more a means to secure a future higher income than about learning. However, the worship of the market is very dangerous for the British. It assumes that everything of value has a price in pounds. But when and if the rationing of certain goods becomes necessary, the wealthy may find that even they lose out.

Characterising other countries as places that have bigger problems than the UK, as has been done frequently with Italy, is a standard British right-wing trope. On the right of politics, patriotism demands that you believe your own country is somehow, and is destined to remain, the best. The fact that it obviously is not, so the argument goes, is because it has 'lost its way' and needs to look inside itself to find the so-called traitors within – the scroungers (at the bottom, not at the top), the exhausted poor who are supposedly lazy, and any minority (whether by colour, creed, birthplace, disability or sexuality).

There are also immigrants to be blamed (except American immigrants and, inexplicably, rich Russians) and evils elsewhere (especially within the EU). The right claims that Britain needs to look back to a supposedly more glorious past to find its way again – to be Great Britain once more. However, when we look back at our past, we are often presented with highly contrived accounts that not only tell us it was wonderful when in fact it was harsh, but that also disguise what it is we have actually lost and the influences that helped to create that loss.

There is a tendency to overlook the influence America has had on UK social policies for the past forty years. Thatcher adopted extreme right-leaning tendencies in everything related to the costs of the state, and effectively opened the door to US companies, allowing them to profit from changes being made to social policy and the NHS. Thatcher's successor, Conservative prime minister John Major, invited a discredited American health insurance giant to design social policies to limit access to disability benefits. His successor, the 'New' Labour prime minister Tony Blair, adopted US social and labour market policies that guaranteed the low-waged were intimidated and blamed for the fact they were employed in a low-waged job. Blair's successor, Gordon Brown, introduced a fatally flawed disability assessment model that successfully terrorised those in greatest need. Brown's successor, David Cameron, escalated the harshest sanctions introduced with austerity measures, also influenced by US social policies, which meant that those in greatest need would live in fear when unfit to work or unemployed.[42]

The present reality is also often made more obscure than it needs to be. Official government bodies tend to be very selective with the evidence they present – often doing so in ways that can make it appear that the UK is not doing as badly as it is. For example, in its 2022 *State of the Nation* report, the government's Social Mobility Commission included only one international comparison in its data tables. It showed the percentage of adults who earn more in absolute terms than their parents did at age thirty. By this measure the UK ranked equal second best with Norway out of eight countries compared. Only the Netherlands had a higher percentage.[43] However, the source they used also showed that if the very same calculations are repeated at age forty, then the UK is ranked second worst out of the eight, just above the United States, and the gap between the UK and the US was narrowing. For most countries it makes little difference whether age thirty or forty is used, but not so for the UK.[44]

Although the Social Mobility Commission report was obviously looking for good news, the choice of example just mentioned may have been inadvertent. The researcher who selected this data may not have read on to page 74 of the academic paper they took it from. If they had, they would have noticed that the UK was unusual and ranked so much differently when age forty was the comparator. But the fact that they did not include any other international comparisons, when the majority of such comparisons are so damning, suggests that at the very least they were subconsciously aware that those who would be signing off their work would not be happy with them if they did so. This is how ideologues most influence policy: by limiting what others are prepared to say and do, by reframing the debate into one that serves their interests, by promoting omissions and thus misleading – or at least failing to fully inform – their audience.

Distractions

Power protects itself through deflection, scapegoating and making systemic issues look like individual failures – you didn't work hard enough, there's something wrong with you, or, if you are claiming benefits, you're playing the system. This drives people further and further into social exclusion and all the perils that this brings. Paradoxically, problems are said to have been created both by people not working hard enough, and by people coming to Britain to work hard. People buy into such stories at the expense of seeing our problems in perspective. Internalising these tropes of personal failure helps to keep them alive, and creates collective misguidance.

A failing state blames outsiders and internal traitors, despite its failures being largely home-grown by misguided patriots. The story it tells its own people – that in future they will prosper and that there is opportunity for all – is a compelling myth. Because more successful and equitable countries in Europe have less space at the bottom of their societies, due to fewer poorly paid jobs, they tend to attract and retain fewer migrants from abroad – but those who opt to stay are found to be happier, according to international surveys of citizen happiness. In contrast, as the British state falls deeper into failure, part of the current government's plan is to increase the flow of guest-worker labour – people who stay for a while, but do not remain for too long. This is the country-house-servant model of the future.

In May 2004 the EU welcomed ten new member states from Central and Eastern Europe. At first, however, only the UK, Sweden and Ireland allowed migration from these new member states. The majority of people who left those countries came to the UK. Life expectancy for women in the UK rose significantly after 2004. In hindsight, it appeared that the women who came may well have been some of the most energetic and healthy, young and well educated. This will not be the whole story, but the picture changed abruptly once people in these EU accession states had the option to move to a wider range of Western European countries.

The improvement in health in those early years may have also been aided by the care work that many of those migrants did. However, the in-migration did not last, and it was frequently very geographically focused.[45] For example, Southampton has one of the largest Polish populations outside London, alongside Slough and the Erdington district of Birmingham. People migrate to where there is work, but also to places where they know there will be others who speak their mother tongue.[46]

On the first anniversary of the June 2016 advisory referendum on leaving the EU, the Office for National Statistics released their annual population estimates of how many people had been born, how many had died, and how many had migrated in and out of every part of England. Those migration numbers told an interesting story.

In terms of the proportion of the population in June 2016 who had arrived from abroad within the previous twelve months, the local authority districts of England and the boroughs of London could be ordered from the lows of South Staffordshire (0.11 per cent) and Staffordshire Moorlands (0.13 per cent) up to the highs of Westminster (5.9 per cent) and the City of London (8.5 per cent).[47] Almost no one came from overseas to live in those two districts of Staffordshire between June 2015 and June 2016. In contrast, one in every seventeen residents in Westminster at the time of the EU referendum was a very recent arrival, as were more than one in twelve of the residents of the City of London, many of them living on the Barbican Estate. In Westminster and the City of London, less than a third of those who voted in the referendum voted to leave the EU. In contrast, in both of those two Staffordshire districts with the lowest international immigration rates of all, some 65 per cent of all those who voted wanted to leave.

The strongest geographical correlation to predict the size of the leave vote in an area was with migration. The fewer migrants an area had, the more people in that area were likely to vote leave – partly because they had been told about the terrible problems migrants were causing elsewhere. Surveys in 2014 had already shown that overall only 20 per cent of people thought that immigration was a problem in their local area, but 75 per cent thought it was a problem for Britain.[48]

Migrants tend not to migrate to poorer rural areas unless there is demand for them – there are generally not enough opportunities in those areas. Migrants tend to have get-up-and-go. On the very same day the result of the EU referendum was announced in 2016, the official mid-year UK population estimates were published for the year ending June 2015. They revealed the most remarkable rise in mortality for that year. Although it was little commented upon at the time, there was one anomaly in the results – death rates for people aged twenty-five to twenty-nine had not risen at all. This was the age group of highest net in-migration to the UK at the time.[49]

The crash of 2008 and the great recession that followed it; the austerity that was enacted from 2010 onwards; the decades-long debate about immigration; the blaming of the EU for everything; the announcement of a referendum in 2015; the final Brexit decision at the end of 2019; the controversies over how the pandemic was dealt with in 2020–21; the arguments over the cost of living, the 'mini-budget' and then the major budget crisis of 2022 – these were all distractions from the overall reality. The truth was that the state was falling apart, with rising resentment in the 'peripheral regions and nations', a fall in Conservative support in the Home Counties, a tacit acceptance of huge levels of inequality as normal, and a general floundering about in the dark as one crisis morphed into the next.

Such distractions always appear to be of overriding importance. Often they are indeed very important, but if they are nearly continuous and absorb the majority of media attention, then the country's slow and steady falling down the ranks on health, education and the economy goes largely unnoticed, or is ascribed to the distractions themselves. A media that focuses mostly on the distractions will not encourage debate on the issues of growing fragmentation. Politicians, elected because of their party affiliation rather than for their personal qualities, highlight particular distractions as being terribly important, but often do not want society's growing fragmentation highlighted. Ideologues, who see inequality as essential, need distractions so that their motives and underlying beliefs are not questioned. This is what failing looks like.

9.

Conclusion

In 2022, the man who had served as chair of the National Trust from 2008 to 2014 wrote: 'If I were Northern Irish, I would vote to rejoin the prospering south. If I were Scottish, I would wonder why I was once richer than Ireland and Denmark but am now poorer, and would opt for independence, whatever the pain.'[1] He didn't say what he would do if he were Welsh, but he did quote the words once used to stir the Welsh rugby team into action when they took on the English: 'bastards . . . taking our coal, our water, our steel . . . They exploited, raped, controlled and punished us – that's who you are playing.' To the list of what the English took, slate could have been added. You can see Welsh slate on roofs all over England.

It is remarkable how little wealth flowed back into Wales, for all that was removed by the English. Huge empty slate caverns remain. Some are now 'attractions' for the entertainment of (mainly English) tourists. Former coal mines are too dingy to make good attractions because the tunnels are too low and dirty. When visiting a former Welsh slate mine, tourists learn about the exploitation, but not who the owners were, or who they still are, or who the money from tourism is going to.

Papering over the cracks of this shattered state requires constantly rewriting history and presenting a still very partial picture after each rewrite, often in order to prevent any greater understanding. One example is the recent controversy over mentioning the money derived from overseas slavery – money that was used directly or indirectly to build so many of the stately homes and country estates now run by the National Trust. In October 2022, the *Telegraph* claimed that 1,700 National Trust curators had been sacked by the Trust as it tried to promote what the newspaper called an anti-British skewing of history. In fact only eight curators had left, half of them voluntarily. The historical or even very recent facts did not matter to the *Telegraph*, although the newspaper was forced to apologise.[2]

Couple that dispute with the fervent arguments for keeping statues of people such as Cecil Rhodes in place and it becomes clear just how strongly felt is the conservative desire to maintain a fantasy of past glory and, by inference, of a glorious future to come. In August 2022, Rishi Sunak, then one of the final two contenders for leadership of the Conservative Party, proposed that people who '*vilify the UK*' should be referred to the Prevent counter-terrorism scheme for re-education. In November 2022, Jeremy Hunt, speaking as Sunak's chancellor of the Exchequer, stated without equivocation that 'the United Kingdom is and has always been a force for good in the world'.[3]

Dystopia

What will most likely occur if nothing is done to end the shattering? What dystopian nightmare scenario awaits us, if current trends continue? Complacency is our greatest enemy, so we need to ask how things could get worse. This is especially true of those of us among the shrinking number of people in Britain still able to afford to buy a book and have the time to read it. They (most of you) have more to lose because they have lost less so far. It is already clear that destitution is the fate of a growing number of people, but what will the better-off personally lose? Can they ignore the question of what is to be done?

This is a question that the main opposition party is not addressing, other than by making vague promises of 'growth'. The Labour Party proposes only more tinkering, but such tinkering failed to reverse the trends described in this book when it was attempted between 1997 and 2010, years in which inequality did not fall significantly in any single year. Under New Labour, wealth and opportunity (social mobility) divides deepened, the privatisation of public provision was extended, and the take of the 1 per cent carried on rising.

The dystopian future is not one of formal re-education camps for university professors who 'vilify the UK'. Rather, it is one in which such voices will be silenced, where academics will become ever so careful about what they say in a lecture for fear of a complaint about their 'bias'. It is a future in which a whole range of people – from academics to filmmakers, recording artists, poets and sports figures – will know to hold their tongues on an increasing range of issues if they wish any of their commentary to be carried by the media. If they speak out, they risk being shunned.

This is a future in which people will still quietly discuss their opinions, but only when they believe they can really trust those they are speaking to, in places where they are not being recorded and cannot be overheard. In this dystopia, many people will increasingly avoid using social media, for fear of being made outcasts. In public, the story will increasingly be one of national success, of how well our athletes are doing in some sporting event, of how bravely our soldiers are fighting in whatever war we have just joined or started. We will hear more tales about how everything ever done in the name of the UK was done for the good of all in the world. We will find new things to be 'world leaders' in, and forget the equality and social innovation that we were once so good at. Those past achievements will be repainted as failures.

As the UK has fallen in numerous international rankings of what is good, it has also risen in the OECD league tables of what is bad – from England being worse at teaching its children about reasoning and deep learning (it is now worse than China in this ranking[4]), to the UK as a whole now imprisoning many more people than any other country in Europe bar two others on its periphery: Russia and Turkey.[5] The UK prison population was the same in 1945 as in 1900. But it doubled in the forty-five years between 1945 and 1990, after which it doubled again in just eighteen years, between 1990 and 2008. The rise only stalled with the financial crash and Covid-19. The UK was not always a force for good in the world, especially not at the height of its power in 1900. We don't need to lament our falling down the ranks. But one way to better understand our history is to look at how things have changed over time, the direction of travel, and to consider the international geographical rankings, what our actual place now is and what we could be.

As recounted earlier in this book, the much-maligned 1970s were a time when the UK often ranked first in Europe in measures of quality of life. It had the best provision of social housing, and enjoyed (with just a few other similar states) the lowest income inequality worldwide. It had the lowest infant mortality rates, was far more progressive in education than it is today, had extremely low rates of homelessness, most of its people enjoyed good wages, and its prison population was just a third of the size it is now.[6]

The fall of the UK is, in part, the story of the fall of a junior partner. Britain's fate is closely intertwined with that of the United States, more closely than that of any other state in Europe. The US may have been declining in status for decades, but its most abrupt fall from grace occurred between the years 2000 and 2010. In 2000, over three-quarters of all countries in the world traded more goods with the US than with China. Just ten years later that situation was reversed. China is now the more important trading partner for nearly three-quarters of all nations. The article in which this was revealed was titled 'Joe Biden is determined that China should not displace America'.[7] It contained a graph showing that (in terms of trade at least) this displacement had already occurred. The US is now very widely acknowledged to be a divided and shattered state. A couple of decades ago it was racism that most divided the US, and although that division remains, there are now many more new divisions to see today.

Is the shattering really worse in Britain than elsewhere in Europe? And if so, when did it start to become worse?

The preceding chapters have been full of statistical examples of how the UK currently fares badly in terms of its pensions, benefit levels, income inequality, education outcomes (despite huge costs), health (despite high spending) and housing (despite it being so expensive). But there is more to life than what can be measured by numbers and then ranked. As a state shatters, something even more important subtly changes for the worse. People change, and what is considered normal and what is outlandish shifts. The underlying ethos changes, behaviour changes, and what is acceptable changes. In 2011 the polling company Ipsos MORI produced a report for UNICEF comparing three European countries. One of its qualitative findings struck a chord with many who read the report:

> Families in the UK, more so than in Sweden and Spain, use the purchase
> of new material objects (particularly new technology) in an attempt to
> compensate for relationship problems and social insecurity. The children
> themselves across the three countries had a very ambivalent attitude to
> those who appear to be able to afford the latest status goods, simulta-
> neously deriding them and envying them. However, the response by
> parents was quite different. Whilst many UK parents were complicit
> in purchasing status goods – indeed almost seemed to be compelled to
> do so – this behaviour was almost totally absent in Spain and Sweden.[8]

Seven years after these words were printed, the managing director of the Social Research Institute at Ipsos MORI found himself
trying to explain why, despite a narrow majority voting for Brexit
in the referendum, so many of those who voted remain were flab-
bergasted and confused by the result. Polling companies have a
hard time explaining people's views and behaviour as a country
shatters.

As that shattering occurs, even people who are in many ways
very similar more often take up very opposing positions. As we
are pulled apart we begin to become different people, and what we
become then increasingly determines our views and beliefs. More
and more, we begin to have misconceptions about each other and
about what is true. In the Ipsos MORI managing director's words,
rather than mine:

> These misperceptions are not just about us being misled by politicians
> or the media – they are more emotional than that. We exaggerate what
> we worry about, so what we get wrong is as much a reflection of our
> concerns as a cause of them. Attempting to change people's views
> of Brexit solely with a more evidence-based description won't land,
> because it misses a large part of the point: our allegiances affect our

view of reality as much as the other way round. Our misperceptions are, in the end, an incredibly direct measure of how divided the country is: that groups of fellow citizens can see the same realities so differently shows the monumental task we face in finding any common ground.[9]

A task becomes monumental both when it is huge in size but also when it takes on what appears to be a near-permanent form – when it becomes a monument. A shattered UK is now the reality; it is not just a broken mould that can be stuck together again with the reintroduction of some form of one-nation politics, but a testament to what happens when people are forced so far apart that society breaks. A series of policy sticking-plasters are applied to address each new crisis, but following the application of each sticking-plaster, other weaknesses quickly become apparent. Eventually there is a complete mess of disorganised and contradictory policy. The divides become so wide that an easily agreed reunification becomes much less likely, because to come together again some groups will have to lose out so much.

Nevertheless, in the past, it was at times like this that the reunification behind the scenes began. William Beveridge was no radical. He was a Liberal elitist whose views were altered during the 1930s by the untenable situation he witnessed, and by the arguments of others.[10] Similarly, the Conservative minister of health in 1943, Henry Willink, had by then become persuaded by others that a National Health Service was essential.[11]

Debt

When a government borrows more and more money, it eventually finds it harder to get people to buy government bonds, which in the

UK are called gilts. The UK's pension regulator insists that private pension providers buy gilts to reduce the risk that the government might have to bail out pensioners later. However, the interest rates paid on those gilts are too low to safely build up the private pension pots. The value of those pensions falls, and the guarantees for their future become weaker. Pensions will not necessarily rise with inflation in future, if inflation is too high. These private pensions exist because better-off people want a much better-off retirement. Now those people will not get as much as they thought they would. That is because their pension funds have had to buy government debt, a debt that accrues because the government is not willing to overtly tax the better-off more. So it ends up taxing them covertly.

The average UK pensioner saw their real-terms weekly income (after housing costs) rise by only £12 between 2010 and 2020 to £331 a week.[12] That is only an extra £1.71 a day, and pensioners were the one demographic group whose weekly income grew in that decade! Such a small rise may be surprising, given that the state pension was protected after 2010 by a triple lock that promised it would always increase in line with whichever was the highest of the rise in prices, the rise in wages or 2.5 per cent. The reason pensioners' income hardly rose at all during these years was that the other state benefits they received and relied upon to cope were reduced in real terms. The proportion of pensioners receiving disability payments fell from 23 per cent to 19 per cent between 2010 and 2020.[13] Pensioners have not won out at the expense of others. Today, almost everyone is losing out. And the contemporary equivalents of Beveridge and Willink are beginning to notice this too.

In the dystopian future the UK is currently heading for, not only are the poor poorer but many of the affluent are too. A tiny number of people with sufficient wealth not to have to rely on a pension might be OK, if they are lucky, devious, cunning or willing to do what it takes to make sure their money 'makes' more money – at least enough to rise in value faster than other costs. But how much is enough?

For those who are wealthy but fearful, there is never enough money to guarantee financial security. Gross inequality creates destructive uncaring competitiveness. In highly unequal societies, status is all important to those who have made it to the top financially. Houses, cars, children's education and holidays – everything needs to reflect their status for the wealthy to feel wealthy. Almost everything the very well-off purchase will be the most expensive that can be afforded. They always need more, and become incapable of coping on less. The more divided the UK becomes, the more fearful those at the top become.

Just as economic policy failed to address the UK's economic woes in the 1930s, so too is it failing today. Although the average UK pensioner saw their income rise by just £1.71 a day by the end of the past decade, a very small group of people saw their wealth grow hugely. Quantitative easing post-2008 (the buying of government and some corporate bonds by the Bank of England) resulted in a great rise in the wealth of the already best-off people in the UK, but no one can be sure by how much. Estimates by the ONS suggest that quantitative easing inflated not only the value of stocks and shares, but also the nominal value of property. By 2013, the best-off tenth of households were likely to have gained on average between £128,000 and £322,000 in the value of their properties, financial assets and pensions, due to the wider effects of the policy. But they did not feel safer.[14]

The realisation that our current course of travel cannot continue is now becoming more widespread. A 2021 report by the House of Lords Economic Affairs Committee included the claim that 'the richest 10% of households benefited by £350,000 during the first round of quantitative easing, which was more than 100 times the benefit for the poorest'.[15] Several further rounds of this policy will have had similar effects. In its conclusion, the committee noted that there was now an entrenched belief that quantitative easing was being used in 2020 to enable government borrowing, and that 'the Bank of England's ability to control inflation and maintain financial stability could be undermined significantly'.

The committee also noted that there appeared to be no easy way to wind down the quantitative easing policy, which had been brought in as a temporary measure to try to deal with the financial crisis of 2008. Although the Bank of England is supposed to be independent, it operates under a mandate and instructions from the Treasury. The Treasury has itself introduced many other policies that have both held up and increased housing prices. The most public of these was 'help to buy'. This may have helped a few people, but it resulted in house prices rising even further, which creates future problems of affordability. The policy was an attempt to try to sustain something that was ultimately unsustainable.[16]

On 23 September 2022, a raft of new policies were announced in a mini-budget, including a cut in stamp duty to try to keep house prices up. It all backfired and, within days, the Bank of England was forced to resort to quantitative easing again, in order to prop up gilt prices and ensure that private pension companies could continue to pay pensioners. Over 1,000 mortgage products were withdrawn from offer. This was the first house-price crash in British history that began before any prices fell. However, even as the pension and housing wealth reductions lowered wealth inequalities, on that same day the UK almost certainly became the most unequal country in Europe by income, as tax avoidance controls for those at the top were slashed and the cap on bankers' bonuses was removed.[17] The government's subsequent reversal of most of its other mini-budget commitments, including the proposal to lower the top rate of tax, did not, in itself, take the UK back to second place.

Although business-as-usual is ultimately unsustainable, this is no guarantee that we will not be continuing on this rollercoaster course for a few more years to come. Quantitative easing now (it has yet to officially end) appears to be a policy that cannot be unwound without having severe effects. It was being used by the Bank of England again in late 2022, to deal with a new financial emergency. One member of the House of Lords Committee described it as 'state-created financial instability', and used the phrase 'Ponzi scheme' in his description.[18] From the 2008 crash to Brexit to Covid-19 and the war in Ukraine, each new crisis is blamed for the current state of affairs both at home and elsewhere, while the underlying factors that have made the UK so unstable are ignored by those in power a little while longer. Those not currently in power increasingly come to realise that merely tweaking current policy in future, which they had perhaps hoped to do, will not be enough. But they are frightened of being more daring.

The current UK financial system is geared towards helping the middle and wealthy classes to accumulate assets. Tax-free Individual Savings Accounts (ISAs) are designed to do this for top-rate taxpayers, as is pension tax relief. Where we are now, in terms of our succession of repeated crises, looks more like the 1920s and '30s than the 1970s and '80s. However, in the 1930s we were already moving, ever so slightly, towards greater equality compared to the 1920s. The state and economic circumstances then began to make it harder and harder for the few at the top to keep hold of so much. In the 1980s, by contrast, we were moving rapidly away from equality. The 1970s was the decade of the fight to try to keep the greater equality that had been won, but that fight was lost. Today's fightback has yet to begin. When it comes, it will at first be framed by the political right, by some in industry and by the more compliant media as a class war and an 'us or them' battle. But the vast majority of the UK's middle class are now part of the getting-poorer group, no longer part of the truly well-off. That is new, or at the very least has not been seen since the 1930s.

In our dystopian near-future, wealth inequalities will change in their distribution. A smaller and smaller group owning the majority of stocks, shares and rental property *may* become even wealthier. Increasingly, this group includes people who do not live in the UK or at least are not resident here for tax purposes. However, the pension and housing wealth of the large majority of better-off people already appears to be falling. We will continue to hear the myth repeated of how the rich bring 'inward investment' into the country and that part of their wealth will eventually trickle down. But the majority of better-off people are now seeing their private pensions become less safe and their homes less valuable, and they will worry more, spend less and try harder to save. The UK has become an asset-stripped version of its former self. And that makes change more likely.

Division

The FTSE 100 is an index of the top 100 UK companies listed on the London Stock Exchange, as measured by market capitalisation. Today, many of those companies, like many of the richest individuals in the UK, are based offshore, sometimes even in tax havens, and they conduct most of their operations outside of the UK. A company's headquarters need not be in Britain for it to be listed as one of these top 100 British companies. Making high profits is becoming harder as we plunder the earth, so some of these businesses have become ever more dematerialised, piratical and short-termist.

The UK has attracted private equity firms into London by having a low-tax, low-scrutiny regime. Its traditional businesses have increasingly been taken over by these and other opaque entities whose focus is on making short-term gains. In the first half of 2021, private equity firms struck more deals in the UK 'than in the same period in any year on record'.[19] The privatisation and outsourcing over the past four decades was also part of this short-termism. It's hard to make large profits from manufacturing – especially in the UK it seems. Privatisation has been a stopgap for profit-seekers, selling services previously provided by the state back to the population at twice the price. From energy companies to academy trusts, to the growing number of companies selling goods and services to the NHS, many 'providers' are created to make it appear as if there is a market, but the competition is frequently phoney.

Education is becoming even more divided as academisation proceeds, now mostly of primary schools. The remaining state schools are held at arm's length from the state. All new 'state' schools built in England are 'free schools', which are even less part of any collective system.[20] State schools, which were for decades free at the point of use, may begin to charge for books and compulsory expensive uniforms, and may have to find other ways to impose charges in order to weather future funding cuts. Schools in more affluent neighbourhoods are able to charge more, raise more money from parents, and so become better resourced.

Sixth forms are now more frequently selective, excluding children who didn't reach certain grades, but taking in outsiders from other schools (including fully private schools) to falsely inflate their own school's achievements. This is greatly to the detriment of the reputation of other schools, resulting in more separation between those students with well-off parents and those without. Selection may increase if new grammar schools are allowed to open. Existing grammar schools can already expand by building new sites and saying they are part of the same school. Private schools thrive when the publicly supported sector is damaged, as is now happening. A brutal hierarchy is created for children, where state school education in better-off neighbourhoods aided by private tuition produces results almost in direct proportion to the wealth of the parents.

University fees may be allowed to rise again. There are already no effective controls over postgraduate fees, which are often much higher than those for undergraduate degrees. The hunt for overseas students able to pay even higher fees is intensifying. This may sound like a great plan to increase 'export earnings' – selling university degrees internationally in the 2020s, in place of the textiles and other manufactured goods sold abroad in the 1920s – but how safe a plan is it? Few overseas students would be willing to pay a very large amount of money for a university course they might fail. The universities will say that they select and teach ever so carefully, which is why hardly any student who does not drop out fails. At some point, however, these claims will no longer wash.

As long as current trends continue, then our most affluent university cities will welcome in more very affluent overseas students, who will be served by a growing number of local workers living in increased poverty. Even if the workers' wages do not keep falling in relation to prices, local housing costs will be encouraged to rise. Our regime of welfare benefits and low income tax is already a cumbersome mess designed to try to ensure that a large and growing group of people can only just survive while living in or near poverty. In the dystopian future we are heading towards, this group will, if things carry on as they are, come to include a large majority of families with children. We may well hear more and more talk of the plucky few who do well and elevate themselves up from the mass. Proportionately, though, we will hear far less about the steady increase in the numbers of those only just managing, the hardly managing and the not coping – other than that they are (in ever greater numbers apparently) failing to budget properly.

What might the UK look like as a failed state? In some key aspects, it would not look like it did the last time it failed. In the 1930s, some regions of the UK were shattered by mass unemployment, other areas much less so. A bimodal mortality distribution emerged in that decade in Britain, with a majority of neighbourhoods being areas in which you were more likely to die earlier than average, a smaller group of neighbourhoods where you were much less likely to, and an even smaller group in between.[21] If a similar pattern were to occur in the UK today, it would more likely be shown by a rise in deaths of despair than by a new phase of mass unemployment.

The United States provides the best model for where the UK is currently heading. Life expectancy for most Americans is lower than in the UK. Many factors contribute to this, including a more lax attitude to people dying through car crashes, much higher deaths from guns (including a very large number of suicides by gun), and poor healthcare for a very large section of the population. However, those issues have been the case for a long time. The key reason today why people live shorter lives in the US is deaths from drugs, particularly opiates, which have reduced life expectancy for American men by almost a year. This problem increased greatly during the pandemic.[22] The United States is now widely recognised as an affluent state that is failing. The UK is not yet failing as much, but it is moving rapidly towards the same position. Between 2014 and 2018 life expectancy fell by a fraction more in the UK than it did in the US.[23]

Today capitalism has evolved into many different flavours. We no longer have the simple vanilla Victorian variety, the one in which all rich countries became so very similar – where, roughly a century ago, almost all of them saw just 1 per cent of their populations take a fifth of all income. Today, the rich countries of the world have fanned out to produce many different variants of capitalism.

It is now more widely accepted that the current UK version of capitalism produces failure. As one professor of politics noted in 2022: 'A common denominator in so many policy challenges facing the current government, from sewage in rivers to energy prices, rail strikes to university fees/admissions, is that market forces plus weak regulation is now so clearly running into deep trouble as a policy formula.'[24] In November 2022, the third chancellor of that year produced the third budget of the year and the reality began to sink in. The fantasy that there was some easy way out had evaporated. But this did not produce some sudden shift to a more understanding and able government. There is still great incompetence.

The rail strike, similarly to many other strikes in autumn 2022, continued to be exacerbated by the government stepping in to prevent supposedly private rail companies awarding their workers a pay rise better aligned with inflation, just so that their real wages did not fall so much. It was as if the government wanted the strikes. The same professor of politics, commenting on the strikes, thought that the government's intervention suffered not from being weak, but from being so very blunt and clumsy. His is just one example of thousands of similar conclusions being drawn in the early 2020s.

Notwithstanding our many divisions, we are beginning perhaps to agree that something has gone wrong on a very fundamental level. Once that conclusion is reached more widely then, and only then, might more significant changes begin to be discussed as real possibilities, or even inevitabilities.

Deliverance

One might argue that although the UK may be an exception within Europe, its inequality is not exceptional internationally, and many other parts of Europe are almost as bad. However, today, comparisons between the UK and some unlikely far-off places are not very flattering. In China, the top 1 per cent now receive 14 per cent of all income and hold 31 per cent of all wealth. By the same measure in 2022, the UK's richest 1 per cent received 13 per cent of all income and 21 per cent of all wealth.[25] When it comes to the take of the top 1 per cent, the UK is more similar to China than it is to most of the rest of Western Europe. As both China and the UK are so very unequal, it is not surprising that both are big climate polluters, although the UK's pollution is higher per capita. Worldwide, people in the top 1 per cent of the income distribution emit 100 times more carbon than those in the bottom half, and the best-off 1 per cent have been responsible for a greater total rise in emissions since 1990 than the rise caused by the entire bottom half of humanity (three times greater, in fact).[26]

If we consider legacy emissions of carbon – emissions in the past – then the position of the UK appears to be even worse. This will even itself out a little in future. Economically, China is on an upward trajectory and the UK on a long downward one. But both states need to become more equal for many reasons, only one of which is to reduce carbon emissions. What happens if we take the story currently being told in China about reducing inequality and try to apply that to the UK?

In China there is now little talk of a rising tide lifting all boats; instead, the talk is of mountains. For the Chinese, there are two mountains that currently appear immovable, but that have to be shifted if any progress is to be made.[27] These are the mountains of greed and indifference. If a state cannot rein in its most greedy, it faces becoming a failed state. Indifference means not caring enough about others, or even ourselves, to do anything much about the state we are in. This is how the current president of China describes the problem of inequality in his country: inequality is a problem of too much greed and too much indifference.[28] He uses the 'two mountains' as his analogy because it has previously been used before – with great effect.

Today, the two new mountains of greed and indifference are as big as the two original very different mountains identified in China in 1942, the very same year that the Beveridge report was published in Britain. The two mountains that then held back progress in China were feudalism and colonialism. Both seemed to be immovable, but both were pushed aside. In 1942, in place of two mountains, the UK had its five giants of social evil to confront. In very different ways, both China and the UK successfully overcame their worst evils in the years that followed. Today, however, they are more similar in terms of income inequality than they have ever been before, despite having such different political systems. It is hard to imagine any UK prime minister suggesting that the biggest problems the UK faces are caused by greed and indifference – but it would be equally true.

China had been geopolitically, economically and socially shattered for more than a century before 1942, and the UK was complicit in that shattering (directly, at the very start, through the opium wars – so much for the UK having 'always been a force for good in the world'). Today, the tables are turned, although China has much less interest in the UK than the UK once had in China. Shattering always comes to an end. Outside of Xinjiang, China is becoming less shattered geopolitically, with Hong Kong rejoining the country in 1997 and Macau in 1999. For the UK, the end of the shattering may well involve the break-up of the state rather than its coming together, with Northern Ireland and Scotland the most likely to exit. But whether or not that happens is not what matters most. What matters most is that hunger, precarity, waste, exploitation and fear are confronted and reduced.

The fall of the UK into ever growing divisions since the early 1970s was impossible to predict. Few people back then might have believed how things could have got so much worse by the 2020s – that the public services we once took for granted would no longer exist as free and universal, or that we would see the return of landlordism, mass poverty and widespread despair. The precise future consequences of the shattering we have been through, and continue to go through, are unknowable. But they are not inevitable.

Already we can see plenty of signs of a growing understanding that this cannot go on. If even China, with all its economic success, can see that both greed and indifference must be reduced, surely the UK, with all its economic failure, might find that possible too? We can all influence whether, as a society, we become more dystopian, or change tack and slowly begin to heal our wounds. Whether we do, and the extent to which we each do our part, depends on what we are now still willing to tolerate. It depends on whose accounts we believe – on how what has occurred comes to be understood. Think back again to where you grew up. How has it changed? Why do you think it has changed in that way? What

stories have you been told that claim to account for the changes?
Do you believe them?

By October 2022, only four weeks after Liz Truss became prime
minister, and two weeks before she would be forced to resign, it
became obvious to the majority of voters and MPs that her government was incapable of responding adequately to the many
crises facing the country. Truss was so obviously wrong on so
many things. Her thinking had been irreparably deluded by the
right-wing think-tanks discussed in the previous chapter. The
Financial Times published an analysis that month suggesting that,
of all the economic policies of all the political parties in the affluent
and emerging economies of the world, the British Conservative
Party's had become the most far-right worldwide.[29] In the same
analysis, Labour was sitting just to the right of the US Democrats,
the latter having shifted slightly leftwards. The Labour Party in
2022, unlike in 2017, was no longer calling for public ownership of
water, Royal Mail, the energy networks or the national grid, but
it was still committed to covering day-to-day public spending by
taxes – which implied raising taxes on the wealthy.[30]

In early October, the BBC's political editor gave his verdict on
the new prime minister: 'what has happened in the last 10 days will
leave an indelible mark on her – it is unrecoverably bad'.[31] Within
hours the chancellor announced he would no longer be bringing
the top tax rate down from 45 per cent. The BBC's economics
correspondent explained that, despite this, the rest of his proposed package, 'including the reversal of the National Insurance
hike, will still benefit the better-off more in cash terms. The same,
broadly, is true of the energy help package – for the further up the
income scale you are, the more energy you're likely to use.'[32] The
chancellor was then sacked, and very shortly afterwards the prime
minister was forced to resign.

In mid-October reports began to circulate in the UK car industry that the huge growth in reliance on debt to buy new cars had created a bubble that could burst, leaving buyers with debts they could not repay even after returning the car. Some nine out of ten new cars, and most second-hand vehicles, were being bought with debt.[33] A week later, school heads explained that most state-funded schools would become bankrupt in a short time given current funding levels: 'At this burn rate, in under three years we will be bankrupt. No one is in a position to keep going for very long eating their reserves.'[34] Rishi Sunak, whose family is among the richest 250 families in the UK, became prime minister on 25 October 2022. We knew little about him, other than that he appeared to hold very similar views to his many predecessors and, on a personal note released to try to make him seem relatable, is a *Star Wars* fan who has amassed a large collection of lightsabres. Spending cuts and tax rises followed, all targeted above all else at trying to ensure the short-term survival of the Conservative Party.

The bad news stories began to arrive more quickly. In November we learnt that the number of women in the UK dying during pregnancy or shortly after giving birth had risen by a fifth. The leading cause of the rise was suicide. Those new or expectant mothers in the poorest areas were twice as likely to die compared to mothers in better-off areas, and that gap was widening.[35] On the same day another report was published detailing the overall rise in anxiety in Britain. It revealed that by every single measure this rise had resulted in anxiety being much worse for those renting their homes, sometimes more than twice as bad as for homeowners. The measures included losing sleep, being unable to make decisions, being under strain, becoming depressed, feeling worthless, lacking happiness, becoming downhearted and, above all else, lacking energy.[36]

The UK has been speeding in the wrong direction for over forty years and that has resulted in growing disillusion, despair and apathy. But recognition of this is also fuelling a now widespread acceptance that a great shift in priorities will soon be required. Will this shift occur due to the election of a political party that is willing to make it, or will it simply be forced on whichever party is in office at some point, rather than being planned? The turnout in the general election held immediately after the First World War – when we were last at an inequality peak – was only 57 per cent, but following that it was always over 70 per cent up to 1997. In 1950, after five years of Labour government, it rose as high as 84 per cent, and Labour were re-elected. However, after five years of the 1997 New Labour government, turnout fell in 2001 to 59 per cent. Many people could not see the point of voting. Turnout slowly picked up until the 2017 election, when it peaked at 69 per cent. In calling that election, Theresa May, full of confidence, had wanted to increase her twelve-seat majority. Unexpectedly, she lost seventeen seats, staggered on but later resigned in ignominy to be replaced by Boris Johnson. Then voter turnout once again started to fall, to just two-thirds of the electorate in 2019.[37]

Planned progressive change will only happen if and when enough people think it is worthwhile voting and have options worth voting for. The Conservatives are now putting new hurdles in the way of people both registering to vote and voting. However, there is huge potential for current non-voters to produce a sea change when people who previously thought of themselves as comfortably off, and who did not vote, realise they are being taken for a ride. When opposition parties more obviously stand for the many, rather than the few, turnout rises. Any sea change that comes might not end the shattering of the nations, and it may well accelerate the geographical break-up of the UK. But it could start the long, slow process of reconstruction that is required. Other than through the ballot box, it is hard to imagine how else this could be done in any way that was not even more chaotic and disastrous than the continuation of business as usual.

It would be usual, at this point, to end on a positive note concerning what should be done. Phrases such as hope and solidarity and the common good could be used, and a positive vision of courage and inclusiveness described – a vision of people voting in hope not fear, voting for a better world in difficult times. Other countries could be listed, ones that have overcome enduring hopelessness and right-wing or otherwise authoritarian oppression. The widespread support for the workers' strikes in 2022 and 2023 could be cited. That might all sound relevant, but I don't think it is what someone reading this book most needs to know.

What may help most at this point is to realise that if there is no planned progressive change – change of the kind that last began in 1942 during the Second World War – then in each year from here on there will be more crises. No revolution will occur that will deliver some kind of a rapturous transformation. It is even possible that inequalities could fall within the large majority of the population, while rising overall because just a tiny few at the top are allowed to keep taking more. Housing could become even more precarious than it already is, pension funds could fail, the health and social care crisis could deepen, education may become even more unaffordable and mental health become even worse. The people who will lose out the most – if we just try to stagger on with a few minor remedial actions – are not the poorest. They are already suffering the most. Instead, it will be you, the reader of this book, and more and more people like you.

Acknowledgements

Thanks are due to Leo Hollis at Verso for encouraging this book along its path, a journey which began with many meetings over many years in London. At each meeting Leo would give me another book Verso were about to publish to take away and read. Often they concerned a particular aspect of some of the crises described in these pages. He said he wanted a manifesto, not a description. This is a mixture of both. Seeing the change that is needed is only possible if you have a better idea of what it is you are trying to change.

I am greatly indebted to Lorenza Antonucci, John Bowers, Ian Curtis , Alison Dorling, David Dorling, John Drummond, Mubin Haq, Stacy Hewitt, Bill Kerry, Anna Linsel, Penny Ormerod, David Partridge, Adam Peggs, Amanda Ramsay, Khadija Rouf, Karen Shook, Mo Stewart, Frances Tomlinson and Karel Williams, all of whom kindly read through parts of the book, including in many cases through the entirety of earlier much messier drafts. They made me think more carefully about what I was saying and how I was trying to say it. The idea for the book crystallised during the worst months of the first year of the pandemic. Living through that period meant seeing sudden changes to the way we live, changes that we don't tend to notice when they occur over longer time frames.

I am also very grateful to Mark Martin at Verso who managed the book through production, and to Tim Clark for his careful copy-editing of the text. The final revisions to the manuscript were made during the autumn and winter of 2022/23. During these months economic and political changes appeared to be sudden, but the longer-term factors that had led to the crisis were less carefully examined at the time. The UK had been shattered long before the international money markets finally lost their faith in the Conservative government's economic plans. But in the cold dark of that winter it became much more widely accepted that something had changed in the UK, and that the shattering of previous hopes and dreams was no temporary hiatus.

Everything changes and is always changing. But is it for better or for worse, and how do we try to change what we think of as better or worse? When the dominant ideology of a state has held up the wrong values as being the right values for such a long time – for example that high levels of inequality are necessary to sustain competition, the rewards from which lie just around the corner – it can be hard to argue against the usual prescriptions and platitudes. So my final acknowledgement is to all those people who kept on struggling even when the struggle appeared fruitless and futile. They gave me hope. And that hope and commitment are not only essential – they can, when the times are right, become infectious and spread. Without hope we succumb to greed and indifference.

Notes

1. The Roundabout

1 Barry White, 'Old ways win at ailing Belfast shipyard', *New York Times*, 9 February 1975.

2 Danny Dorling, 'How much does place matter?', *Environment and Planning A*, vol. 33, no. 8, 2001, pp. 1335–40.

3 There were 1,500 places offered in 2020 in Oxford. They are now often better hidden so the local council cannot identify them so easily. See David Lynch, 'Oxford landlord banned from letting out house via Airbnb', *Oxford Mail*, 19 August 2020.

4 John Burn-Murdoch, 'Britain and the US are poor societies with some very rich people', *Financial Times*, 16 September 2022.

5 The Mini car plant used to contribute as much as a whole percentage point to the UK's industrial export earnings. In late 2022 it was announced that production of the electric Mini will move to Leipzig and to China. The Oxford factory will continue, mainly automated, to produce petrol Minis for seven years, until 2030. See Sophie Zeldin-O'Neill, 'BMW to axe UK production of electric Mini and relocate to China', *Guardian*, 15 October 2022. In March 2023 it was rumoured the decision might be reversed.

6 Danny Dorling, 'Houses, not homelessness', *European Journal of Homelessness*, vol. 15, no. 3, 2021, pp. 87–96.

7 John Lanchester, 'Fraudpocalypse', *London Review of Books*, vol. 44, no. 15, 4 August 2022, p. 3.

8 As I write, this policy has not yet been overturned, although there is

speculation it might be. See Justin Cash, 'Banker bonus cap may still be scrapped despite Jeremy Hunt's U-turn on most of UK mini-budget', *Financial News*, fnlondon.com, 17 October 2022.

9   Danny Dorling and Annika Koljonen, *Finntopia: What We Can Learn from the World's Happiest Country*, Newcastle: Agenda, 2021.

10 Danny Dorling and Sally Tomlinson, *Rule Britannia: Brexit and the End of Empire*, London: Biteback, 2019.

11 Danny Dorling, *Slowdown: The End of the Great Acceleration – and Why It's Good for the Planet, the Economy, and Our Lives*, New Haven: Yale University Press, 2021.

12 Conor Burns, 'Margaret Thatcher's greatest achievement: New Labour', *Conservative Home*, 11 April 2008.

13 The Conservatives had only nineteen MEPs at the time, but UKIP had twenty-four, aligned with another small far-right European parliamentary group that included the Danish People's Party and Italy's Lega Nord.

14 New Labour also took the UK into the Iraq War of 2003 as an enthusiastic partner with the United States. The only other European nation involved was Poland. By 2020 Poland had the highest number of far-right members in the European Parliament of all EU countries, replacing the UK in that position.

15 Lorenza Antonucci and Simone Varriale, 'Unequal Europe, unequal Brexit: how intra-European inequalities shape the unfolding and framing of Brexit', *Current Sociology*, vol. 68, no. 1, 2020, pp. 41–59.

16 Ben Zimmer, 'The roots of the "what about?" ploy', *Wall Street Journal*, 9 June 2017.

17 Lydia Stephens, 'British diplomats told to call UK one country instead of a union of four nations', *Wales Online*, 6 June 2021.

18 Select your local area, BBC webpage, accessed 16 August 2022.

19 Tim Davie, 'The BBC across the UK: the BBC 2022–2027', bbc.co.uk, March 2021.

20 Mark Sweney, 'BBC appoints insider Tim Davie as director general', *Guardian*, 5 June 2020.

21 Between 2022 and 2025 the BBC will produce two new long-running dramas. One will be based in the North of England, the other in a yet-to-be specified 'nation'. Another hundred one-off TV shows will 'reflect the lives and communities of audiences outside London'. See Jon Creamer, 'BBC unveils nations and regions plan', *Televisual News*, 18 March 2021.

22 'Slough Borough Council faces assets sell-off after bankruptcy', BBC News, 25 May 2022.

23 Danny Dorling, 'The share of people working in public service', *Public Sector Focus*, May/June 2022, pp. 12–15.

24 Danny Dorling, 'Public spending in the UK, and elsewhere in Europe, 1980–2026', *Public Sector Focus*, July/August 2021, pp. 16–19.

25 The UK still has an unelected House of Lords and a first-past-the-post electoral system.

26 Not including Ireland and Switzerland, because in both cases their GDP is inflated due to firms locating their headquarters there to benefit from low taxes or, in the case of Switzerland, to be at the heart of Europe while avoiding being in the EU. Because of their small populations this can make public spending in both countries look low in GDP percentage terms, when it is actually quite high. Switzerland spends some of the highest sums in Europe on healthcare. Like in the rest of the EU, universities in Ireland are almost entirely publicly funded.

27 'YouGov Jubilee results – public views on the monarchy', YouGov, 16–17 May 2022.

28 Eir Nolsoe, 'Young Britons are turning their backs on the monarchy', YouGov, 21 May 2021.

2. Growing Divides

1 'Hovis "boy on bike" advert filmed at Gold Hill back on TV', *Bournemouth Daily Echo*, 3 June 2019. The original advert can be found on YouTube.

2 See the Wikipedia entry for Ridley Scott.

3 The New Economics Foundation, 'Chasing progress: beyond measuring economic growth', 2004.

4 Although other countries were catching up on Britain's record health improvements at this time (see Chapter 7).

5 Danny Dorling, 'The trickle up of fear', *Public Sector Focus*, March/April, 2022, pp. 12–15.

6 See the Wikipedia entry for 'Gold Hill, Shaftesbury'.

7 See vis.oobrien.com/booth, the work of cartographer Oliver O'Brien. It shows the deprivation map of England, but you can click an option on the webpage to see Scotland instead, or look at the method O'Brien used in the

detailed maps of household deprivation from the 2021 census on the ONS census maps webpages.

8 Daniel Dorling, Jan Rigby, Ben Wheeler, Dimitris Ballas, Bethan Thomas, Eldin Fahmy, David Gordon and Ruth Lupton, *Poverty and Wealth across Britain 1968 to 2005: A Look at How the Geographical Distribution of Poor and Wealthy People in Britain Has Changed in the Last 40 Years*, York: Joseph Rowntree Foundation, 2007.

9 Tim Nudd, 'Ridley Scott's classic 1973 Hovis ad "Boy on a Bike" has been beautifully remastered', *MuseByClio*, 3 June 2019.

10 George Monbiot, 'Our quality of life peaked in 1974 – it's all downhill now', *Guardian*, 31 December 2002.

11 As one review of his next book explained: 'Sandbrook is not an isolated figure. Alongside such figures as David Starkey and Tom Holland, he has secured a conservative ascendancy in British public history which is not reflective of the research produced by university departments.' Ewan Gibbs, 'We're still living in Margaret Thatcher's Britain', *Jacobin*, 5 May 2020.

12 The 5th Viscount Ridley went to Eton, is an expert on the mating system of the common pheasant, and was chairman of the UK bank Northern Rock when it experienced the first run on a British bank in 130 years.

13 Chris Haynes, 'Cracked open Britannia Unchained in light of the looming prospect of PM Liz Truss, and boy is this book densely researched' – tweeting ironically on 20 July 2022.

14 Nicholas Henderson, 'Britain's decline: its causes and consequences (leaked document not published in full)', *Economist*, 2 June 1979. Available in full on margaretthatcher.org.

15 Although, to be fair, he was only repeating almost word for word remarks made earlier by the prime minister, James Callaghan, in 1976 in the Ruskin College speech referred to in Chapter 6 of this book.

16 Much of his missive was a lament about Britain having earlier failed to join the European Community and the negative effects of that decision. Once the UK had finally joined, he recommended that its politicians should behave '*as though* we were fully and irrevocably committed to Europe' (paragraph 28, emphasis added). Those two words 'as though' were telling, and partly explain why the memorandum was marked confidential.

17 Mark Green, Danny Dorling and Richard Mitchell, 'Updating Edwin Chadwick's seminal work on geographical inequalities by occupation', *Social Science and Medicine*, vol. 197, 2018, pp. 59–62.

18 These ratios are as calculated from Table 2 of Green et al., 'Updating Edwin Chadwick's seminal work' (see note 17 above).

19 Danny Dorling and Sally Tomlinson, *Rule Britannia: Brexit and the End of Empire*, London: Biteback, 2019, Figure 9.1, derived in turn from Valentina Romei, 'How wages fell in the UK while the economy grew', *Financial Times*, 2 March 2017.

20 See the Wikipedia entry for 'List of Scottish National Party MPs'.

21 Morwenna Ferrier, 'Nicola Sturgeon says Liz Truss asked her "how to get into *Vogue*"', *Guardian*, 10 August 2022. Torcuil Crichton, 'Liz Truss as PM makes Scottish independence more likely, poll finds', *Daily Record*, 21 August 2022.

22 See the Wikipedia entry for 'List of Plaid Cymru MPs'.

23 'Council tax triples for holiday home landlords (Wales)', Guild of Residential Landlords, 3 March 2022.

24 Tom Edgington, 'Brexit: what is the Northern Ireland Protocol?', BBC News, 10 October 2022.

25 Bethan Thomas and Danny Dorling, *Identity in Britain: A Cradle-to-Grave Atlas*, Bristol: Policy Press, 2007.

26 Danny Dorling and Bethan Thomas, *Bankrupt Britain: An Atlas of Social Change*, Bristol: Policy Press, 2011.

27 Danny Dorling and Bethan Thomas, *People and Places: A 21st-Century Atlas*, Bristol: Policy Press, 2016.

28 Rory Scothorne, 'It's our turn', *London Review of Books*, vol. 44, no. 15, 4 August 2022, pp. 33–6.

29 Ipsos MORI, '8 in 10 dissatisfied with how the government is running the country', 30 September 2019.

30 Danny Dorling, 'Voting intention Autumn 2019: what do we know of what the public think?', *Public Sector Focus*, October/November 2019, pp. 18–19.

31 'Guidance: UK Shared Prosperity Fund: prospectus', Department for Levelling Up, Housing and Communities, 1 August 2022.

32 Alex Wickham, 'Sunak under fire over boast he moved funding from deprived areas', *Bloomberg News*, 5 August 2022.

33 Danny Dorling, 'Counting words in the manifestos', *Public Sector Focus*, November/December 2019, pp. 14–15.

34 This included two national newspapers, the *Guardian* and the *Mirror*, several now online-only affairs such as the *Independent*, and a couple of magazines of dubious loyalty to the left, such as the *New Statesman*.

35 Daniel Finn, 'The *Sun* is going to get people killed', *Tribune*, 9 December 2019.

36 Incidentally, that constituency contains the Roundhay ward and the school Liz Truss attended.

37 Danny Dorling, 'Brexit: the decision of a divided country', *BMJ*, 6 July 2016.

38 Michael Ashcroft, 'Why I'm for Brexit', lordashcroftpolls.com, 22 June 2016.

39 Danny Dorling, 'Would you let this man drive your daughter home?', *Public Sector Focus*, August/September 2019, pp. 14–17.

40 Adam Bienkov, '"The Brexit Party rebadged": Boris Johnson expels 21 Conservative moderate MPs, including 2 former chancellors and Winston Churchill's grandson', *Business Insider*, 4 September 2019.

41 See the four maps given in Danny Dorling, 'So, how did we end up with this government?', *Public Sector Focus*, January/February 2020, pp. 14–17.

42 Julian Coman, '*Broken Heartlands* by Sebastian Payne review – a tour of the red wall's ruins', *Guardian*, 12 September 2021.

43 See Figure 2.12.2 in Danny Dorling, *Peak Inequality*, Bristol: Policy Press, 2018.

44 'Election results 2019: analysis in maps and charts', BBC News, 13 December 2019.

3. Hunger

1 The Trussell Trust, 'Our story: how we got to where we are today . . .', trusselltrust.org.

2 Bethany Dawson, 'Many in the UK face a grim choice this winter between eating and heating as a cost-of-living crisis grips the nation', *Business Insider*, 9 October 2022.

3 Oya Celasun, Dora Iakova and Ian Parry, 'How Europe can protect the poor from surging energy prices', blogs.imf.org, 3 August 2022.

4 OECD, Income inequality online statistics, data.oecd.org, 2022.

5 Department for Work and Pensions, 'Households below average income: an analysis of the income distribution FYE [Financial Year Ending] 1995 to FYE 2020', gov.uk, 25 March 2021. Relying in turn on the Institute for

Fiscal Studies. See section 11 on long-term trends (data prior to FYE 1995 are not National Statistics).

6 In Bulgaria income inequality has been higher than in the UK since 2013, although it fell in the most recent year recorded. In Lithuania it was lower in the latest year reported (2019) than in any year since 2014. In Romania it reached a high point in 2017, but has fallen since. Moreover, like in Lithuania, Romania's inequality was still below the level the UK reached in 2017. Similarly, in every other Eastern European country inequality is also lower, sometimes much lower, than in the UK. In October 2022 the UK reported that there had been a fall in its income inequality in 2020, but it was still higher than that of any other European country reporting at that time. See: OECD, Income inequality, online statistics, data.oecd.org.

7 Michael Savage and Dulcie Lee, '"I regularly see rickets": diseases of Victorian-era poverty return to UK', *Guardian*, 23 December 2017.

8 The UK has been the most unequal Western European country since 2007, when it became more unequal than Portugal by income inequality, as reported by the OECD.

9 Mubin Haq, 'Nearly 60% increase in UK households in serious financial difficulties', Financial Fairness Trust, 11 July 2022. Five months later there had been a: 'huge increase (77%) in people with no confidence in their financial futures', Karen Barker, Financial Fairness Trust Tracker, 14 December 2022, financialfairness.org.

10 J. Neumann and John Kington, 'Great historical events that were significantly affected by the weather: part 10, crop failure in Britain in 1799 and 1800 and the British decision to send a naval force to the Baltic early in 1801', *Bulletin of the American Meteorological Society*, vol. 73, no. 2, 1992, pp. 187–99.

11 Figure 12 in Torsten Bell, Emily Fry, Gavin Kelly, Louise Murphy, Greg Thwaites and Daniel Tomlinson, 'Stagnation nation: navigating a route to a fairer and more prosperous Britain', *The Economy 2030 Inquiry*, 13 July 2022.

12 Levi Winchester, 'Three million households not paid the £150 council tax rebate – how to claim your payment', *Mirror*, 24 August 2022.

13 Rupert Neate, 'Over £5.5bn of Covid support funds lost to fraud or error', *Guardian*, 4 November 2022.

14 'Marcus Rashford: government changes decision on free school meals', *BBC Newsround*, 8 November 2020.

15 Katie Grant, 'Free school meals: vouchers for summer holidays cut to as little as £1.66 a day for millions of children', *Inews*, 16 July 2022.

16 See the Wikipedia entry for the Joseph Rowntree Foundation.

17 Michael Jacobs, 'Thatcherite mythology: eight Tory leadership candidates in search of an economic policy', *LSE British Politics and Policy Blogs*, 13 July 2022.

18 Nikoleta Kalmouki, 'Price ceiling for products sold in beaches', *Greek Reporter*, 30 July 2014. British newspapers took a long time to realise what was happening in Greece and sometimes reported the protection of prices with criticism: Helena Smith, 'The fixed-price shopping basket: Greece's answer to cost of living crisis', *Guardian*, 8 December 2022.

19 E.K.POI.ZO, Canteen prices: consumer rights, ekpizo.gr, 11 January 2022.

20 'Children can eat for just £1 at Asda cafés across England and Wales this summer', Asda corporate news release, 7 July 2022.

21 Olaf van Vliet and Koen Caminada, 'Unemployment replacement rates dataset among 34 welfare states, 1971–2009: an update, extension and modi-fication of the Scruggs' welfare state entitlements data set', Leiden Law School, Department of Economics, NEUJOBS Special Report no. 2, 2012, Table 2, p. 7.

22 See page 16 of Brigid Francis-Devine, *National Minimum Wage Statistics*, House of Commons Library, research briefings files, 13 June 2022.

23 David Webster, 'Briefing: benefit sanctions statistics', Child Poverty Action Group, 24 August 2022.

24 Danny Dorling, *Inequality and the 1%*, 3rd edition, London: Verso, 2019, p. 188.

25 Patrick Butler, 'Spending cuts breach UK's human rights obligations, says report', *Guardian*, 28 November 2018.

26 Danny Dorling, 'Economics and compassion', in Matt Hawkins and Jennifer Nadel (eds.), *How Compassion Can Transform Our Politics, Economy and Society*, Abingdon: Routledge, 2021; Robert Schultz and Anna Stansbury, 'US economics PhDs are less socioeconomically and racially diverse than other major fields', Working Paper 22-4, Peterson Institute for International Economics, 31 March 2022.

27 The exact ratio was 9.3 to 1. This is a fraction above the ratio of the next most privileged social science: geography, with a ratio of 8.7 to 1, although human geography alone has a ratio of 12 to 1 (compared to physical geog-raphy at 6.4 to 1). In social policy undergraduate degrees the ratio is 1 to

1; in sociology it is 1.2 to 1; in maths 4.7 to 1; in medicine 7.2 to 1 – all less elitist than economics. See Table 8.1 in Danny Dorling, 'The post-pandemic provision of education in the UK', in Patrick Allen, Suzanne Konzelmann and Jan Toporowski (eds.), *Return of the State: Restructuring Britain for the Common Good*, Newcastle upon Tyne: Agenda, 2021, and Table 3 in Danny Dorling, 'Where are we heading? The example of generational change in British academic geography', *Environment and Planning F*, 19 March 2022.

28 Patrick Butler, 'Millions forced to skip meals as UK cost of living crisis deepens', *Guardian*, 18 October 2022.

29 Mary Reader, Jonathan Portes and Ruth Patrick, 'Does cutting child benefits reduce fertility in larger families? Evidence from the UK's two-child limit', largerfamilies.study, 6 April 2022.

30. Scottish Environment Protection Agency, '99% of Scotland's bathing waters passed environmental water quality standards this summer', sepa.org.uk, 13 December 2021.

31 Olivia Marshall, 'Wage woe: pay cut for millions as real wages fall by record 3% – what it means for your money', *Sun*, 16 August 2022.

32 Assuming they were internet savvy and had online access. See gov.uk/winter-fuel-payment.

33 Danny Dorling, 'A letter from Helsinki', *Public Sector Focus*, July/August 2022, pp. 12–15.

34 Calculation made using the Households below Basic Incomes data series, after housing costs were deducted and income equivalised for household size, benefits received and taxes paid: DWP, 'Households below average income: for financial years ending 1995 to 2020', Department for Work and Pensions, 25 March 2021.

35 See page 8 of Eurostat, *Regional GDP per Capita Ranged from 31% to 626% of the EU Average in 2017*, ec.europa.eu, 26 February 2019.

36 Louise Everett, Reply of the deputy director, policy and performance, Disability and Health Support Directorate, Department for Work and Pensions, to Mo Stewart, 15 August 2022, personal correspondence.

37 See 'Informing the Disability Unit', independentliving.co.uk, 22 August 2022.

38 Mo Stewart, 'Shaping future support: the health and disability green paper. A briefing', Preventable Harm Project, citizen-network.org, September 2021. In March 2023 the abolition of the WCA was announced.

39 Mo Stewart, 'The public health crisis created by UK social policy reforms', *Justice, Power and Resistance*, 28 July 2022.

40 Danny Dorling, *Injustice*, Bristol: Policy Press, 2010.

41 HMRC, 'Tax credits: 2 child limit policy', revenuebenefits.org.uk, 1 July 2022.

42 Trussell Trust, 'Our story: how we got to where we are today . . .'

43 See the Wikipedia entry for 'Seebohm Rowntree, third York study (1951)'.

4. Precarity

1 'Taking action on cost emergency: Scottish Government Resilience Room convened', gov.scot, 11 August 2022.

2 Maps from a decade ago look very similar to more recent ones. Compare Olly O'Brien's maps of 2013 (at oobrien.com), the 2022 Scottish census (when released) and the most recent release of the SIMD (Scottish Index of Multiple Deprivation).

3 ONS, 'People in households by housing tenure and combined economic activity status of household members', 29 September 2022, Table 1.

4 Becky Tunstall, 'The deresidualisation of social housing in England: change in the relative income, employment status and social class of social housing tenants since the 1990s', *Housing Studies*, 19 April 2021.

5 Simon Lambert, 'The average home in the UK cost £1,891 in 1952: how much would it be now if house prices had only risen in line with inflation?', *This Is Money* (*Daily Mail*), 17 June 2022.

6 The 2021 census data on dwellings became available at the time of writing. However, even if the number of additional bedrooms built had been lower than expected, it would still be higher than the increase in people. The 2010s were the first decade since records began in which the average new-built British home had slightly less than three bedrooms. See Aaron O'Neill, 'Average number of bedrooms in new British houses 1930–2020', statista.com, 21 June 2022.

7 The first UK census was held in 1801 just as the new state was formed. The 2021/22 census could be the last. See David Martin, 'Looking to the future of the UK censuses', blog.ukdataservice.ac.uk, 21 June 2022.

8 Danny Dorling, *All That Is Solid: The Great Housing Disaster*, London: Allen Lane, 2016, pp. 196–7.

9 Citizens Information, *Housing Taxes and Reliefs*, citizensinformation.ie.

10 Liam Geraghty, 'Social housing tenants should get compensation for living in homes "unfit for human habitation", say MPs', *Big Issue*, 20 July 2022.

11 Abigail O'Leary, 'Homeless single mum in one room B&B with three children says lockdown is "unbearable"', *Mirror*, 14 April 2020.

12 Sarah Wilson, 'Revealed: at least 30,000 people have waited 10 years for social housing', *Big Issue*, 12 July 2022.

13 Danny Dorling, 'The price we pay for housing is too high', *Public Sector Focus*, September/October 2016, p. 72.

14 Richard Ault and Hannah Cottrell, 'London property: over 1,000 renters and families thrown out onto streets with huge rise in landlord evictions', *My London News*, 16 August 2022.

15 Callum Cant, 'Taking what's ours: an ACORN inquiry', *Notes from Below*, 16 August 2018.

16 A few very nasty people might even argue that some people do not deserve to have toothpaste or soap.

17 The UK delivery and courier market is estimated to be worth £13 billion. It is made up of almost 10,000 businesses which employ around 112,000 people in total. See Mark Dean, 'UK delivery and courier industry statistics', shiply.com, 19 August 2022.

18 Katie Collins, 'What the US can learn from Europe about broadband affordability (and what it can't)', CNET, 23 June 2021.

19 Candice Cyrus, 'Failed UK energy suppliers update', *Forbes*, 18 February 2022.

20 The Rothschild Archive, 'Exhibition – "If you see Sid . . . tell him!"', rothschildarchive.org.

21 'Rail travel in Germany increases by 42% following introduction of €9 train tickets', *Schengenvisa News*, 12 July 2022.

22 Claudia Hille and Matthias Gather, 'Study proves: 9-euro ticket strengthens the social participation of people with low incomes', Institute for Transport and Space, Erfurt University of Applied Sciences, 24 October 2022.

23 Joshua Manning, 'Pedro Sanchez announces free Renfe train tickets at Spain's national debate', *EuroWeekly News*, 12 July 2022. And Dale Peterson, 'You can travel through Spain for free by train for all of 2023', *Travel Off Path*, 15 October 2022.

24 Roselyne Min, 'Free public transport in Europe: is the social experiment working or is it just a gimmick?', *Euronews*, 17 September 2022.

25 Nicole Kobie, 'The case for making public transit free everywhere', *Wired*, 29 July 2022.

26 Richard Partington, 'Labour explores plans to ban private jets from UK airports from 2025', *Guardian*, 4 November 2019.

27 Christian Brand and Brenda Boardman, 'Taming of the few: the unequal distribution of greenhouse gas emissions from personal travel in the UK', *Energy Policy*, vol. 36, no. 1, 2008, pp. 224–38.

28 Mary Shepperson, 'Why hasn't there been a single new reservoir built for over 30 years in the UK? We used to build loads', Twitter, 29 July 2022.

29 Joseph Baines and Sandy Brian Hager, 'Profiting amid the energy crisis: the distribution networks at the heart of the UK's gas and electricity system', common-wealth.co.uk, 14 March 2022.

30 David Hall and Vera Weghmann, 'Nationalisation would save UK billions, Greenwich research reveals', gre.ac.uk, 15 November 2019.

31 See preface to the third edition of Danny Dorling, *Inequality and the 1%*, London: Verso, 2019.

32 The data is in *Inequality and the 1%*, third edition, in the section titled 'New figures in the 3rd edition', at dannydorling.org.

33 Paul Kiel and Hannah Fresques, 'Where in the US are you most likely to be audited by the IRS?', *ProPublica*, 1 April 2019.

34 Anoosh Chakelian, 'You're 23 times more likely to be prosecuted for benefit fraud than tax fraud in the UK: yet tax crimes cost the economy nine times more', *New Statesman*, 25 July 2021.

35 Danny Dorling, 'Top "remuneration": have we reached peak inequality?', *Public Sector Focus*, January/February 2018, pp. 54–5.

36 Danny Dorling, 'Peak inequality: the gap between the very rich and the rest is wider in Britain than in any other large country in Europe, and society is the most unequal it has been since shortly after the First World War. But is great change coming?', *New Statesman*, 4 July 2018.

37 High Pay Centre analysis of FTSE 350 pay ratios, highpaycentre.org, 23 May 2022.

38 'CEO pay survey 2022: CEO pay surges 39%', highpaycentre.org, 22 August 2022.

39 Andy Hoffman, 'Swiss watch exports to China slump again as US stays strong', *Bloomberg News*, 21 June 2022.

40 According to the *Sunday Times* Rich List, their wealth fell in 2020, and after that the Rich List excluded them!

41 Danny Dorling, 'Britain is a segregated society – the isolation of the richest', *Public Sector Focus*, May/June 2018, pp. 16–17; Theresa May, 'Integrated communities strategy: green paper', DHCLG, March 2018.

42 Ajay Singh Chaudhary, 'We're not in this together: there is no universal politics of climate change', *Baffler*, no. 51, April 2020.

43 Jack Monroe, 'The curse of the poverty hangover, ten years on', *Cooking on a Bootstrap* blog, 31 July 2022.

44 Leo Schulz, 'Housing as a human right', letter to the editor, *Times Literary Supplement*, 12 August 2022.

45 Danny Dorling, 'Twelve facts you may have missed as the UK missed its first Brexit deadline', *Public Sector Focus*, March/April 2019, pp. 12–14.

46 See Figure 19b in ONS, 'Detailed assessment of changes to sector and financial accounts', 7 September 2020 (note, this change was realised by the ONS when they included better new estimates of the value of pensions).

47 Danny Dorling, *Slowdown: The End of the Great Acceleration and Why It's Good for the Planet, the Economy, and Our Lives*, New Haven: Yale University Press, 2021.

48 'UK workers' pension funds now own just 6% of UK listed shares', tuc.org.uk, 6 January 2022.

49 Ibid.

50 'Immediate freeze on rent increases plus eviction ban', Scottish Association of Landlords, 6 September 2022.

51 Part 1 and Schedule 17 of the Housing Act 1988; see also Danny Dorling, 'Lessons from more equitable European countries: rent regulation', *Public Sector Focus*, March/April 2017, p. 54.

5. Waste

1 Sean Illing, 'Bullshit jobs: why they exist and why you might have one. And why this professor thinks we need a revolution', *Vox*, 9 November 2019.

2 ONS, 'Regional gross value added (balanced) by industry: UK and all ITL regions', 30 May 2022. To compare years use Table 1c: current price estimates and share of total economy within each year.

3 ONS, 'Changes to national accounts: imputed rental', 23 March 2016.

4 Usually attributed to Napoleon but first mentioned in Adam Smith's *The*

Wealth of Nations. See Sita Balani, 'Britain: a history of shopkeeping, empire and racial tensions', *Media Diversified*, 7 October 2013.

5 Some 6 per cent more (excluding the motor trade). See ONS, 'JOBS03: employee jobs by industry', 14 June 2022.

6 If you want to know what is in each industry see ONS, 'UK SIC 2007', 24 January 2022.

7 Kevin Peachy, 'Funeral costs drop for first time in 18 years', BBC News, 17 January 2022.

8 The cut is undoubtedly huge, but hard to quantify. For just one 'player', the *Financial Times* explains: 'Tracing the finances at Four Seasons is all but impossible; the company's sprawling structure consists of 200 companies arranged in 12 layers in at least five jurisdictions, including several offshore territories.' Gill Plimmer, 'Private equity and Britain's care home crisis', *Financial Times*, 8 February 2020.

9 Lucy White, 'Loss-making care home firm HC-One pays £1.8m dividend to its private equity owners', *Daily Mail*, 11 July 2022.

10 Automation does not in itself reduce the amount of useful work people can do, but when it comes to automated factories being moved to other countries, which can better look after and service the robots, the UK does have a significant problem. See 'BMW to move electric Mini production from Oxford to China', ITV News, 17 October 2022. This move may have been averted in March 2023. In other economic activities, such as car washing, what was once automated has become increasingly now done by hand by very cheap labour, on otherwise disused urban land.

11 This comparison relies on Table 1b from the ONS 2022 source referred to in note 2 above, 'Regional gross value added (balanced) by industry' (chained volume measures in 2019 money value, pounds million).

12 Peggy Hollinger and Sarah Neville, 'Drug wars: how AstraZeneca overtook GSK in UK pharma', *Financial Times*, 7 May 2020.

13 The figures are 0.783 million in December 2019, 3.1 million by 2039 and 15.7 million by 2059. Although entirely fanciful and impossible, by March 2022 there were 0.896 million people in these jobs – so the figures were still rising quickly.

14 Minouche Shafik, Clive Cowdery, Adam Tooze, Dani Rodrik, Carolyn Fairbairn, Frances O'Grady and Nicholas Stern, 'Stagnation nation: navigating a route to a fairer and more prosperous Britain', *The Economy 2030 Inquiry*, Resolution Foundation, 2022, p. 8.

15 British workers putting in longest hours in the EU, TUC analysis finds, tuc. org.uk, 17 April 2019.

16 Mo Stewart, 'The public health crisis created by UK social policy reforms', *Justice, Power and Resistance*, 28 July 2022.

17 'Peter Dowd MP calls for four-day working week without pay cut', BBC News, 18 October 2022.

18 The nominal GVA worked in both Oxford and Blackpool was £28.70 per hour in 2018, the last year for which hourly rates were published by local authority districts as I write (in late 2022). These were the rates used to identify areas for 'levelling up' from: ONS, 'Subregional productivity in the UK', 28 February 2022.

19 ONS, 'Regional gross value added (balanced) per head and income components', 20 May 2022.

20 Marcus Johns and Ryan Swift, 'Levelling up was business as usual, but that has to change', Institute for Public Policy Research North, press release, 26 July 2022.

21 Danny Dorling, 'Brexit – the Ides of March', *Public Sector Focus*, January/ February 2019, pp. 14–16.

22 Martin McKee and Lucinda Hiam, 'Britain's not working', *BMJ*, 29 July 2022.

23 Figure 17 in Molly Broome and Jack Leslie, 'Arrears fears: the distribution of UK household wealth and the impact on families', Resolution Foundation, 20 July 2022.

24 Pip Murrison, 'Boris Johnson says he "can't live" on £157,000 a year – PM's salary woes exposed', *Express*, 12 January 2022.

25 See 'How much does the poverty premium cost your constituency?', fairbydesign.com.

26 Boris Johnson, resignation speech, 7 July 2022, youtube.com (recording and transcript differ slightly, see note 27 for transcript).

27 Boris Johnson, 'Full text: Boris Johnson's resignation speech', *Spectator*, 7 July 2022.

28 Paul Fitzpatrick, 'Situationism and rock', furious.com, October 2000.

29 Danny Dorling, 'Please sir, can I have more?', *Public Sector Focus*, November/ December 2020, pp. 14–16.

30 Danny Dorling, 'Income inequality in the UK: comparisons with five large Western European countries and the USA', *Applied Geography*, vol. 61, 2015, pp. 24–34.

31 Danny Dorling, *The Equality Effect: Improving Life for Everyone*, Oxford: New Internationalist, 2017.

32 See Figure A.2.2, p. 74 in Robert Manduca et al., 'Trends in absolute income mobility in North America and Europe', IZA Discussion Paper 13456, July 2020.

33 ONS, 'UK standard industrial classification of economic activities 2007 (SIC 2007)', 2009.

6. Exploitation

1 William Makepeace Thackeray, *The Book of Snobs: By One of Themselves*, London: Punch, 1848.

2 Enter 'snobbery' as a search term into the Google Books Ngram Viewer.

3 ONS, 'JOBS03: employee jobs by industry', Table 5 (UK female), 13 September 2022.

4 To see when we began pulling apart, see Figure 3 in Danny Dorling, 'Public sector spending and living standards in the long run', *Public Sector Focus*, November/December 2021, pp. 12–14.

5 Richard Wilkinson and Kate Pickett, *The Inner Level: How More Equal Societies Reduce Stress, Restore Sanity and Improve Everyone's Well-Being*, London: Allen Lane, 2018.

6 Jenny Colgan, 'Book clubs are nothing to do with reading. They are just get-togethers for sad middle-class women', *Guardian*, 3 May 2002.

7 Enter 'reverse/inverted snobbery' as a search term in the Google Books Ngram Viewer.

8 Entirely free again from 2008 when the SNP scrapped what was called 'the graduate endowment'. See 'Sturgeon's claim that SNP scrapped tuition fees is mostly true', theferret.scot, 6 August 2017.

9 Jim Knight, 'England is bottom of the league when it comes to deep learning. And top for drill and practice. It's no coincidence', *Times Educational Supplement*, 8 March 2016.

10 Martin Armstrong, 'The world's highest and lowest tuition fees', Statista, 17 September 2022.

11 Edel Blake, 'New research reveals the cost of international education around the world in 2021', International Schools Database, 6 December 2021.

12 PISA 2018 ranking summary – available from many sources, but it is most simply laid out in Wikipedia.

13 They may be higher now; type 'Edinburgh overseas student fees' into Google to find out.

14 In medicine, dentistry, science, engineering, technology and subjects with a studio, laboratory or fieldwork element (including maths and modern languages). University of Manchester website, as of November 2022.

15 Manchester Metropolitan University, 'Tuition fees for international students, as of November 2022'.

16 'Eight reasons why Manchester is a great place to be a student', British Council, Study UK, n.d.

17 Jessica Shepherd, 'Academies to become a majority among state secondary schools', *Guardian*, 5 April 2012.

18 Liz Lightfoot, 'Nepotism, fraud, waste and cheating . . . welcome to England's school system. A Nottingham professor has collated 3,800 examples of bad practice she says go to the heart of government. Now she has written a book', *Guardian*, 8 September 2020.

19 'Open academies, free schools, studio schools, UTCs and academy projects in development', Department for Education, open data, last updated 21 October 2022.

20 'Key UK education statistics', British Educational Suppliers Association, 2022.

21 James Callaghan, 'A rational debate based on the facts', Ruskin College speech, 18 October 1976.

22 Eversheds Sutherland, 'Articles of Association of Ruskin College: a private company limited by guarantee', Ruskin College website, March 2022.

23 Richard Adams, 'Oxford Brookes doing worse than University of Oxford on state school admissions', *Guardian*, 13 February 2020.

24 University of Oxford, 'Undergraduate admission statistics current', ox.ac.uk.

25 Christine Farquharson, Sandra McNally and Imran Tahir, 'Education inequalities', chapter in the IFS Deaton review of inequality, Institute for Fiscal Studies, 16 August 2022.

26 Charlotte Lynch, '"She's lying through her teeth": Leeds residents blast Truss over tough upbringing claims', *LBC*, 29 July 2022.

27 '41% of young adults hold a tertiary degree', Eurostat, 24 May 2022.

28 OECD, 'Population with tertiary education (indicator)', data.oecd.org, November 2022.

29 Ashley Cowburn, 'Liz Truss cabinet has highest proportion of privately educated ministers since John Major', *Mirror*, 7 September 2022.

30 Luke Sibieta, 'School spending in England: trends over time and future outlook', Institute for Fiscal Studies, 2 September 2021.

31 Jim Dickinson, 'Yes, international students are displacing home students', *WonkHE*, 19 August 2022.

32 Sian Griffiths, 'Universities push for "vital" tuition fee rise: UK students must pay closer to £24,000 a year or lose their places to foreigners, argue bosses', *Sunday Times*, 21 August 2022.

33 Amar Mehta, 'Exam regulator to review why some students are still waiting for their BTEC results. Exam board Pearson apologised for the delays, which has meant that students have been unable to confirm university places', Sky News, 22 August 2022.

34 Scott Beasley, 'And here's that chart – showing the change in real terms per pupil funding for state and private schools', Sky News on Twitter, source: Institute for Fiscal Studies, 27 March 2022.

35 Luke Sibieta, 'The growing gap between state school and private school spending', observation, Institute for Fiscal Studies, 8 October 2021.

36 Patricia Sanchez, 'Getting a university degree might make people more socially liberal and economically conservative', *PsyPost*, 26 June 2022.

37 Ralph Scott, 'Does university make you more liberal? Estimating the within-individual effects of higher education on political values', *Electoral Studies*, vol. 77, 26 April 2022.

38 Amory Gethin, Clara Martínez-Toledano and Thomas Piketty, 'Brahmin left versus merchant right: changing political cleavages in 21 western democracies, 1948–2020', *Quarterly Journal of Economics*, vol. 137, no. 1, 2022, pp. 1–48.

39 'Invariably the reason why the person has the antisocial behaviour injunction is because of their mental health and if they come [to prison] for short periods of time, we don't have them long enough to stabilise them [and] their antisocial behaviour becomes worse. They can become very psychotic when they come into prison and we do not have the facilities to manage them. Putting people in prison for short periods of time for a civil offence is just crazy.' Maeve McClenaghan, 'Sent to jail for feeding the pigeons: the broken system of antisocial behaviour laws', Bureau of Investigative Journalism, 21 August 2022.

40 There were 600 playgroups in 1966; thousands more started in the years that

followed, but private nurseries later increased greatly in number in their place. See the Wikipedia entry for 'Pre-school Learning Alliance'.

41 Paying a weekly fee to attend a state grammar school for example (in my grandparents' time), keeping the school leaving age lower than it need be (in my parents' time), or endorsing corporal punishment in schools (when I was at school). None of these policies were missed as soon as they were ended.

42 Natasha Hinde, '"Complete devastation": this is the real-time impact of nursery closures', *Huffington Post*, 19 August 2022.

43 Jack Fifield and Helen Pidd, 'Manchester electronic ad boards each use electricity of three households', *Guardian*, 9 January 2022.

7. Fear

1 Registrar General, 'Birth- and death-rates for 1936 in England', *Nature*, vol. 139, 1937, p. 189.

2 Lu Hiam and Danny Dorling, 'The end of great expectations? The pandemic inquiry must account for stalling life expectancy before the pandemic', editorial, *BMJ*, 6 May 2022.

3 No estimate has been made for Northern Ireland. See Patrick Butler, 'Over 330,000 excess deaths in Great Britain linked to austerity, finds study', *Guardian*, 5 October 2022.

4 See Deborah Harrington, 'Aneurin Bevan's 1952 essay on the NHS – Chapter 5 of "In Place of Fear"', *Public Matters*, 5 February 2019.

5 Richard Partington, 'Life in the home counties brings 16 more years of good health', *Guardian*, 15 September 2019.

6 Google Books Ngram Viewer of 'illness' and 'disease' 1500–2019.

7 Poor nutrition and healthcare matter, but polio also returns because of effluent in waterways. See Ian Sample, 'National incident declared over polio virus findings in London sewage', *Guardian*, 22 June 2022.

8 Sebastien Peytrignet, Jay Hughes, Ellen Coughlan, Josh Keith, Tim Gardner and Charles Tallack, 'Waiting for NHS hospital care: the role of the independent sector', Health Foundation, 22 July 2022.

9 Denis Campbell, 'Far more NHS contracts going to private firms than ministers admit, figures show', *Guardian*, 25 April 2015.

10 Denis Campbell, 'Private firms handed £15bn in NHS contracts over past five years', *Guardian*, 29 November 2019.

11 See the Wikipedia entry for Aneurin Bevan.

12 David Walsh, Gerry McCartney, Jon Minton, Jane Parkinson, Deborah Shipton and Bruce Whyte, 'Deaths from "diseases of despair" in Britain: comparing suicide, alcohol-related and drug-related mortality for birth cohorts in Scotland, England and Wales, and selected cities', *Journal of Epidemiology and Community Health*, vol. 75, no. 12, 2021, pp. 1195–201.

13 Lucy Johnstone et al., 'Power Threat Meaning Framework (PTMF)', bps.org.uk, 2022.

14 Sanah Ahsan, 'I'm a psychologist – and I believe we've been told devastating lies about mental health', *Guardian*, 6 September 2022.

15 Christopher Snowdon, 'No, life expectancy is NOT falling', Institute for Economic Affairs, 19 December 2019.

16 There are many studies in press and the figure continues to rise. An estimate in 2019 of 130,000 was given by the IPPR in terms of preventable deaths not being avoided since 2012. See Dean Hochlaf, Harry Quilter-Pinner and Tom Kibasi, 'Ending the blame game: the case for a new approach to public health and prevention', ippr.org, June 2019.

17 ONS, 'National population projections: 2016-based statistical bulletin', 26 October 2017; Danny Dorling, '120,000 additional premature deaths in the UK 2010–2017', *Public Sector Focus*, November/December 2017, pp. 14–15.

18 Statement on visit to the United Kingdom, by Professor Philip Alston, United Nations special rapporteur on extreme poverty and human rights, ohchr.org, 16 November 2018.

19 CIPFA, Adult Social Care Performance Tracker, Institute for Government, 2019.

20 Danny Dorling, 'Public inquiry into rising mortality in England announced', *Public Sector Focus*, July/August 2018, pp. 14–15.

21 Public Health England, *A Review of Recent Trends in Mortality in England*, London: Wellington House, 2018.

22 See the Wikipedia entry for 'List of countries by past life expectancy'.

23 The figures through to 2015 are available from the same UN source as those for 1950–55.

24 The ranking is thirty-fourth if countries not included in the early data are also excluded.

25 John Burn-Murdoch, 'The NHS is being squeezed in a vice: excess deaths not related to Covid are rising in a system under almost intolerable strain', *Financial Times*, 22 August 2022.

26 The UK's 2021 life expectancy was the tiniest fraction above Germany's because of men still doing poorly in eastern Germany. That will be the next milestone to be passed.

27 ONS, 'UK drops in European child mortality rankings', 13 October 2017.

28 WHO, 'Neonatal mortality rate (0 to 27 days) per 1000 live births (SDG 3.2.2)', who.int, 18 January 2022.

29 WHO, 'Under-five mortality rate (per 1000 live births) (SDG 3.2.1)', who. int, 18 January 2022.

30 Lucinda Hiam and Danny Dorling, 'The end of great expectations?', *BMJ*, 6 May 2022.

31 Sarah Knapton, 'Excess deaths are on the rise – but not because of Covid', *Telegraph*, 5 July 2022.

32 You can find this data in the World Health Organization Global Health Observatory, November 2022.

33 Toby Watt, Ann Raymond and Laurie Rachet-Jacquet, 'Quantifying health inequalities in England', Health Foundation, 15 August 2022. The quote was from the press release of this report, titled 'Major study outlines wide health inequalities in England' and released on the same day by the foundation.

34 Louise Marshall, David Finch and Jo Bibby, 'Mortality and life expectancy trends in the UK: stalling progress', Health Foundation, 14 November 2019.

35 Veena Raleigh, 'What is happening to life expectancy in England?', King's Fund, 10 August 2022. The Internet Wayback Machine can be used to see the original if that version is updated.

36 Commission on the Future of Health and Social Care, 'The UK private health market', King's Fund, 2 April 2014.

37 'How the Health Foundation is funded', health.org.uk.

38 'The history of the King's Fund', kingsfund.org.uk.

39 Mo Stewart, *Cash Not Care: The Planned Demolition of the UK Welfare State*, London: New Generation Publishing, 2016.

40 See the Wikipedia entry for 'List of countries by past life expectancy'.

41 Mary Shaw and Danny Dorling, 'Who cares in England and Wales? The Positive Care Law: cross-sectional study', *British Journal of General Practice*, vol. 54, no. 409, 2004, pp. 899–903.

42 Ruth Green, Harriet Agerholm and Libby Rogers, 'Full extent of NHS dentistry shortage revealed by far-reaching BBC research', BBC News, 8 August 2022.

43 Lucy White, 'Loss-making care home firm HC-One pays £1.8m dividend to its private equity owners', *Daily Mail*, 11 July 2022.

44 Josh Layton, 'Care home operator calling for state aid put on spot over boss's purported £800k salary', *Coventry Telegraph*, 22 May 2020.

45 Brian Bell and John Van Reenen, 'Extreme wage inequality: pay at the very top', Centre for Economic Performance, LSE, occasional paper 34, February 2013.

46 OECD, 'Health spending: total, government, compulsory, voluntary, out-of-pocket, % of GDP, 1970–2021', data.oecd.org.

47 Hannah Brown, 'Tony Blair's legacy for the UK's National Health Service', *Lancet*, 19 May 2007.

48 Kalyeena Makortoff and Jasper Jolly, 'How the UK government lost £4.9bn to Covid loan fraud', *Guardian*, 29 January 2022.

49 Clare Dyer, 'Covid-19: government's use of VIP lane for awarding PPE contracts was unlawful, says judge', *BMJ*, 13 January 2022.

50 All these figures were derived from the OECD health spending data referenced in note 46 above. Choose out-of-pocket expenses, data as a percentage of GDP, and data back to 1970 to download the table to find that data.

51 Which would include many *Guardian* readers. See Andrew Gregory, 'Millions of UK patients forced to go private amid record NHS waiting lists: 10% of adults turned to private sector or independent healthcare in past year', *Guardian*, 11 September 2022.

52 John Burn-Murdoch, 'Chronic illness makes UK workforce the sickest in developed world. Every country saw economic inactivity spike during Covid but only in Britain is a rise in worklessness continuing', *Financial Times*, 21 July 2022.

53 Adrian O'Dowd, 'Fifth of coalition MPs have links to private healthcare firms', *BMJ*, 19 November 2014.

54 Danny Dorling, 'Why are the old dying before their time? How austerity has affected mortality rates', *New Statesman*, 7 February 2014.

55 Danny Dorling, 'How quickly might we forget the lessons of Covid-19?', *Public Sector Focus*, March/April 2020, pp. 14–16.

56 Danny Dorling, 'So what do we know now about Covid-19 in the UK?', *Public Sector Focus*, May/June 2020, pp. 12–15.

57 What would the alternative have been? Would people have welcomed strangers – discharged, unrelated, elderly, frail and confused patients –

into their homes in 2020 in the same way and number that some took younger and much more able refugees from Ukraine into spare rooms in 2022?

58 Maggie Baska, 'Third of employees asked to work while furloughed, survey finds', *People Management*, 18 June 2020.

59 Danny Dorling, 'COVID-19: the rise in destitution and inequality in the UK', *Public Sector Focus*, July/August 2020, pp. 14–17.

60 Danny Dorling, 'Who should be vaccinated before others?', *Public Sector Focus*, January/February 2021, pp. 12–15.

61 Danny Dorling, 'The ever ending never ending pandemic', *Public Sector Focus*, January/February 2022, pp. 12–14.

62 Saima May Sidik, 'Heart disease after COVID: what the data say', *Nature*, 2 August 2022.

63 All these figures are from the United Nations World Population Prospect dataset released in July 2022.

64 Kat Lay, 'Antidepressant use in England rises by a fifth', *The Times*, 8 July 2022.

65 Jonathan Cribb, Tom Waters, Thomas Wernham and Xiaowei Xu, 'Living standards, poverty and inequality in the UK: 2022', Institute for Fiscal Studies, 14 July 2022.

66 Debórah Dwork, *War Is Good for Babies and Other Young Children: A History of the Infant and Child Welfare Movement in England 1898–1918*, New York: Tavistock Publications, 1987.

67 DWP, 'Households below average income: an analysis of the income distribution FYE 1995 to FYE 2020', 25 March 2021, section 11: long-term trends.

68 A couple of other small Eastern European countries are also worth watching: OECD, 'Income inequality', online statistics, data.oecd.org.

69 See Table 4 and supplementary material in Thomas Crossley, Paul Fisher and Hamish Low, 'The heterogeneous and regressive consequences of COVID-19: evidence from high quality panel data', *Journal of Public Economics*, vol. 193, 2021. And also Danny Dorling, 'Who is being hurt the most?', *Public Sector Focus*, November/December 2022, pp. 12–15.

70 David Finch and Adam Tinson, 'The continuing impact of COVID-19 on health and inequalities', Health Foundation, 24 August 2022.

71 They appear in Figure 6 in Finch and Tinson's 2022 report cited in the previous note.

72 'Timeline: Covid contracts and accusations of "chumocracy"', BBC News, 15 March 2021.

73 Pippa Medcalf, 'Helping homeless people in hospital', Royal College of Physicians, rcplondon.ac.uk, 26 October 2020.

74 Haider Warraich, Pankaj Kumar, Khurram Nasir, Karen Joynt Maddox and Rishi Wadhera, 'Political environment and mortality rates in the United States 2001–19', *BMJ*, 7 June 2022.

75 Theo Rashid, James Bennett, Christopher Paciorek et al., 'Life expectancy and risk of death in 6791 communities in England from 2002 to 2019', *Lancet Public Health*, vol. 6, no. 11, 2021, pp. 805–16.

8. A Failing State

1 Vere Gordon Childe, *Man Makes Himself*, London: Watts, 1946.

2 Mark Honigsbaum, 'Revisiting the 1957 and 1968 influenza pandemics', *Lancet*, vol. 395, 2020, pp. 1824–6.

3 See 'country data' at fragilestatesindex.org.

4 See 'indicators c2' at fragilestatesindex.org.

5 'Bulgaria gov't falls after losing confidence vote. Bulgaria now faces the fourth national election since April 2021 amid disagreements on budget spending and the EU', *Al Jazeera News*, 22 June 2022.

6 Ibid.

7 Reporters without Borders, Press Freedom Index, rsf.org.

8 Reporters without Borders, '2022 World Press Freedom Index: a new era of polarisation', rsf.org.

9 Ibid.

10 Jessica Shepherd, 'Michael Gove: public school domination "morally inde-fensible"', *Guardian*, 10 May 2012.

11 Chloe Chaplain, 'Boris Johnson pictured running with *Sun* editor Tony Gallagher', *Evening Standard*, 2 October 2017.

12 Owen Gibson, 'Most leading journalists went to private schools, says study', *Guardian*, 15 June 2006.

13 Jonathan Haidt, 'Why the past 10 years of American life have been uniquely stupid', *Atlantic*, 11 April 2022.

14 Ezra Klein, 'Why a middle-class lifestyle remains out of reach for so many', *New York Times*, 17 July 2022.

15 See the Wikipedia entry for 'Michael Gove journalistic career'.

16 Danny Dorling, 'The changing political shape of the UK: May 2019', *Public Sector Focus*, May/June 2019, pp. 14–17.

17 Sutton Trust, 'Elitist Britain 2019: the educational backgrounds of Britain's leading people', published jointly with the Social Mobility Commission, 2019.

18 Michael Savage, 'Just one in 100 Tory MPs came from a working-class job, new study shows', *Guardian*, 24 July 2022.

19 Will Black, 'Michael Gove's brave new world', *Huffington Post*, 23 January 2014.

20 Craig Meighan, 'Giles Coren slammed for "sickening" comment after death of journalist Dawn Foster', *National*, 21 July 2021.

21 Martin Williams, 'A quarter of Tory MPs are private landlords', *Opendemocracy*, 22 July 2021. It is also thanks to our MPs that today 'the UK is the world's biggest regulated online gambling market, with British players having lost more than £14 billion on online casino games, sports betting, and other forms of gambling over four of the past five years'. Gavin Finch, 'How the UK got hooked on online gambling', *Bloomberg News*, 1 December 2022.

22 And of the donors who own key addresses. See Tom Bawden, 'The address where Eurosceptics and climate change sceptics rub shoulders', *Independent*, 10 February 2016.

23 Deputy PM Nick Clegg suggested ways businessman could split donation, *Channel 4 News*, 21 March 2015.

24 'Unprecedented leak exposes inner workings of UK Labour Party', Al Jazeera Investigative Unit, 23 September 2022.

25 Martin Forde, *The Forde Report*, paragraphs C1.8 and C1.32, fordeinquiry.org, 2022.

26 See the Wikipedia entry for '55 Tufton Street'. It is also closely associated with the Institute of Economic Affairs, located very nearby at 2 Lord North Street.

27 55 Tufton Street, desmog.com; see also the entry for Tufton Street at wikiwand.com.

28 There are some that do tend towards the right, and Poland has had an Adam Smith Centre since 1997.

29 For examples of how and why far-right think-tanks in the US work so well to direct others' thinking, including influencing politicians in the UK, see the far-right Heritage Foundation: heritage.org/solutions.

30 Nancy Kwak, *A World of Homeowners: American Power and the Politics of Housing Aid*, Chicago: University of Chicago Press, 2015.

31 Adam Peggs, 'What is housing policy for? And why we need a radical approach', *Labour List*, 21 September 2022.

32 Jane Mayer, *Dark Money: How a Secretive Group of Billionaires Is Trying to Buy Political Control in the US*, London: Scribe UK, 2016.

33 Jamie Grierson, 'Priti Patel appoints ex-Taxpayers' Alliance head as new aide', *Guardian*, 12 August 2021.

34 Hamish Morrison, 'Nadhim Zahawi appoints TaxPayers' Alliance member as new special adviser', *National*, 16 August 2022.

35 Guy Shrubsole, 'Matthew Sinclair, former head of the TaxPayers' Alliance, has been appointed Truss' chief economic advisor', Twitter, 6 September 2022.

36 BBC, 'Tom Scholar: former top civil servants hit out at Treasury boss sacking', BBC News, 11 September 2022.

37 Basit Mahmood, 'The think tanks closely linked to Liz Truss who cheered the disastrous mini-budget', *Left Foot Forward*, 30 September 2022.

38 Kristian Niemietz, 'Politically active left-wingers are the equivalent of the tribal football fan', 1828.org.uk, blog (managed by IEA Forum), 31 August 2022.

39 Aris Roussinos, 'Britain needs Macmillan, not Thatcher: none of the Tory candidates inspires hope for the future', *UnHerd*, 13 July 2022.

40 Danny Dorling, 'A tale of three elections', *Public Sector Focus*, September/October 2022, pp. 12–15.

41 Nick Schifrin and Phoebe Natanson, 'Ferrari crackdown: Italy declaring war on tax cheats', *ABC News*, 22 May 2012.

42 Mo Stewart, 'Influences and consequences, Centre for Welfare Reform', citizen-network.org, November 2019.

43 Social Mobility Commission, *State of the Nation*, 2022, Chapter 2, Figure 2.5 in data tables.

44 Figure A.2.2, on page 74 of Robert Manduca et al., 'Trends in absolute income mobility in North America and Europe', IZA Discussion Paper 13456, July 2020.

45 Danny Dorling, 'Things fall apart: Brexit, immigration, crime, health and wages', *Public Sector Focus*, November/December 2018, pp. 20–1.

46 'Here's where Polish people are buying houses in the UK', *Kafkadesk*, 12 June 2020.

47 ONS, 'Population estimates for UK, England and Wales, Scotland and Northern Ireland: mid-year estimates 2016', 22 June 2017.

48 Bobby Duffy, 'Perceptions and reality: ten things we should know about attitudes to immigration in the UK', *LSE Politics and Policy* blog, 26 November 2014.

49 ONS, 'Changing trends in mortality: an international comparison, 2000 to 2016', 7 August 2018.

9. Conclusion

1 Simon Jenkins, 'The United Kingdom is broken. It's time for a new British federation', *Guardian*, 5 July 2022.

2 Basit Mahmood, '*Telegraph* issues jaw-dropping correction for printing falsehood about National Trust', *Left Foot Forward*, 20 October 2022.

3 Susie Boniface, 'Sorry Rishi Sunak, but it's time to vilify the UK and its fundamental values: the way those in charge are doing things is just flat wrong . . . We need change', *Mirror*, 15 August 2022. And Jeremy Hunt, The Autumn Statement 2022 speech, His Majesty's Treasury, 17 November 2022.

4 Jim Knight, 'England is bottom of the league when it comes to deep learning. And top for drill and practice. It's no coincidence', *Times Educational Supplement*, 8 March 2016.

5 Noah Robinson, 'UK prison population third highest in Europe and suicide rate twice the average', *The Justice Gap*, 13 April 2021. There are many rankings of imprisonment rates, and they tend to be very similar to each other; see the Wikipedia entry for 'List of countries by incarceration rate'.

6 Georgina Sturge and Richard Tunnicliffe, *Uk Prison Population Statistics*, House of Commons Library, 29 October 2021.

7 'Joe Biden is determined that China should not displace America', *Economist*, 17 July 2021.

8 Ipsos MORI and Agnes Nairn, 'Children's well-being in UK, Sweden and Spain: the role of inequality and materialism', ipsos.com, June 2011.

9 Bobby Duffy, 'The public is shockingly wrong in its perception of Brexit – and there's a simple reason why', *Independent*, 28 October 2018.

10 Not least his brother-in-law, R. H. Tawney, who in turn was influenced by many others at a time when, among a large majority of the rest of the elite, it was widely presumed that there was no good alternative to the status quo.

11 Conservatives do not like to admit that good ideas can come from others. Here is one Tory take on this which suggests that the NHS was entirely Willink's idea: Andrew Grimson, 'Profile: Henry Willink, the Conservative who proposed a National Health Service before Bevan created one', *Conservative Home*, 5 January 2018.

12 Pensioners' Incomes Series: financial year 2019 to 2020, Department for Work and Pensions, 25 March 2021.

13 Danny Dorling, 'Austerity led to twice as many excess UK deaths as previously thought – here's what that means for future cuts', *Conversation*, 6 October 2022.

14 Josh Ryan-Collins, Richard Werner, Tony Greenham and Giovanni Bernardo, 'Strategic quantitative easing', New Economics Foundation, July 2013.

15 Economic Affairs Committee, 'Quantitative easing: a dangerous addiction?', House of Lords, 1st Report of Session 2021–22, 16 July 2012.

16 Danny Dorling, 'House prices: should we welcome a crash?', *UK in a Changing Europe*, 24 July 2012.

17 Danny Dorling, 'The "mini-budget" will make the UK the most unequal country in Europe', *BMJ*, 26 September 2022.

18 Robert Skidelsky, 'Where has all the money gone?', *Project Syndicate*, 15 September 2021.

19 Kaye Wiggins, Harriet Agnew and Daniel Thomas, 'Private equity and the raid on corporate Britain', *Financial Times*, 11 July 2012.

20 Oxford's new free school temporarily excluded 11 per cent of its pupils in the most recent year, or a quarter if multiple exclusions are counted, more than any other school in the county. It had a particular ethos of discipline and cannot be much influenced by the community around it because it is a free school. Sophie Perry, 'Revealed: which Oxfordshire school excludes pupils most often', *Oxford Mail*, 14 September 2022.

21 Danny Dorling, *A New Social Atlas of Britain*, London: John Wiley and Sons, 1995, Chapter 5: Health.

22 John Burn-Murdoch, 'How US life expectancy fell off a cliff', *Financial Times*, 26 August 2022.

23 The overall falls were slight, but did not happen in any other affluent country in the world. In the US, life expectancy fell from 79.02 years in 2014 to 78.99 years in 2018, and in the UK from 81.16 to 81.13 years. UN global data, July 2022, accessed from population.un.org in August 2022.

24 Stuart Wilks-Heeg, in a tweet on 22 August 2022.

25 Lucas Chancel, Thomas Piketty, Emmanuel Saez and Gabriel Zucman, *World Inequality Report 2022*, wir2022.wid.world, pages 191 and 227. By other measures the take of the UK 1 per cent is nearer 16 per cent.

26 Tim Gore, 'Confronting carbon inequality', Oxfam International, 21 September 2020.

27 In one version of the story there are three mountains: education, healthcare and housing, but that is a very different telling of the story from the translation used here. For that version see Jonathan Cheng, 'To achieve "common prosperity", Xi Jinping seeks to scale China's "three big mountains"', *Wall Street Journal*, 2 February 2022.

28 Branko Milanović, 'Socialism with Chinese characteristics for the young person', *Brave New Europe*, 15 August 2022.

29 John Burn-Murdoch, 'The Tories have become unmoored from the British people', *Financial Times*, 30 September 2022.

30 Danny Dorling, 'Let them eat growth?', tribunemps.org, 29 September 2022.

31 Chris Mason, 'Anguish at conference that should be Truss's victory lap', BBC News, 3 October 2022.

32 Dharshini David, 'U-turn will only counter some mini-budget criticism', BBC News, 3 October 2022.

33 Stuart Masson, 'Endless growth in car finance threatens household budgets', *Car Expert*, 12 October 2022.

34 Anna Fazackerley, 'Exclusive: 90% of UK schools will run out of money next year, heads warn', *Guardian*, 22 October 2022.

35 Hannah Devlin, 'Maternal mortality rises by nearly 20% in UK, report finds', *Guardian*, 10 November 2022.

36 See Figure S1: Home truths: every indicator of mental distress is higher for renters than for homeowners, in Tom Clark and Andrew Wenham, *Anxiety Nation? Economic Insecurity and Mental Distress in 2020s Britain*, York: Joseph Rowntree Foundation, November 2022.

37 D. Clark, 'Voter turnout in general elections and in the Brexit referendum in the United Kingdom from 1918 to 2019', Statista, 22 June 2022.

Index

academy schools (UK), 143–4
adult mortality, 31–2, 87, 168–9
advertising, 72, 119; Hovis bread, 22–3, 26, 27–8
Airbnb, including former social housing, 4–5
apathy. *See* complacency and indifference
Ashcroft, Michael, 42
Australia, 182
Austria, 18, 95
automation, 120, 246n5, 259n10
automobile industry, 4, 246n5

Bank of England, 82, 106, 229, 230, 231
banks and banking. *See* Bank of England; financial services
BBC, 15–16, 19, 197, 202
Belgium, 18, 167
Bevan, Aneurin, 164, 165
Beveridge, William, 47, 51, 59, 80, 110
Beveridge Report, 47, 51–2, 80
Biden, Joe, 225
Birmingham, 111–12, 134–5; immigrants, 217
Blackpool: GVA, 128, 260n18
Blair, Tony, 12, 13, 20, 215
Brexit, 34–7 passim, 42, 46, 54, 113, 129, 218, 219, 226; dentistry and, 174; financial services and, 121; Northern Ireland and, 26; party opposition, 13
Britannia Unchained: Global Lessons for Growth and Prosperity (Kwarteng et al.), 29
British crown dependencies. *See* crown dependencies (UK)
British Empire, 30, 31, 136, 207, 209. *See also* former British colonies
British Overseas Territories, 14–15, 36, 104
Brown, Gordon, 79, 207, 215
Bulgaria, 79, 195, 196; inequality, 20, 52, 184, 196, 252n6; life expectancy, 182; neonatal mortality, 168

Callaghan, James, 145, 156
Cameron, David, 66, 215
Canada, 139–40, 183
carbon dioxide emissions, 96, 104, 134, 237
care homes, 112, 118, 119, 180; chains, 174
CEO pay, 102, 174–5
Chaudhary, Ajay Singh, 103–4
child benefits, 68, 70, 78; Scotland, 58, 59, 64–5
childcare, 156, 161, 260n40
Childe, V. Gordon, 193

child homelessness, 52, 89

child mortality. _See_ infant mortality

childhood nutrition and children's meals, 54, 60, 62, 63, 78, 153

Chile, 149

China, 225, 237–9; auto industry, 246n5; Covid-19, 183; education, 224; international schools, 140; Swiss watch imports, 102

Clegg, Nick, 41

climate change, 8, 104, 237, 258n42, 270n22

clothing, 55, 71; manufacturing, 114, 117. _See also_ school uniforms

Club Med, 132–3

community colleges, 160

complacency and indifference, 222, 238

comprehensive schools (UK), 145, 148

Conservative Party (UK), 12–14 passim, 29, 37–47 passim, 65, 75, 122, 187, 206–7, 240; BBC and, 202; class makeup, 203; _Guardian_ and, 198; health spending, 175; house prices and, 106; 'levelling up', 112; segregation index, 47; tax policy, 131; Truss, 29, 34, 378. _See also_ Johnson, Boris

conspicuous consumption, 200, 226, 229

consumer spending, 56–7

Corbyn, Jeremy, 43, 45, 46, 47, 90, 186, 240, 242 passim; 'Corbynism from Below', 91

corruption: in academy schools, 144; in financial services, 10

cost-of-living crises, 66, 80–2, 95, 184, 212

council housing, 17, 83, 84, 88, 210

Covid-19 pandemic, 58, 75, 81, 102–3, 113, 129, 179–85; care homes, 174; education and, 135, 153; effect on jobs, 133, 180; health spending and, 176; housing and, 88, 89, 90; life expectancy and, 163, 168; lockdowns, 107, 183; long-term health effects (long Covid), 181, 185

Croatia, 168

crown dependencies (UK), 36

Cummings, Dominic, 181

Cyprus, 36, 129

Czech Republic, 53, 195

Davie, Tim, 16

debt. _See_ mortgages; national debt; personal debt

deindustrialisation, 4, 111, 141

Denmark: life expectancy, 173; public services spending, 18; rent control, 109; social mobility and taxation, 134

dentistry, 75, 173–4

Department for Levelling Up, Housing and Communities (UK), 39, 65–6, 112

Department for Work and Pensions (UK): Work Capabilities Assessment (WCA), 76–7

deprivation maps, 26, 44, 82, 247n7, 250n32

deregulation of financial markets, 123

disabled people, 76–7

disease, 31, 54, 162–4 passim; 'diseases of despair', 165. _See also_ Covid-19 pandemic

domestic servants, 137, 217

downsizing (housing), 105–7

drug abuse, 165, 235

economic growth, 107, 108, 124, 131

Edinburgh, 82, 139. _See also_ University of Edinburgh

education, 140–60 passim; adult and continuing, 159–60; 'alternative provision', 160–1. _See also_ schools; university education

elder care, 173; 133, 169, 172, 267n57 passim. _See also_ care homes

elections, 243; Barbados, 19; Bulgaria, 196; Italy, 213; UK, 34–47 passim, 90, 154, 175, 186, 196, 202, 242

electricity, 93–7 passim; Northern Ireland, 33

emergency medical care (A&E), 168, 187

energy costs, 53–7; 66, 72–3, 93–6, 254n34 passim

Estonia, 53, 95

eugenics, 78, 204

European Community, 25

European Union: internet provision, 93; new members (2004), 217. *See also* Brexit

eviction and evictions, 81, 89–90; bans, 109

family size: third (and subsequent) children, 64, 68, 70, 78

financial crisis of 2008, 46, 230

Financial Fairness Trust Report, 57

financial services, 9–11, 26, 118, 121. *See also* offshore banking

Finland, 11, 53, 74, 195; health services, 177; public services spending, 18, 177; school meals, 153

'five great evils' (Beveridge), 47, 51, 59

food banks, 52, 53, 60, 79, 119

food crises, 55, 56, 58–63 passim, 68, 116. *See also* hunger

food prices, 55, 56, 62–3

former British colonies, 19. *See also* British Overseas Territories

Fragile States Index, 194–6

France, 29–30, 133, 188; energy nationalisation, 93; income inequality, 73–4; leisure, 124; public services spending, 18; public transport, 95; rent control, 109; revolution, 56; university education, 140

freedom of the press. *See* press freedom

FTSE 100, 232–3

fuel, 108; prices, 55–6, 66, 72–3, 93–4; rationing, 70

funeral directing, 118–19, 127

gambling industry, 205, 270n21

gas. *See* natural gas

gasoline. *See* oil

gentrification, 4

Germany, 133; automobile industry, 246n5; cost-of-living crisis, 212; Covid-19, 180; federal structure, 33; income inequality, 73–4; leisure, 124; public services spending, 18; public transit, 95; rent control, 109; university education, 140

gilts (gilt-edged securities), 227–8, 230

Gini index, 184

global population, 7, 70

global warming. *See* climate change

Gold Hill, Shaftesbury, Dorset, 22, 26, 27

Goldsmith, Zac, 39–40

Gove, Michael, 39, 198, 201–2, 204

government bonds, 227–8. *See also* gilts

grammar schools, 35, 145, 234

Greece, 17–18; food price caps, 62, 253n18; public services spending, 18; taxing and spending, 38; wages, 32

greenhouse gases, 96. *See also* carbon dioxide emissions

Green Party (UK), 38

Gross Domestic Product (GDP): Germany, 123; UK, 32, 76, 100, 123, 124

gross value added (GVA), 121, 128, 260n18

Guardian, 137, 178, 197, 198, 199, 201

Haidt, Jonathan, 200

health and healthcare, 21, 31, 163–88 passim; United States, 235. *See also* life expectancy

Health Foundation, 172

health insurance, private. *See* medical insurance, private

Heath, Edward, 196

Henderson, Nicholas, 29–30, 31, 188

historiography, 222

HM Revenue and Customs (HMRC), 101

HM Treasury, 9, 180, 210, 230

holidays, 132–3

home heating, 26, 66, 67, 73, 75, 213
homelessness, 6, 69, 87, 88, 89, 187;
Bulgaria, 52; Finland, 11
home ownership, 114–15; multiple
homes, 83–4, 85–6. *See also*
mortgages
Hong Kong, 19, 239
household borrowing, 107. *See also*
personal debt
house prices, 85, 86–7, 91, 106, 115, 230
housing: UK, 3–6 passim, 20, 21, 30,
36, 80–91, 105–7, 114–15, 210. *See
also* council housing; eviction and
evictions; homelessness; mortgages
housing associations, 87–8
Hovis bread adverts, 22–3, 26, 27–8
hunger, 51, 58–63 passim, 67, 69, 79
Hunt, Jeremy, 42–3, 222

IMF. *See* International Monetary Fund
(IMF)
immigrants, 217–19
Immigration Act (UK), 24, 25
income tax, 60, 74, 100, 234
India, 100, 136
Inequality, 7, 11, 13, 30, 52, 54, 102, 169,
173, 185, 225, 238
infant mortality, 7, 31, 168, 224; Finland,
11
inflation, 26, 55, 61, 64, 72, 82, 230;
pensions and, 228
information asymmetry, 71
inheritance tax, 100
Inland Revenue, 101
insurance, 57, 104. *See also* medical
insurance, private; National
Insurance (UK)
interest rates, 82, 84, 107, 115, 228
International Monetary Fund (IMF),
18, 53
internet provision, 92–3
Ireland, 33, 35, 44, 248n26; Brexit, 129;
immigration, 217; property taxation,
87; school uniforms, 71; university
education, 148

Isaby, Jonathan, 210
Italy: inequality, 213; public transport,
95; tax evasion, 213; UK
comparison, 213, 214; university
education, 140, 148; wages, 32

Japan, 139
Johnson, Boris, 37, 40, 47, 80, 103, 130,
132, 186, 242; public opinion, 42–3;
salary, 131
Joseph, Keith, 41
judiciary: UK, 203

King's Fund, 172
Klein, Ezra, 200–1
Kwarteng, Kwasi, 52, 99; *Britannia
Unchained*, 29

Labour Party (UK), 12–13, 37–47
passim, 65, 79, 90, 206–7, 240, 242;
BBC and, 202; education policy,
145, 155; *Guardian* and, 198; health
spending, 175; Wales, 33–4, 35
Lanchester, John, 9–10, 11
landlords, 81, 83, 90, 106–7, 108, 115,
205; MPs as, 205
Latvia, 54
Leeds: adult mortality, 31–2;
Conservative enclave, 41; housing,
89; life expectancy (eighteenth-
century), 31
leisure, 124, 134
Levelling Up Department. *See*
Department for Levelling Up,
Housing and Communities (UK)
Levelling Up the United Kingdom, 36–7
Levinson, Charles, 169
Leyen, Ursula von der. *See* Von der
Leyen, Ursula
Liberal Democrats (UK), 13, 38, 46,
154, 198
life expectancy, 31, 42, 163, 166–73
passim, 188, 235–6; women, 166–7,
188, 217
Lithuania, 252n6

Liverpool, 41; adult mortality, 31–2; life expectancy (eighteenth-century), 31; 'managed decline', 112

loans: personal debt. *See* personal debt

Luxembourg: Brexit, 129; public transport, 95

Macmillan, Harold, 194

Major, John, 37, 38, 207, 215

malnutrition, 74–5, 78

Malta, 71, 129, 168

'managed decline', 112

Manchester: adult mortality, 31; life expectancy (eighteenth-century), 31; minimum wage, 64; Osborne, 41; schools and universities, 141–3

manufacturing, 113–17 passim, 233, 234; Birmingham, 111, 134; food, 116; triangular trade, 33; unemployment, 4. *See also* auto industry

May, Theresa, 37, 103, 186, 242

McIntyre, Robert, 34

media, 197–202, 232. *See also* newspapers; social media; television

medical insurance, private, 171–2, 177

mental health, 162, 163, 165–6; antidepressant use, 183; anxiety, 185, 241; prison and, 263n39; welfare sanctions and, 67

military spending, 18

minimum wage, 64, 65

mining and quarrying, 113, 119–20, 221

monarchy: public opinion 19

monopolies, 71, 92–4 passim, 107, 108, 127

Mordaunt, Penny, 212

mortality, 75, 163, 166, 167, 172, 219, 235; 'diseases of despair' and, 165, 235; homelessness and, 187; pregnant women and new mothers, 241. *See also* adult mortality; infant mortality; suicide

mortgages, 81–91 passim, 106, 114–15, 230; landlords', 81, 91; repossession orders, 90

Murty, Akshata, 98

national debt (UK), 227–8

National Health Service (NHS), 165, 169, 171, 175–6, 227; dentistry and, 174

National Insurance (UK), 60, 240

nationalisation, 93, 94, 98, 107, 240

natural gas, 55–6, 93–4

neonatal mortality. *See* infant mortality

Netherlands: housing, 109; life expectancy, 173; public services spending, 18; social mobility, 215

New Economics Foundation (NEF), 24–5

New Labour. *See* Labour

newspapers, 99, 137, 197–202 passim, 222

NHS. *See* National Health Service (NHS)

NIMBYism, 88

Northern Ireland, 25–6, 33, 35–6, 58, 221, 239; minimum wage, 64

Northern Ireland Protocol, 35–6

Norway: Covid-19, 183; life expectancy, 173; public services spending, 18; social mobility, 215

nursing homes. *See* care homes

offshore banking, 104

oil, 26, 28, 108, 113, 246n5

Oman, 182

Osborne, George, 41, 78, 122, 132

'outdoor' and 'indoor' relief, 73

Oxford, England, 4–6, 187, 273n20; colleges and universities, 141, 146, 198; deaths from homelessness, 6; GVA, 128;

Oxford Brookes University, 146

Oxfordshire, 16, 45, 187

pandemics, 194. *See also* Covid-19 pandemic

Patel, Priti, 210
pay. *See* wages and salaries
Pearson, Karl, 78
pensions and pensioners, 89, 107, 108, 228, 229, 232; tax relief, 231. *See also* state pension (UK)
personal debt, 57, 131, 184, 241; student debt, 135. *See also* mortgages
personal savings. *See* savings
petrol. *See* oil
Plaid Cymru, 35
Poland, 64, 209–10, 247n14; emigrants, 217
pollution, carbon dioxide. *See* carbon dioxide emissions
Poor Law of 1834 (UK), 73, 78
Portugal, 18, 32
postal services, 92
pound: trade, 82; value, 18, 114, 116, 143. *See also* inflation
poverty, 7, 13, 21, 25, 27, 54, 60, 79, 101, 112, 125, 146, 165, 183, 193, 235. *See also* outdoor
premature deaths. *See* mortality
press freedom, 197–8
primary schools, 4, 144, 233
prisons and imprisonment, 159, 224, 263n39
private equity firms, 233
Private Finance Initiative (PFI) (UK), 38–9
Private health. *See* medical insurance
private schools, 131, 138–45 passim, 149–55 passim, 234; judiciary and, 203; newspapers and, 198–9
private transport, 96
privatisation, 17, 92, 95, 210, 233; of council housing, 83; electricity, 97; NHS, 35, 176; schools, 144–5; universities, 135, 143; water, 70, 95, 97
Preston, Lancashire, 65
productivity, 112–20
public health. *See* health and healthcare
public opinion: UK, 23, 34, 37, 40, 42–3

public sector workers, 17–18
public transport, 95–6

quantitative easing, 229, 230, 231

radio: BBC, 202
rail transportation, 69, 95; strikes, 236
Rashford, Marcus, 58
rationing, 70, 71, 72, 214
Reagan, Ronald, 211
'Red Wall' myth (UK), 40–1, 45
relief. *See* 'outdoor' and 'indoor' relief; welfare
rent and rents, 81–5 passim, 91, 106, 127, 184; Manchester, 143; rent control, 90, 109
residualisation of council housing, 83
retail, 113, 115–16
rickets, 54, 164, 252n7
Ridley, Matt, 29, 249n12
right-wing think-tanks. *See* think-tanks, right-wing
Romania, 168, 252n6
Rothschild & Co., 95
Rowntree, Joseph, 59, 79
Rowntree, Seebohm, 79
Royal Tunbridge Wells, Kent, 39–40
Ruskin College, 146
Russia, 182, 196, 212, 224
Rutland: public health, 31

salaries. *See* wages and salaries
Sandbrook, Dominic, 29, 249n11
savings, 72, 92, 130–1, 150, 179, 231
Scholar, Tom, 210
school meal programmes, 62, 153
school milk programmes, 60
schools, 140–60 passim, 198, 205, 207, 233–4; Slough, 17. *See also* academy schools; primary schools; state schools (UK); university education
school uniforms, 71, 161, 233
Scotland, 15, 33–7 passim, 46–7, 80–2 passim, 108–9, 156, 221, 239; child benefits, 58, 59, 64–5; 'diseases of

despair', 165; GDP, 76; minimum wage, 64; private schools, 139; tax rebates, 58; university education, 69, 139, 142; water and sewage, 71; youth voting, 43

Scott, Ridley, 22–4, 27

Scottish National Party (SNP), 33, 34, 46–7

second homes, 35, 84, 85–6

self-censorship, 223

segregation index of Conservative voters, 47

servants. *See* domestic servants

Shaftesbury, Dorset, 22, 26

Sheffield, 41, 89, 142

Shepperson, Mary, 97

Simpson, Duncan, 210

Sinclair, Matthew, 210

Sinn Féin, 33, 35

Slough, Berkshire, 17, 217

Slovakia, 53, 168

Slovenia, 167

snobbery, 136–8, 150, 152

social housing, 89, 91. *See also* council housing; housing associations

social mobility and immobility, 134, 158, 202–3, 215–16

Social Mobility Commission (UK), 215–16

'Social Insurance and Allied Services' report (1942). *See* Beveridge Report

social media, 199–200, 223

soup kitchens, 59, 79

South Korea, 140

Spain, 17–18, 133, 226; Civil War, 193; public services spending, 18; public transit, 95; university education, 140

state pension (UK), 21, 64, 73, 108, 170, 228

state schools (UK), 123, 138, 144–55 passim, 233, 234, 241; Gove comment on, 198, 201

status goods, 200, 226, 229

Stewart, Mo, 76–7

strikes, 236, 243

Sturgeon, Nicola, 34

suicide, 165, 235, 241

Sunak, Rishi, 9, 20, 39–41 passim, 98, 122, 133, 212, 222, 241

supermarkets, 61, 62

superrich, 99, 104–5

Sweden: consumer behaviour, 226; immigration, 217; life expectancy, 173; public services spending, 18; university education, 140

Switzerland, 248n26; international schools, 140; watches, 102–3

taxation, 60–1, 100–102 passim, 131, 228, 230–1, 231; avoidance and evasion, 98, 100, 213, 230; private schools, 150; property, 86–7, 88–9; rebates, 57–8; Thatcher policies, 60; VAT, 60, 61

TaxPayers' Alliance, 210

television, 19, 197; BBC, 15, 16

tenants' organisations, 90–1

Thackeray, William Makepeace, 136

Thatcher, Margaret, 12, 20, 59–60, 215; death, 211; education policy, 145; financial market deregulation, 123; housing policy, 83

think-tanks, right-wing, 209–10, 212, 240; left-wing 25, 28, 265n16, 124, 259n14, 260n23 passim

third child benefits, 70, 78

Torquay, Devon, 128

Tory party (UK). *See* Conservative Party (UK)

Tower Hamlets, London, 128

transportation. *See* private transport; public transport; rail transportation

Treasury (UK). *See* HM Treasury

Truss, Liz, 20, 29, 37, 99, 121–2, 207–8, 211–12, 240; appointees, 210; comprehensive schooling, 148; on Nicola Sturgeon, 34; Thatcher influence on, 211

Trussell Trust, 52, 79
Tufton Street. See right-wing think tanks
Tunbridge Wells. See Royal Tunbridge Wells, Kent
Turkey, 196, 224

UK Department for Levelling Up, Housing and Communities. See Department for Levelling Up, Housing and Communities (UK)
UK Department for Work and Pensions. See Department for Work and Pensions (UK): Work Capabilities Assessment (WCA)
Ukraine, Russian invasion of, 8, 193, 231, 268n57
unemployment: EU, 178; UK, 4, 63–4, 110
United States, 196, 215, 225, 235–6; California wildfires, 103–4; deaths of despair, 235; health gap, 187–8; housing policy, 210; international schools, 140; media, 199–200; Reagan, 211; social mobility, 134, 158, 215; university education, 139, 158, 200; wage and price freeze of 1971, 56
university education, 69–70, 135, 148, 151, 154, 157–8, 204–5; tuition, 13, 139–41, 154, 234; United States, 139, 158, 200. See also community colleges
University of Edinburgh, 142, 193
University of Manchester, 142–3

University of Oxford, 146, 198
utilities, 92–8. See also water

vacation. See holidays (vacation)
Von der Leyen, Ursula, 93

wages and salaries, 26, 32, 56, 116, 124, 147; Boris Johnson, 131. See also CEO pay; minimum wage
Wales, 15, 33–4, 35, 65, 221; Bevan, 164; child support, 58, 59; GDP, 76; housing, 86; minimum wage, 64; youth voting, 43
water, 70, 71, 94–8 passim; heating cost, 66
welfare, 52, 63–9, 74, 75, 79; as a business activity, 133–5; means-tested benefits, 52, 72; sanctions, 66–7
'whataboutery', 14
wildfires: California, 103–4
Willink, Henry, 227
Workers' Educational Association, 160
workforce statistics, 17, 64, 116, 122, 130
workhouses (nineteenth-century UK), 73, 77
workweek, 126–7

Xenophobia, 195
Xi Jinping, 274n27

York, 79
Yorkshire, 76, 89, 142

Zahawi, Nadhim, 210